ROLLED & TOLD ™

Published by Oni-Lion Forge Publishing Group, LLC

James Lucas Jones, president & publisher • Sarah Gaydos, editor in chief • Charlie Chu, e.v.p. of creative & business development • Brad Rooks, director of operations • Amber O'Neill, special projects manager • Harris Fish, events manager • Margot Wood, director of marketing & sales • Jeremy Atkins, director of brand communications • Devin Funches, sales & marketing manager • Katie Sainz, marketing manager • Tara Lehmann, marketing & publicity associate • Troy Look, director of design & production • Kate Z. Stone, senior graphic designer • Sonja Synak, graphic designer • Hilary Thompson, graphic designer • Sarah Rockwell, junior graphic designer • Angie Knowles, digital prepress lead • Vincent Kukua, digital prepress technician • Shawna Gore, senior editor • Robin Herrera, senior editor • Amanda Meadows, senior editor • Jasmine Amiri, editor • Grace Bornhoft, editor • Zack Soto, editor • Steve Ellis, vice president of games • Ben Eisner, game developer • Michelle Nguyen, executive assistant • Jung Lee, logistics coordinator

Joe Nozemack, publisher emeritus

onipress.com | lionforge.com
facebook.com/onipress | facebook.com/lionforge
twitter.com/onipress | twitter.com/lionforge
instagram.com/onipress | instagram.com/lionforge

First Edition: June 2020
ISBN 978-1-62010-745-4
eISBN 978-1-62010-749-2

Printed in China.
Library of Congress Control Number: 2019955394

1 2 3 4 5 6 7 8 9 10

VOLUME 2

ROLLED & TOLD ™

CONTENTS

7 Adventures

EDITOR
STEENZ

ASSISTING EDITORS
KAT VENDETTI
ZOE MAFFITT

LEAD GAME DESIGNER
E.L. THOMAS

CREATIVE DIRECTOR
ANNIE MONETTE

DESIGNER
ROBIN ALLEN

**CREATIVE EDITOR
ISSUES 11 AND 12**
ANDREW E.C. GASKA

ADVENTURES

VAULT OF THE MAD CRAFTER

WRITTEN BY E.L. THOMAS, ILLUSTRATED BY TABBY FREEMAN

A 5E Adventure for Levels 4–6 | You will need a copy of the 5E core rulebooks to fully utilize this adventure. You also should familiarize yourself with the adventure and the map to fully enjoy this adventure. You should familiarize yourself with the spells used by the foes prior to playing the adventure.

Glossary | PC: Playable Characters | GM: Game Master | DC: Difficulty Class
HP: Hit Points | NPC: Non-Player Character

Adventure Scaling | This adventure is designed to be highly challenging for a group of 3rd- to 5th-level level players, though it can easily be challenging for a larger group or a group of upper 2nd-tier characters by giving all the foes maximum hit points and adding +2 to the DC of tests and saves.

GEAROK'S VAULT

A   A KNIGHTLY WELCOME
B   THE LIGHTNING HALL
C   THE DESTROYED PORTAL CHAMBER
D   STOCK AND SCRAP
E   THE ARTIFICE FORGE WORKS
F   GUARD ROOM
G   TELEPORT MECHANISM
H   THE KNIGHT OF THE VAULT
J   GEAROK'S CHAMBERS
K   THE TRUE VAULT
K   THE STOREROOM/ LARDER
L   THE WORKSHOP

- TELEPORT ENTRY SPOT
- SECRET DOOR
- DOUBLE STONE DOOR
- 10 FT.

PLOT

The PCs are hired by a temple of pacifist monks, The Order of the Still Hand, to seek out and raid the maze-like vault of Gearok the Mad Crafter—a long-dead wizard obsessed with magical constructs. They are to seek out and recover the *Clockwork Codex*, a tome of instructions for manufacturing clockwork constructs. The monks require the tome so they can craft clockwork golems to protect their isolated temple from the growing orc tribes in the area. The PCs must best the Mad Crafter's maze-like vault, survive its many traps and guardian clockwork constructs, locate the tome, and find the teleportation mechanism to escape the sealed underground complex.

BACKGROUND

Over a century ago, when The Order of the Still Hand sought to remove themselves from the violence of the world by raising a temple in the wilderness, a broken, but ingenious young wizard named Gearok came to them. The youthful mage's creativity had all but consumed him. The monks thought they could heal Gearok's broken mind by letting him aid in the construction of their temple, but little did they know that they only further fueled his obsession. While building the temple, the young wizard was also constructing a secret complex below the temple, a complex only accessible by magical teleportation. In that secret complex, Gearok continued his experimentation

with clockwork golems. In only a short time, Gearok began spending more and more time away from the temple in a misguided effort to solve what he saw as the problem of protecting the pacifist monks. Gearok knew that one day danger would come for the temple, isolated as it was, and the monks' beliefs would bar them from defending themselves. So the young wizard created clockwork golems to do the defending for them. He recorded all the instructions for making those golems in a tome of knowledge he called the *Clockwork Codex,* so that even after his own death the monks would have the means of making their protectors. When Gearok presented his plans to the monks, they shunned him for what they took as the ravings of broken man. Gearok took his codex and retreated into his complex. There, deep beneath the earth, away from monks he saw as betraying him, Gearok threw himself into his work and his madness. Years passed, and with those years Gearok's madness shattered his already broken mind and he died with his creations. Eventually, the Mad Crafter's predictions of danger to the temple became reality as massive orc tribes now see the grand temple as a great prize, and the monks need defenses. The monks need the codex, and only adventurers have a chance of retrieving it. The monks have managed to find and activate the teleportation circle that can gain entry to the Mad Crafter's vault. Now all that is required are heroes brave enough to raid it and bring back the *Clockwork Codex.*

SAVE THE TEMPLE...
SAVE THE TEMPLE...
HEHEHE SAVE THE TEMPLE...
WHAT IN THE WORLD...
MASTER WU LONG! HAVE YOU COME TO SEE MY BABIES! DO YOU LIKE THEM?!?!
TAO... LOCK MASTER GEAROK IN THE FORBIDDEN TEMPLE.
Y-YES... SIR...

RULES OF THE MAZE COMPLEX

ENTRY AND EXIT

The teleportation circle from the temple gives only one-way entry into the maze complex. Anyone entering must find, and then figure out how to operate, the Teleport Mechanism (in Area G) to escape the maze complex.

SECRET DOORS

All the secret doors in the maze complex are difficult to locate, requiring a Wisdom (Perception) check at DC 20, or an Intelligence (Investigation) DC 25 [(made with advantage if *detect magic* is used)], and are magically locked. They can only be opened in one of three ways: if the lock is disabled using Thieves' Tools + Intelligence DC 20; a *dispel magic* spell against 7th-level magic; or smearing five hit points' worth of blood from any humanoid with spellcasting ability. The secret doors only stay open and unlocked for one minute before they automatically close and relock.

OTHER DOORS

The doors of the maze complex are all alchemically treated stone, AC 17, 27 hit points with resistance to all but force damage, and are locked with a complicated combination lock using arcane symbols that requires three consecutive Intelligence (Arcana) DC 12 tests or a single Thieves' Tools

(Dexterity) DC 20. Should the PC fail any of the tests, the DCs for any test increase by +5 until they max out at DC 30. An Intelligence (Investigation) DC 15 (made with advantage if the PC that makes it is also trained in Arcana) will reveal the increase of difficulty for failing to successfully open the combination locks.

STARTING THE ADVENTURE

You have found your way to the temple of the Order of the Still Hand, a place of peace and tranquility. The order of pacifist monks has managed to build a place of beauty and serenity in the isolated wilderness. The grand temple is in the calm eye of an wildly raging orcish maelstrom. Now, the many warring tribes have been united under one banner and their new king sees the temple to his liking. The monks are beings of peace and stand no chance against the orcish forces. While the monks will not physically raise a hand in their own defense, they do have a solution to their woes. That solution lies beneath their very temple, but it will take heroes such as you to see it to their hands. It seems that the wizard who aided in raising the temple also made a secret complex below it. That wizard is none other than the Mad Crafter, Gearok, an unparalleled maker of golems, amongst other arcane inventions. Though long dead, the Mad Crafter was said to have left behind a tome of how to make his magnificent golems, the Clockwork Codex. The monks believe that with the codex they could construct guardians that would keep them safe from the coming orc violence. This dire need is what brought you to the temple and to the aid of these monks.

GM | The monks offer the PCs 5,000 gp in coin, a *periapt of health,* and three *potions of greater healing.* They offer this sum because their need is great, and going into the vault could be a one-way trip.

The monks will be sheepish if asked direct questions about how they know about the codex, unless asked by a lawful good character or the PCs can succeed at a Charisma (Persuasion) DC 15.

Any PC that can succeed at an Intelligence (History) DC 20 (any monk or bard gains advantage on this roll) receives the information in the background section.

If the PCs are still not willing to aid the monks, they will add five more *potions of greater healing* to try and convince them.

ONCE THE PCS AGREE, READ THE FOLLOWING:

The monks bring you deep into the halls of the temple and reveal a glowing circle inlayed into the very floor. Azure runes glow with arcane power, unmistakably marking the magic circle as some form of teleport.

GM | Any PC trained in the Arcana skill can easily operate the teleportation circle, simply by using an action to activate it. The character and any creatures in the circle (up to four Medium-sized creatures at a time can fit on the portal) are instantly teleported to Area A.

An Intelligence (Arcana) DC 10 reveals that the teleport is indeed one-way only.

AREA A
A KNIGHTLY WELCOME

A bright flash of magic and you are instantly standing in the center of large circular chamber. At opposite sides of the round chamber are matching arched stone doors. A pair of massive, ogre-sized hulking forms encased in heavy plate armor stand, weapons at the ready. Almost as soon as you arrive, both towering knights begin swinging deadly-looking spiked flails as they wordlessly stomp towards you with grim purpose.

GM | The massive clockwork knights attack as soon as the PCs arrive. They will fight until destroyed. The stone doors (see "Other Doors" entry in the rules section for info) are currently closed and locked.

- **Threats**: 2 clockwork knights (see stat blocks)

STABBING SPIKE FLOOR
Mechanical trap

This trap is triggered as soon as either of the two doors are opened. When triggered, and on initiative count 20 each round until the doors are closed, spear-like spikes stab up from the floor throughout the entirety of Area A.

- **Spikes**. *Melee Attack*: +6 to hit. *Hit*: 4 (1d8) piercing damage to any creature touching the floor.

A successful DC 10 Wisdom (Perception) notices the holes in the stone floor (though made at disadvantage if combat with the clockwork knights is still occurring). An Intelligence (Investigation) DC 20 reveals that opening one of the doors will trigger the trap and closing it again will stop it.

AREA B
THE LIGHTNING HALL

Eldritch runes in mad, haphazard patterns line the walls, floor, and ceiling of this C-shaped hall. All the runes glow with a pale white light, washing the area in an eerie illumination.

GM | Four clockwork spiders patrol the area, though they are currently at the dead end of the C-shaped hall, furthest away from the door. As soon as any PC triggers the lightning hall trap (see below), the spiders will come

to investigate, and they will fight until destroyed or any trespassers are eliminated, whichever comes first.

- **Threats**: 4 clockwork spiders

LIGHTNING HALL TRAP
Magic trap

The entire hall is a deadly lightning trap that is activated by motion. Any living creature that does any of the following in this area of the map—starts their turn, moves through, is forced to move through, takes an action (that requires physical motion) in, or ends their turn in the area—must succeed on a Dexterity (Stealth) DC 15 or be targeted by an arc of magic lightning. This also means that a living creature could be targeted multiple times in a single round (if they take more than one move or action while in the area).

- **Lightning Arc**. *Ranged Spell Attack*: +8 to hit, range anywhere within the trap area, one living target. *Hit*: 7 (2d6) lightning damage.

  An Intelligence (Arcana or Investigation) DC 15 reveals the nature and danger of the rune covered hall, and that the movement of living creatures is what causes the runes to throw lightning.

- **Countermeasures**: So numerous are the runes that the process of deactivating each one would be time consuming and deadly, though it is possible. Wisdom (Thieves' Tools) DC 25 (made with advantage if trained in Arcana, made at disadvantage if trying to do it stealthily), clears a 5-foot square. Clearing the square will likely cause others to go off. Additionally, a *dispel magic* spell could be used to suppress the runes in a number of 5-foot areas, equal to the level the spell would normally dispel (see core rulebooks) for a number of combat rounds equal to the spellcaster's spell attack bonus. Example: a caster's spell attack bonus of +6 would suppress the runes for six combat rounds.

AREA C
THE DESTROYED PORTAL CHAMBER

The shattered remains of what was once a massive stone gateway dominates this chamber. What part of the ring-like gate that remains standing is reminiscent of a crescent moon. Intricately hewn symbols run along its cracked and blackened surface. Heaped, scattered, and embedded into the walls about the chamber are the blackened and crumpled remains of its other half. It is plain to see that some great and very explosive mishap occurred here.

GM | An Intelligence (Arcana) DC 15 identifies the symbols of being planar in nature. A DC 18+ reveals that the gate was usable to access any of the Elemental Planes.

Once that is discovered, a Wisdom (Insight) DC 15 or Intelligence (Investigation) DC 12 lets the PCs surmise that perhaps this gate was how the Mad Crafter acquired the raw materials and arcane energy required to make his creations in such an isolated place.

An Intelligence (Investigation) DC 15 of the rubble uncovers the shattered remains of some form of automaton (a clockwork drone), a small locked DC 15 chest containing 20 rubies (valued at 25 gp each) in a small pouch, and two vials of *oil of slipperiness* (see core rulebooks) protectively wrapped in silk.

AREA D
STOCK AND SCRAP

This area is chock-full of organized piles of coal, iron ingots, iron filings, and rusted scrap metal in every shape and size imaginable. Numerous hand carts, racks of basic tools, buckets, and barrels sit rotting, as if they were abandoned in the midst of a day's work left unfinished. A heavy coating of dust covers everything in this oddly shaped area.

GM | A Wisdom (Perception) DC 10 shows numerous small-sized and square-toed footprints in the dust. Unless encountered already in this adventure, the PCs will have no idea they belong to the clockwork drones hiding in this area.

The 10 clockwork drones are well hidden throughout the labyrinthine collection of piles and tools. A Wisdom (Perception) DC 13 is needed to spot the drones before they attack. The drones rush from hiding, and try to swarm the PCs and engage as many of the PCs as possible.

There are 2d6 + 6 basic tools (spades, hammers, shovels, and the like) that have not fully succumbed to age and are still useable, as well as 12 barrels of fetid water, and four barrels of lamp oil. The iron ingots are of a high quality, though in their current form they are worth around two copper pieces each, and there are literally a few thousand.

- **Threats**: 10 clockwork drones (see stat blocks)

AREA E
THE ARTIFICE FORGE WORKS

Before you lies an expansive and partially segmented chamber shrouded in shadow. Huge smelting furnaces, long since gone cold, and forge works fill up much of the wide area. Carts of raw ore and tools lay scattered and abandoned. Though deep towards what looks to be center-most furnace, the dim glow of smoldering fire pushes back the coal-stained gloom.

GM | This is indeed where the raw materials were turned into useable metal. The glow is from a fire elemental that was once bound to the furnace and is now free and angry. It will attack as soon as any living creature approaches more than 10 feet into the massive chamber.

- **Threat**: Fire elemental (see core rulebooks for stats)

- **Loot**: In an iron-bound, locked DC 20 chest are the following items: 620 cp, a silvered longsword, 2 silvered daggers, a set of adamantine thieves' tools (making them virtually unbreakable), and 12 odd pieces of silver plates, utensils, and serving dishes (total value of 60 gp).

AREA F
GUARD ROOM

The hall seemingly dead-ends in a large open area. A large stone brazier, crackling with a heatless, emerald, magical fire sits in each corner of the room. The flickering green light washes the whole room in a sickly pallor, along with the four hulking, ironclad forms of clockwork knights. Unlike your first meeting with these constructs, these make no move to engage you, or even seem to take note of your presence.

GM | The fire in the stone braziers is the same as a *continual flame* spell (see core rulebooks).

The clockwork knights will do nothing and seem nonfunctional, unless a Wisdom (Perception) DC 20 or a Wisdom (Insight) DC 15 can be made. If the check is successful, the PC can see that they each have a readied attack action and are more than ready to attack should anything trigger their long-ago-given orders.

The clockwork knights will attack if any of the following happens:

- Any of the four knights are attacked.

- Any living creature begins looking for secret doors via Investigation. You would have to approach the doors closely to investigate them.

- Anyone tries to open one of the secret doors.

Other than these listed triggers, the clockwork knights stay as still as statues.

- **Threats**: 4 clockwork knights

AREA G
TELEPORT MECHANISM

Beyond the secret door is a room filled, floor to ceiling, with strange arcane machinery, arranged encircling a runic pattern that dominates the center of the chamber. All manner of levers, wheels, tumblers, dials, and gauges cover

the bronze thing of mechanical-made genius. The runes of the floor pattern mirror those of the teleport circle that brought you into this accursed place. So perhaps you have located your way of escape. . .

GM | This strange device is indeed the only way out of the maze complex, without access to another magical travel device. Though like the teleport that granted entry, this teleport will only fit up to four Medium-sized creatures at a time per activation. If successfully activated, the creatures and anything they are carrying are instantly returned to the temple above and are safe. If activated incorrectly, though, there can be dire consequences (see below).

There are four tasks that need to be completed on the machinery to make the teleport function work. The results of the four tasks (required test and checks) will set the Teleport Escape Arcana Check DC, which begins at a base of DC 30. By the numerous tasks that must be completed, it is evident that many personnel are required to operate the machine. To reflect this, all the tasks must be attempted and completed in order, within three rounds, and each requires an action. This means multiple players must make the attempts.

1. All the needed numbers and information dials, wheels, and levers are written in a maddening combination of different languages: Abyssal, Common, Draconic, Dwarvish, and Elvish. To decipher the mingled

languages and symbols, the PCs must succeed on a DC 30 Intelligence check, gaining a proficiency bonus to the roll for each language they have access to. It also grants an advantage for any character making the check who is trained in Arcana and has at least three of the languages already. Any PC trying to make the check who is not trained in Arcana makes the roll at disadvantage. If successful, reduce the Teleport Escape Arcana Check DC by 5 (see below).

2. Activating the stability runes (the runes that keep anyone from being ripped apart when teleporting) in the correct order: This is accomplished by a Wisdom (Insight) DC 20 (made at disadvantage if the creature making the check is not trained in Arcana). If successful, reduce the Teleport Escape Arcana Check DC by 5.

3. Precisely calibrate the energy flow-path emitters: This is accomplished by a Dexterity (Sleight of Hand) DC 20 (made at disadvantage if the creature making the check is not trained in Arcana). If successful, reduce the Teleport Escape Arcana Check DC by 5. If failed, increase the DC by 5.

4. Engage all the safety switches: This is accomplished by a Strength (Athletics) DC 15. If successful, reduce the Teleport Escape Arcana Check DC by 5.

After the above listed four tasks are completed (success or failure), the party can make the Teleport Escape Check using Intelligence (Arcana) DC 30 modified as listed above. If the Intelligence (Arcana) for the Teleport Escape Check is successful, go to ending the adventure. If the PCs have the *Clockwork Codex* from the Area J, use "Escape with the *Codex*," if not, use "Escape without the *Codex*." Whether they succeed or fail on the Teleport Escape Arcana Check, the PCs are still teleported out of the maze complex. Though on a failure, all the PCs who are teleported for that trip must roll on the Botched Teleport Chart below.

BOTCHED TELEPORT CHART (ROLL 1D20)

1: Searing pain rips through your body as the teleport engages. In the blink of an eye, you find yourself returned to the temple above in a crumpled and broken heap. Creature suffers 21 (6d6) force damage.

2–10: Something definitely went wrong with the teleport and you are returned to the temple above, though as if a giant hand slapped you to the ground. Creature suffers 10 (3d6) force damage.

11–19: It was painful, but you are returned to the temple in a blinding flash, though every one of your joints ache. Creature suffers 3 (1d6) force damage.

20: Even though it felt as if your body would be ripped apart as the flash of magic fills your vision, you miraculously are safely returned to the exact spot in the temple above where you first began your adventure.

AREA H
THE KNIGHT OF THE VAULT

A single clockwork knight stands as a vigilant sentinel, though this construct appears even more armored and is covered in more sword-length spikes than clockwork knights previously encountered.

GM | The lone clockwork knight uses the same stats as those found in the stat block section, with the following additions: AC 20 and defensive sword-spikes: As a reaction the clockwork knight may force any creature that makes a melee attack against it to succeed at a DC 17 Dexterity saving throw or suffer 9 (1d8 + 5) piercing damage.

- **Threat**: modified clockwork knight (see stat block section and above modifications)

AREA I
GEAROK'S CHAMBERS

This longish chamber is arranged in a maddening array of age-rotted and burnt furnishing meaning to have functioned as a personal workshop, study, sitting room, and bed chamber. Strewn about it are charred, rotted, and unreadable tomes that number in the thousands. The entire place looks as if a deadly spell battle and melee had taken place here years ago. Just as you are taking in the vast destruction before you, a wholly mad cackling cuts the hushed silence as a glowing green apparition of a tall, too-lean man garbed in translucent tatters of wizards' robes and a bronze face mask slips into near solidified existence, floating above the ruins of the room.

GM | The apparition is Gearok, The Mad Crafter's ghost, and he means to destroy any living thing that dares enter his chambers. He will pursue any who flee and will slay any living creature he can find until he is destroyed.

Battle in the chamber is made even more difficult because any land-based movement counts as difficult terrain, due to the vast array of burnt books and furnishing that cover the entire floor.

- **Threat**: Gearok the Mad Crafter's ghost (see stat block section)
- **Loot**: The following items still survive and are scattered about the ruins of the room. Finding each requires a separate Wisdom (Perception) DC 18 check. *Immovable rod, potion of resistance,* and a *wand of lightning bolts.*

AREA J
THE TRUE VAULT

The walls of this chamber are lined, floor to ceiling, with shelves and alcoves, stuffed with tomes, scrolls, and potion vials. At its open center is an ornately carved stone lectern. Atop the reading stand sits a bronze-plated tome covered in seemingly constantly moving magic runes. This must be the vault of the Mad Crafter, and the bronze tome is surely the codex you seek.

GM | All the tome and scrolls stuffing the shelves are filled with mad rambling and nonsense. Most of these are not even legible, having been written by a broken mind. The *Clockwork Codex* is indeed the bronze-plated tome. The *Codex* is heavy, being the size of a backpack and weighing about the same as a suit of plate mail. The lectern is not trapped in any way. The potion vials are mostly worthless failed experiments, but amongst the hundreds of mixtures there are 6d6 magic potions. The PCs can choose any combination of potions they wish of common or uncommon rarity (see core rulebooks for choices).

- **Loot**: 6d6 common or uncommon potions and the *Clockwork Codex*

AREA K
THE STOREROOM/ LARDER

Crates of long-turned-to-dust foodstuff and barrels of once-wine-now-vinegar mostly fill this room.

GM | Searching through the ruined food stores using an Intelligence (Investigation) DC 15 uncovers a *bag of holding* (see core rulebooks) that still has 10 days of rations and a water skin.

AREA L
THE WORKSHOP

This chamber is a collection of forges, bellows, anvils, and workbenches cluttered with a mass assortment of rusty smithing and metalworking tools, along with half-finished projects, including the framework of a clockwork knight.

GM | Concealed amongst the numerous workspaces are a collection of 10 clockwork spiders.

- **Threats**: 10 clockwork spiders (see stat block section)
- **Loot**: Scattered with rusty tools are a set of nearly indestructible adamantine smithing tools, valued the same as an uncommon magic item.

ENDING THE ADVENTURE

ESCAPE WITH THE *CODEX*

In a gut-wrenching rush and blinding flash of magic, you find yourself once more in the chamber with the teleportation circle, though now the runes no longer glow with power. Even with the Clockwork Codex, the orcish threat is far from dealt with. But at the very least, you have

given the monks of the Order of the Still Hand a chance to defend themselves and still maintain their vows of pacifism. Sometimes, the best a hero can do is to give someone a chance...

ESCAPE WITHOUT THE *CODEX*

In a gut-wrenching rush and blinding flash of magic, you find yourself once more in the chamber with the teleportation circle, though now the runes no longer glow with power. The taste of your failure will not soon fade, nor will the memories of the foulness that can be found below. Without the Codex, the monks must seek out other means of defense from the growing orc threat. This failure may mean many will pay a deadly price, but nothing is ever certain in an adventurer's life...

REWARDS

- Reward the PCs XP for the foes they faced.
- 150 Bonus XP per surviving PC for the danger of the mission.
- If they recovered the *Clockwork Codex*, reward each surviving PC an additional 250 XP.
- If all the PCs survived, grant each another 100 XP for good play and teamwork. ⊛

NEW MONSTERS

CLOCKWORK DRONE
Small construct, unaligned

Armor Class 17 (natural armor)
Hit Points 13 (2d6 + 6)
Speed 30 ft.

STR	DEX	CON	INT	WIS	CHA
16 (+3)	6 (–2)	16 (+3)	6 (–2)	10 (+0)	1 (–5)

Damage Resistances bludgeoning, piercing, and slashing from nonmagical attacks

Damage Immunities poison, psychic

Condition Immunities blinded, charmed, deafened, exhaustion, frightened, paralyzed, petrified, poisoned

Senses blindsight 60 ft. (blind beyond this radius); passive Perception 10

Languages understands Common, but can't speak

Challenge 1/4 (50 XP)

Antimagic Susceptibility. The clockwork drone is incapacitated while in an antimagic field. If targeted by *dispel magic*, the drone must succeed on a Constitution saving throw against the caster's spell DC or fall inactive for one minute.

Enduring Construct. Anytime the clockwork drone is reduced to zero or fewer hit points, it must make a Constitution saving throw at a DC of 5 + the damage taken. On a successful saving throw, it drops to one hit point instead.

Magic Resistance. The clockwork drone has advantage on saving throws against spells and other magical effects.

Pack Tactics. The clockwork drone has advantage on attack rolls against targets if at least one of the drone's allies is within five feet of the target and isn't incapacitated.

ACTIONS

Slam. *Melee Weapon Attack:* +5 to hit, reach 5 ft., one creature. *Hit:* 6 (1d6 + 3) bludgeoning damage.

CLOCKWORK KNIGHT
Large construct, unaligned

Armor Class 18 (natural armor)
Hit Points 85 (9d10 + 36)
Speed 30 ft.

STR	DEX	CON	INT	WIS	CHA
20 (+5)	6 (–2)	18 (+4)	6 (–2)	10 (+0)	1 (–5)

Saving Throws Str +7

Damage Resistances bludgeoning, piercing, and slashing from nonmagical attacks

Damage Immunities poison, psychic

Condition Immunities blinded, charmed, deafened, exhaustion, frightened, paralyzed, petrified, poisoned

Senses blindsight 120 ft. (blind beyond this radius); passive Perception 10

Languages understands Common, but can't speak

Challenge 3 (700 XP)

Antimagic Susceptibility. The clockwork knight is incapacitated while in an antimagic field. If targeted by *dispel magic*, the knight must succeed on a Constitution saving throw against the caster's spell DC or fall inactive for one minute.

Enduring Construct. Anytime the clockwork knight is reduced to zero or fewer hit points, it must make a Constitution saving throw at a DC of 5 + the damage taken. On a successful saving throw, it drops to one hit point instead.

Magic Resistance. The clockwork knight has advantage on saving throws against spells and other magical effects.

Siege Monster. The clockwork knight deals double damage to objects and structures.

ACTIONS

Multiattack. The clockwork knight makes two melee attacks.

Slam. *Melee Weapon Attack:* +7 to hit, reach 10 ft., one creature. *Hit:* 14 (2d8 + 5) bludgeoning damage.

Spiked Flail. *Melee Weapon Attack:* +7 to hit, reach 15 ft., one creature. *Hit:* 18 (3d8 + 5) bludgeoning damage.

Whirlwind Flail Sweep (Recharge 5–6). The clockwork knight makes a single spiked flail attack that targets all targets in reach. Each creature that suffers damage from this attack must make a DC 15 Dexterity saving throw or be thrown back 10 feet and knocked prone.

GEAROK THE MAD CRAFTER'S GHOST *Medium undead, chaotic neutral*

Armor Class 12
Hit Points 54 (12d8)
Speed 0 ft., fly 40 ft.

STR	DEX	CON	INT	WIS	CHA
7 (–2)	14 (+2)	10 (+0)	20 (+5)	14 (+2)	17 (+3)

Damage Resistances acid, fire, lightning, thunder, bludgeoning, piercing, and slashing from nonmagical attacks

Damage Immunities cold, necrotic, poison

Condition Immunities charmed, exhaustion, frightened, grappled, paralyzed, petrified, poisoned, prone, restrained

Senses darkvision 60 ft., passive perception 12

Languages Common, Draconic, Infernal, and the rest were forgotten in madness

Challenge 5 (1,800 XP)

Ethereal Sight. Gearok's ghost can see 60 feet into the Ethereal Plane when it is on the Material Plane, and the other way around.

Incorporeal Movement. Gearok's ghost can move through other creatures and objects as if in difficult terrain. If he ends his turn inside an object, he takes 5 (1d10) force damage.

Magic Resistance. Gearok's ghost has advantage on saving throws against spells and other magical effects.

Immune to Turning. Gearok's ghost cannot be turned so long as he remains in the maze complex.

Spellcasting. Gearok's ghost now counts as an 8th-level spellcaster. His spellcasting ability is Intelligence (spell save DC 16, +8 to hit with spell attacks). He has the following spells prepared:

- **Cantrips** (at will): *acid splash, mage hand, mending, ray of frost*
- **1st level** (4 slots): *burning hands, charm person, magic missile, shield*
- **2nd level** (3 slots): *mirror image, shatter, web*
- **3rd Level** (3 slots): *fireball, lightning bolt, stinking cloud*
- **4th Level** (2 slots): *banishment, blight*

ACTIONS

Withering Touch. Melee Weapon Attack: +5 to hit, reach 5 ft., one creature. *Hit*: 17 (4d6 + 3) necrotic damage.

Etherealness. Gearok's ghost enters the Ethereal or Material Planes, and can only affect and be affected by sources on the same plane.

Share Madness (Recharge 5–6). Gearok's ghost targets one living creature it can see within 30 feet. The target must succeed at a Charisma saving throw DC 16 or suffer 13 (3d6 + 3) psychic damage, and count as stunned until the end of Gearok's ghost's next turn.

CLOCKWORK SPIDER
Medium construct, unaligned

Armor Class 15 (natural armor)
Hit Points 15 (2d8 + 6)
Speed 40 ft., climb 40 ft.

STR	DEX	CON	INT	WIS	CHA
12 (+1)	16 (+3)	16 (+3)	6 (–2)	12 (+1)	1 (–5)

Skills Perception +3, Stealth +5

Damage Resistances bludgeoning, piercing, and slashing from nonmagical attacks

Damage Immunities poison, psychic

Condition Immunities blinded, charmed, deafened, exhaustion, frightened, paralyzed, petrified, poisoned

Senses blindsight 120 ft. (blind beyond this radius); passive Perception 13

Languages understands Common, but can't speak

Challenge 1/2 (100 XP)

Antimagic Susceptibility. The clockwork spider is incapacitated while in the area of an antimagic field. If targeted by *dispel magic*, the spider must succeed on a Constitution saving throw against the caster's spell DC, or fall inactive for one minute.

Enduring Construct. Anytime the clockwork spider is reduced to zero or fewer hit points, it must make a Constitution saving throw at a DC of 5 + the damage taken. On a successful saving throw, it drops to one hit point instead.

Magic Resistance. The clockwork spider has advantage on saving throws against spells and other magical effects.

Spider Climb. The clockwork spider can climb difficult surfaces, including upside down on ceilings and walls, without needing to make ability checks.

ACTIONS

Bite. *Melee Weapon Attack*: +5 to hit, reach 5 ft., one creature. *Hit*: 4 (1d6 + 1) piercing damage, and the target must make a DC 13 Constitution saving throw, taking 7 (2d6) poison damage on a failed save, or half as much damage on a successful one.

Poison Gas Breath (Recharge 5–6). The clockwork spider exhales poison gas in a 15-foot cone. Each creature in that area must succeed on a DC 13 Constitution saving throw, taking 7 (2d6) poison damage on a failed save, or half as much damage on a successful one.

NEW MAGIC ITEM

CLOCKWORK CODEX
Wondrous item, very rare

This tome contains instructions, incantations, and rituals necessary to make clockwork knights and clockwork spiders. To decipher and use the manual, the user must be a spell caster with at least two 5th-level spell slots. Anyone who attempts to use or read the *Codex* suffers 6d6 psychic damage for each attempt or use, and gains a long-term madness (see core rulebooks). In addition, if they do not have the required spell slots, they must succeed on an Intelligence saving throw DC 20 or gain a random indefinite madness (see core rulebooks).

COST IN MATERIALS/TIME REQUIRED

- Clockwork knight: 30,000 gp / 60 days
- Clockwork spider: 20,000 gp / 30 days

THE DRAGON, THE WITCH, AND THE DRYAD

WRITTEN BY PHIL MCCLOREY, ILLUSTRATED BY RACHEL DUKES

A 5E Adventure for Levels 4–6 | You will need a copy of the 5E core rulebooks to fully utilize this adventure. You also should familiarize yourself with the adventure and the map to fully enjoy this adventure. You should familiarize yourself with the spells used by the foes prior to playing the adventure.

Glossary | PC: Playable Characters | GM: Game Master | DC: Difficulty Class
HP: Hit Points | NPC: Non-Player Character

Adventure Scaling | This adventure is designed to be highly challenging for a group of 3rd- to 5th-level players, though it can easily be challenging for a larger group or a group of upper 2nd-tier characters by giving all the foes maximum hit points and adding +2 to the DC of tests and saves.

PLOT

The adventurers traveling through the Moonshadow Wood come upon a ramshackle cottage being repaired by an old woodcutter. The woodcutter has recently returned to his former home following the death of an ancient green dragon that once terrorized the forest. The woodcutter expresses his concern at a rumor that one of the green dragon's eggs has hatched, and a green wyrmling now stalks the forest. He begs the adventurers to find the wyrmling, which is said to lay deep in the wood to the east.

On their journey, the adventurers come upon a group of orcs with an ogre attempting to capture an old centaur. Grateful for her rescue, the centaur takes them to meet a treant who may be able to direct the party to the wyrmling's lair. The treant reveals the location of the wyrmling's lair and tells the player characters that the wyrmling was hatched in secret by a wood elf, and that the wood elf was punished by the fey court for doing so. What that punishment was the treant will not say.

Soon after dealing with a harpy ambush, the adventurers locate the lair and confront the wyrmling, Ragnaw. During the encounter, a dryad appears and uses her *fey charm* to try and prevent the party from harming the wyrmling. The dryad reveals that she was the elf that hatched the wyrmling. The elf believed that the dragon was not predestined to grow to be evil if raised differently. The elf was transformed into a dryad as punishment and bound to a willow tree. Afterwards, the dryad continued to watch over the wyrmling. Discovering the truth, the party leaves the dryad and wyrmling to their fate.

The party returns to the cottage. When the woodcutter is informed of the truth regarding the wyrmling, he becomes enraged and reveals himself to be a green hag! The hag had hoped to trick the party into killing the wyrmling; the thought of a good green dragon roaming the Moonshadow Wood is too repulsive a thought for the hag to allow. The hag disappears after a brief battle, threatening the adventurers that this isn't the last they've seen of Rotten Polly Ringworm.

BACKGROUND

The player characters are traveling through the Moonshadow Wood on their way to their next adventuring contract. The Moonshadow Wood was once a region of great danger, but with the death of the ancient green dragon, Old Venom, travel along the trail is once more possible.

New fears have recently arisen as rumor spreads of the appearance of a green dragon wyrmling. The wyrmling, Ragnaw, was hatched by an elven druidess who found the egg while investigating Old Venom's lair. Discovered by the fey court, the druidess was punished and transformed into a dryad for bringing the spawn of Old Venom into the world.

The dryad reconnected with Ragnaw, and the wyrmling has since made a lair for itself near the willow tree to which the dryad is bound. Now the green hag, Rotten Polly Ringworm, plots to have the wyrmling killed before it can become a force for good in the forest.

Rules

Traveling through the woods presents some problems for the PCs, unless they have a ranger who chose forest as their favored terrain for Natural Explorer (see core rulebooks for more details). If the party leaves the trail, the forest is considered difficult terrain, which slows the party's movement speed by half.

The forest environment is considered lightly obscured, and creatures have disadvantage on Wisdom (Perception) checks that rely on sight (see core rulebooks for more details).

The trees also provide a lot of cover which may come into effect during ranged combat. If a target has half cover they get a +2 bonus to AC and Dexterity saving throws. Three-quarters cover gives a +5 bonus to AC and Dexterity saving throws. Total cover can't be targeted and only takes damage on area effects that reach the target.

STARTING THE ADVENTURE

Dim light filters through the thick foliage of the canopy. Moss covers the giant oaks and elms flanking the trail you find yourself on. For a day and a half, you've been traveling through Moonshadow Wood, listening to the songbirds, and watching them fly from branch to branch while squirrels scurry about their business collecting nuts and acorns from the undergrowth. You still have a couple of days travel ahead as you make your way towards the village of Brendan in the hopes of finding a new adventuring contract.

If the player characters ask for more detail about why they are traveling through the Moonshadow Wood, tell them they heard from a traveling bard that adventurers are being sought in Brendan, located on the other side of the forest, to explore an ancient dungeon that's been recently unearthed.

THE WOODCUTTER'S COTTAGE

Coming around a bend in the trail, you spot a rough-hewn cottage off to the right side, 20 feet into the woods. A fence that has seen better days encircles the cottage, its wooden gate facing the trail. From the stone chimney, a small wisp of smoke curls out.

The cottage looks as though it has been neglected for some years. Green moss covers much of the walls, and holes can be seen in the thatch roof.

GM | A Wisdom (Perception) check 10 allows the player characters to spot the old woodcutter on the roof replacing some of the thatch.

The woodcutter is a green hag in disguise.

- **Threat**: 1 green hag

The green hag, Rotten Polly Ringworm, knows the player characters are approaching from her woodland spies. The hag's goal is to convince the player characters to seek and destroy the green dragon wyrmling, Ragnaw.

If a player character casts *detect evil and good* and gets to within 30 feet of the woodcutter, they will sense he is an evil fey. Award the player character an inspiration point for uncovering something of the woodcutter's true character. The woodcutter's plan won't change. It might become a little

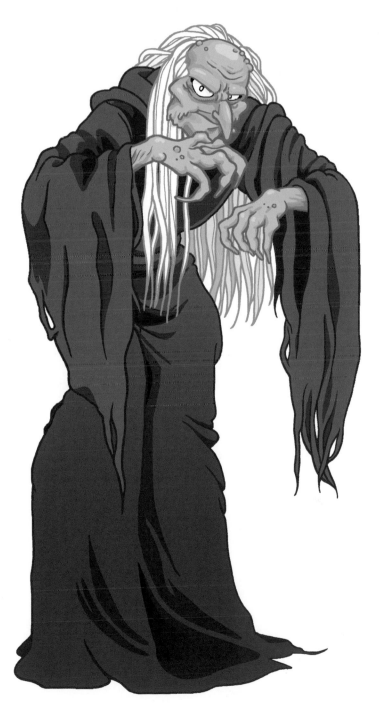

harder to convince the player characters to seek out the green dragon wyrmling. Push the angle of the threat that a green dragon may prove to be in the future, and they could stop it from happening. Appeal to the possibility that a small treasure may be found in the wyrmling's lair. Maybe suggest they are cowards if they refuse.

The woodcutter greets the player characters.

"Well met, travelers! Not many folks make their way through Moonshadow Wood. What business do you have in the forest?"

Provide the player characters an opportunity to tell what they are up to before continuing.

"I've just returned myself. I used to live here, years ago, until an ancient green dragon, Old Venom she was called, came and claimed the forest as her dominion. Traveled to greener pastures after that. I missed these trees something fierce after I left.

When I heard a group of adventurers had killed Old Venom, I thought I'd come back and see the state of the old cottage. It's not in too bad shape. Just needs a little work. This wood always had a special place in my heart. I'm glad to be back.

But this all might be for naught.

I've heard a rumor. A green dragon wyrmling is said to be out in the eastern part of the wood. I don't know, but could Old Venom have laid eggs and now one of 'em's hatched? That could lead to a new nightmare."

GM | Convince the player characters to investigate the rumor by appealing to their adventurous natures. The green dragon may prove to be a threat in the future,

and they could be the ones to stop that from happening. Suggest the possibility of a small treasure being found in the wyrmling's lair. What kind of adventurers would they be if they didn't investigate? Where's your sense of adventure?

If they ask what the woodcutter can offer as reward to investigate, he suggests a bag of valuable mushrooms which could be sold to an alchemist's shop. An Intelligence (Arcana) check 14 identifies they could be used as components in a number of spells and are worth 500 gp.

The woodcutter lets them know that a half mile further down the trail there is a small deer track that leads deeper into the eastern part of the wood and that that would be a good place to start looking for the wyrmling's lair. The deer track will be marked by standing stones, so it is easy to spot. The woodcutter has little other information to provide the player characters.

If the player characters ask questions about the forest, go with your instincts for the answers. The Moonshadow Wood is a fey wood, home to many different types of faerie-like creatures. Feel free to tell outlandish tales; use the map of the Moonshadow Wood as inspiration. The woodcutter is a green hag after all!

DEEPER INTO THE MOONSHADOW WOOD

Just as the woodcutter described, you spot the standing stones marking a small deer trail heading eastward into the forest. Faded, swirling designs of unknown origin are carved into the surface.

GM | If the player characters make an Intelligence (Arcana) check 13, they can determine that the runes look to be Sylvan in origin, but they are too faded to determine the meaning behind them.

You travel deeper into the Moonshadow Wood. The sound of the birds grows less frequent, while each breath feels more stifled, as if unable to penetrate the thick canopy of the wood.

You follow the trail for over a mile as it weaves through the forest before it comes to an abrupt end. Oak, elm, and maple stand before you as you must now leave the trail and venture into the wood.

GM | Refer to the rules on difficult terrain. At your discretion, the party should make a Wisdom (Survival) check DC 15 to determine if they become lost. If they become lost, play up how they are disoriented in the wood and how they can't seem to get their bearings. They seem to be traveling in circles and each moss-covered tree looks identical to another.

Regardless of whether the player characters become lost or not, they will encounter a group of orcs and an ogre surrounding a captured elderly, female centaur (see core rulebooks for statistics). Modify the centaur's current hit points to 15 and reduce her speed to 40 feet.

- **Threats**: 5 orcs, ogre
- **Loot**: Searching the orcs' and ogre's pouches reveals 12 gp, 23 sp, and 46 cp in total.

The sounds from the orcs and ogre capturing the centaur can be heard 180 feet away. The player characters will be able to spot the monsters through the trees for the first time with a Wisdom (Perception) check of DC 15 at a distance of 120 feet due to the tree cover. At 90 feet the DC will drop to 10. Because the monsters are focused on the centaur, the player characters can have advantage on their Dexterity (Stealth) checks versus the orcs' and ogre's Wisdom (Perception) checks to sneak up on them.

Through the trees you spot a group of gray-skinned humanoids snarling and howling, dressed in thick animal hides waving greataxes and javelins in celebration. Standing with them looks to be a small giant with tusks protruding from its lower lip. It holds a spiked greatclub clutched in its monstrous fist; gripped in its other hand is the end of a net.

The creature trapped in the net thrashes about, struggling to escape, as the orcs stab it with their javelins. The ogre swings its club, hitting the creature with a sickening thud, bringing what appears to be a centaur to the ground!

GM | If the player characters do nothing, the ogre will begin to half drag, half carry the trapped centaur back to the orc camp a little over a mile away to the north. The orcs will continue to celebrate. A couple of them will get a fire started, and the centaur will eventually be killed and roasted on a spit. The orcs and ogre are not very vigilant. The player characters still have advantage to sneak up on them.

If the centaur is killed, the PCs won't have a guide to Oakenstep. Modify the way forward. Maybe change the weather so it begins to pour rain. If the player characters are lost, play up on that. But by nightfall, have them stumble upon the glade where Oakenstep is resting.

If the player characters intervene, the orcs and the ogre will immediately attack when they become aware of the player characters. The orcs will throw their javelins at the closest player characters as they use their movement and Aggressive bonus action to close the distance and engage in melee combat as soon as possible. Orcs also have a special hatred for elves, which make them ideal targets when deciding whom to attack. The ogre will target the player character that does a lot of damage to it in the first round of combat. Otherwise, it attacks the closet player character.

The centaur can attempt to free herself from the net on her action requiring a Strength check DC 10. Dealing 5 slashing damage to the net (AC 10) also frees the centaur without harming her, ending the restraint and destroying the net. Once freed, the centaur will pick up her fallen pike, if available. Otherwise, she will grab a fallen branch and aid the player characters in defeating the orcs. Treat the branch as a small club. *Melee Weapon Attack*: +6 to hit, reach 5 ft.; one target. *Hit*: 6 (1d4 + 4) bludgeoning damage.

Once the orcs and ogre are dealt with, Elaho introduces herself. She's covered in fresh blood from orc javelins and her left arm hangs limp from the ogre's blows. Along her hind legs she has a couple of old scars. She would be grateful for any healing by the player characters but won't ask for it. Elaho can only speak Elvish or Sylvan, so she will most likely look to address an elf or half-elf in the party. Otherwise she will thank them in Elven. Hopefully someone in the group speaks it and can translate.

"Thank you for saving my life. My name is Elaho and I am in your debt."

GM | Elaho has grown too old to keep up with her tribe. When that occurs, the custom is for the centaur to leave the tribe and make their own way in the forest, so as not to slow down the group. She was wandering through the wood, traveling southwest, when she was set upon by the orcs.

If asked, Elaho will say she has heard rumors of the appearance of the green dragon wyrmling but does not know where the wyrmling can be found. She offers to take the player characters to one who does, to fulfill her debt. She will not reveal who or what the being is, only that they are old and wise, and know much of what occurs in the forest.

THE TREANT, OAKENSTEP

GM | Elaho leads the player characters southeast. She is familiar with the wood and does not become lost while guiding them.

Elaho leads you deeper into the forest. You travel for many miles, twisting and turning through the dense woods on a general south-easterly course. The shadows cast by the trees intensify as the sun begins to set.

"We shall rest here for the night," Elaho calls as you enter a small glade filled with blooming white trilliums and violets. A small standing stone sits at the centre of the glade, its carvings worn smooth with age.

"The stone marks the glade as a safe space. So long as we bring no harm to the forest, no harm shall befall us here. I will go out and gather wood for a small fire. In the meantime, please rest."

GM | The glade has the effect similar to a *hallow* spell except fey creatures can enter the circle.

Unknown to the player characters, one of the trees surrounding the glade, a giant oak, is the treant Oakenstep (see core rulebooks). Oakenstep remains undetected. So long as he remains motionless he appears indistinguishable from a normal tree. Secretly, Oakenstep is watching and evaluating the player characters. How they behave and what they say might impact how the treant treats them.

Elaho leaves the player characters. She returns after a half hour with a load of wood for a fire. She offers to take the morning watch for the group if they set up a watch schedule. If the player characters decline, Elaho won't push it.

If the game has taken longer than expected to get to this point, you can fast track through the night and jump right into the encounter with Oakenstep.

Otherwise, you could have the player characters observe strange, tiny *dancing lights* flying around the edges of the glade, and hear the occasional giggle or whisper in the woods from a group of four pixies who live nearby. The pixies are curious about the player characters but will avoid direct contact. The pixies use their superior *invisibility* to avoid being seen. If the player characters wake up Elaho during the night to ask her what the lights are, she will tell them it is only pixies and the worst they have to fear are harmless pranks on them.

In the morning, Elaho will get a fire going for the player characters before saying good bye and wishing them well. If the player characters ask when the person they are to meet will appear, Elaho tells them they are already here. She will speak to Oakenstep in Sylvan seeking advice on where to go. The player characters will hear a deep voice in Sylvan suggesting Elaho travel south to the lake looking for an old druid.

Oakenstep now speaks with the player characters.

A giant oak tree on the edge of the glade shakes and stirs as if coming awake. High up the trunk of the tree, the bark separates as two eyes open, staring down at you. A deep, slow voice emanates from the tree.

"Who are you? What business do you have in my wood?"

GM | Below is a list of points Oakenstep is likely to share with the player characters, depending on the questions they ask and what you wish to share. If there is a druid or ranger in the group, Oakenstep is likely to address them.

- "I am Oakenstep, tree guardian of the Moonshadow Wood."

- "I watched acorns grow to saplings, mature, die and fall during Old Venom's reign in the forest. Many parts of the forest remain corrupt, turned to blight and rot because of her presence."

- "It has only been a few seasons since Old Venom was slain by a powerful wizard and his adventuring party. It is said the wizard died casting powerful magic which smote the foul wyrm."

- "A wood elf found a dragon's eggs, and, in secret, allowed it to hatch."

- "The fey court discovered what the elf had done. The court and its peoples suffered greatly at the whims of Old Venom. The thought of the dragon's offspring being brought into the world horrified them."

- "A great trial was held to determine the fate of the elf and wyrmling. The birds sing that even a hag mother was allowed to speak."

- "The elf was punished, their name stricken from the scrolls of history, their fate magically sealed so none who know what judgment was passed may speak of it."

- "The wyrmling was never found by the court, but I believe I know where it lairs. Tiny creatures of the wood chitter and chirp of a place too dangerous to roam, for a cunning predator stalks the area."

- "I have not told the court because they have not asked and it is not my place to pass judgment on the wyrmling. What evil has it yet committed?"

- "If you continue northeast, you will come to a creek. Follow the creek upstream. Look for an old willow tree sundered by lightning yet which still endures. You will find the wyrmling there."

The information provided by Oakenstep partially contradicts what they learned earlier from the old woodcutter. The player characters may pick up on this. It's their first clue that something may be amiss with their quest.

If the player characters express concerns about finding the tree or becoming lost, Oakenstep will offer them the *rod of the eant* (see "New Magic Item" section), provided they made a good impression on him. Oakenstep will ideally give the *rod* to a druid, ranger, or cleric who worships a nature deity. If none exist in the party, Oakenstep will give the *rod* to another magic user. Oakenstep will pull the *rod* out from the folds in his bark when he offers it to the player character. Information on the *rod of the eant* can be found in the "New Magic Item" section.

Once the player characters are done speaking with Oakenstep, he will take his leave and depart, traveling westward.

TO THE CREEK

The weather has changed. A thin mist falls making the air damp and chill. The dense brambles in this part of the forest tug at your cloak and tunic as you seek the creek spoken of by Oakenstep.

GM | It is three miles to the creek from the forest glade.

Once the player characters set off, the wood becomes difficult terrain again. Refer to the rules on difficult terrain.

At your discretion, they should also make Wisdom (Survival) check DC 15 to determine if they become lost. If they become lost, play up how they are disoriented in the wood and they can't seem to get their bearings. They seem to be traveling in circles, and each moss-covered tree looks identical to another. The party's navigator can repeat the check after the party spends 1d6 hours trying to get back on course. If the player characters received the *rod of the eant* from Oakenstep, they can use it to locate the willow tree and prevent themselves from becoming lost. If they did not receive the *rod* and they appear to be growing frustrated, you could introduce a pixie that remains invisible but guides the player characters in the correct direction using *dancing lights*.

HARPY CAVE

The sound of flowing water heralds your approach to the creek. You finally see it ahead, winding its way amongst the trees growing along the stream bank.

Traveling upstream, you soon come to a deep, moss-covered ravine, carved out by the ceaseless flow of the creek over the centuries. The echoes of rushing water surround you as the stream cascades down a series of waterfalls. At the top of the ravine to the right side of the waterfall, you make out a stone tower. The walls appear to be partially collapsed on the left side nearest the top of the waterfall. A narrow trail runs along a stone ledge, up the ravine towards the tower.

GM | The tower is home to a pair of harpies. From inside the tower, the harpies watch for prey traveling through the ravine and use their Luring Song to charm their victims off the dangerous ledges, causing them to fall to their deaths. If they happen to survive the fall, the harpies swoop in and finish them off.

- **Threats**: 2 harpies (see core rulebooks for statistics)

It is 120 feet from the bottom of the ravine along the trail up to the tower. The harpies have three quarters cover, +5 bonus to AC and Dexterity saving throws, while they watch from a perch along the top of the ruined tower. The player characters have disadvantage on Wisdom (Perception) checks to spot the harpies. If the GM uses passive Perception, checks are made with a –5 penalty.

The harpies have a passive Perception 10 to spot the player characters. Once the player characters are spotted traveling up the trail, each harpy will use their Luring Song to try and charm the player characters. Each player character, unless they are immune to charm, will have to make a DC 11 Wisdom saving throw or become charmed by the harpy. The harpy will continue to sing each round, luring the charmed player character higher up the trail. Once the charmed player character is 60 feet up the trail, the harpy will emerge from the tower and fly over the ravine, luring the player character to fall off the trail ledge, taking 6d6 falling damage. Before falling off the ledge, the charmed player character can repeat the Wisdom saving throw.

The harpies are cowards. If they have been unsuccessful at luring any player characters off the ledge, they will flee the tower and fly away. If the harpies had some success, instead of fleeing they may fly down and grapple the remaining player characters on the ledge, trying to physically pull them off. The harpies will make a grapple check instead of an attack roll: use the harpies' Strength (Athletics) check versus the player characters' Strength (Athletics) or Dexterity (Acrobatics) check. Every 10 feet above the bottom of the ravine will result in 1d6 of falling damage to the player character.

The entrance to the tower is on the opposite side of their approach, so the player characters won't be able to see it until they walk around.

Inside the tower, the smell is thick with the stench of decay. The air buzzes with large, black flies swarming amidst the rotted timbers, bones, and hides of the harpies' kills littering the ground.

If the player characters search the walls of the tower, an Intelligence (Investigation) check 15 locates a small alcove in the wall. Inside the wall they find a pouch of gems, six in total, each worth 50 gp.

If the player character searches the floor and the debris, an Intelligence (Investigation) check 15 locates a *potion of greater healing*.

THE SUNDERED WILLOW TREE

At last you see the lightning, sundered willow tree, 90 feet ahead beside the bank of the creek near the base of a rocky hillside. Much of the exposed wood is blackened, yet the tree continues to live, its wispy branches bowed with green leaves.

GM | The dryad, Valina, is resting in the bough of the willow tree. Valina was not her elven name, that name was lost when the wood elf was punished by the fey court. Make opposing Dexterity (Stealth) versus Wisdom (Perception) checks to determine who spots whom first and when. Once the dryad is aware of the player characters, she will use her Tree Stride to magically move 60 feet from one tree to another to hide from the player characters. If the player characters are able to sneak up on the dryad, the dryad will still use Tree Stride once she becomes aware of them, except now the player characters will be aware of her presence in the area.

- **Threat**: Dryad

The dryad will try to remain hidden from the player characters to determine their motivations, though she will suspect they are here for the wyrmling.

An Intelligence (Investigation) check 12 of the willow tree reveals a small hole burrowed beneath the tree. A faint, acrid smell comes from the hole, created when Ragnaw once laired there. A Small-sized creature can crawl into the hole at half their normal rate of movement. It goes down for roughly 15 feet before it opens into a den 5 feet in diameter. Tiny tunnels occupied by a swarm of rats connect to the den. The rats have passive Perception 10 versus the player characters' Dexterity (Stealth) check to detect them in the den. If the player character is detected, the swarm of rats will erupt out of the tiny holes to attack.

- **Threat**: Swarm of rats

The rats will chase the player characters if they attempt to flee out the hole. When the swarm of rats is reduced to half their hit points, they will retreat back into their tiny tunnels.

The wyrmling has grown too large for the den and has since moved on to a rocky cave in the adjacent hillside.

The Medium-sized cave entrance is 60 feet up the hillside and can be observed with a Wisdom (Perception) check 13 from the ground. If the player characters investigate the hillside, they discover the entrance with a Wisdom (Perception) check 10.

When the player characters begin to climb the hill and are 10 feet up the slope, the dryad will send out a warning using a bird call to alert the wyrmling to danger. An Intelligence (Nature) check 12 reveals that that bird call is not native to the region. The player characters won't be able to determine the source of the bird call since the dryad will use her Tree Stride ability to move 60 feet away from where she made the sound.

One round after the bird call, Ragnaw will fly out of his cave. He will not attack the party. He's not evil and doesn't know the purpose of the party. On his action, he will likely move again to put more distance between him and the player characters. If a player character has taken a reaction to make a ranged attack if something comes out of the cave, they can attack when Ragnaw flies out. Ragnaw will not attack back; instead he will demand to know why the player characters have attacked him without just cause, using the trees as half cover.

If he falls to less than half his hit points, he will stop talking with the player characters and fly away. Only the dryad will interact with the player characters from that point on.

So long as Ragnaw has more than half his hit points, he will parlay with the party. The player characters' actions will determine his attitude. If Ragnaw wasn't attacked, he'll express a cautious interest in the player characters—who they are, and why they are here.

- **Threat**: Green dragon wyrmling

Ragnaw does not want to attack the party under any circumstances, unless he needs to defend the life of the dryad, Valina.

Valina has a Fey-harmed brown bear on the other side of the hill, 320 feet away. If Ragnaw is attacked, Valina will Speak with Beasts to call the brown bear to her. It will take four rounds using its action for the bear to reach Valina. The player characters can make passive Perception checks to discern its approach starting when it is 160 feet away. The brown bear will not attack the player characters unless Valina is being attacked. It stands beside her snarling and huffing at the player characters.

- **Threat**: Brown bear

Valina will also use Tree Stride to get within 30 feet of a player character that can see her and will use Fey Charm on them. Because it is a Wisdom saving throw, she won't choose a cleric, druid, monk, paladin, wizard, or warlock as the target, since they get their proficiency bonus to the saving throw roll. If the target fails the roll, they will see the dryad as a friend to be trusted, heeded, and protected. If the player character isn't charmed, Valina will target another player character until finally one of them falls under her spell. She can have only one player character charmed at a time.

Valina will use that player character to listen to her and Ragnaw's arguments and try to persuade the player characters not to attack.

That is the biggest goal for Ragnaw and Valina. They don't want to fight back. They know that if they are to survive long term and not be targets for adventurers, they need to convince the player characters that Ragnaw is not a typical evil dragon, and hope that news will spread throughout the region.

You can have either Ragnaw or Valina test the player characters with the following questions or assumptions:

- "Why are you attacking us?"

- "What have we done to you or anyone else?"

- "Who sent you?"

- "Just because my scales are green does not mean my heart is rotten. There are other ways to live."

If any of the player characters are half-orcs, dragonborns, or tieflings, ask if it would be alright for others to attack them without cause because of what they are, not who they are.

Valina and Ragnaw are guarded regarding their backstories but will provide some information if asked.

- Valina will confirm she was the punished elf. Even she doesn't remember her original name or who she once was due to her magical punishment.

- Valina is Ragnaw's guardian. He is her ward, and it's her responsibility to raise him and teach him to learn respect for the woods and the creatures that inhabit it. He is a good learner.

- Ragnaw knows he is the offspring of Old Venom, but he will not let the legacy of Old Venom define who he is.

- Ragnaw was only newly hatched when Valina was punished. He does not remember who Valina once was due to her magical punishment.

Valina sees Ragnaw as her ward and Ragnaw sees Valina as his surrogate mother, teaching him lessons about the Moonshadow Wood. They've genuinely bonded through their shared experiences. Each would die to save the other.

If the player characters realize this fight was a mistake and leave without killing Valina, Ragnaw, or the brown bear, they can receive half the amount of XP listed in the rewards for each NPC.

ENDING THE ADVENTURE

RETURNING TO THE WOODCUTTER'S COTTAGE

GM | If the conversation becomes amicable, Ragnaw may offer to lead the player characters west back to the trail. Like most dragons, Ragnaw craves knowledge and will ask the player characters to share tales of their adventures. He is only a wyrmling and is childlike in many ways. Otherwise they will have to make their way back to the main trail on their own. The journey will take almost two days.

Once the player characters reach the main trail, a Wisdom (Survival) check 12 identifies they are north of the cottage.

- **Threat**: Green hag

The disguised green hag, Rotten Polly Ringworm, will react in a couple of different ways depending on how the player characters describe their encounter with Ragnaw.

You spot the rough-hewn cottage off in the woods. It appears the woodcutter has moved onto his next project, fixing the fence, as he hammers a nail into a fresh wooden post. He looks up, sees your approach and waves.

"Greetings! How goes your travels? What news from the wood? Were you successful dealing with the wyrmling?"

GM | If Ragnaw is still alive, Rotten Polly Ringworm will be furious and attack the player characters.

"You fools," the woodcutter snarls. "Do you know what you've done? You allowed that thing, that perversion of the

natural order, to live! You broke our bargain. We had a deal. Now you'll pay the cost of your treachery!"

The form of the woodcutter morphs, revealing a hideous, green-skinned figure dressed in a filthy brown robe laden with pouches and bone trinkets. Long, matted, white hair frames her gaunt, malevolent face.

GM | As Rotten Polly Ringworm hurls insults at the player characters, she is secretly casting *vicious mockery* at one of them, ideally whoever has a low Wisdom saving throw, increasing the chance of success. The green hag morphed into her true form using her bonus action.

On her next turn, Rotten Polly will use her claws to attack the nearest player character. She will continue to attack until she has lost half her hit points. On her next turn after that, she will use her action to cast *invisible passage* and flee, letting the player characters know this isn't the last they'll see of Rotten Polly Ringworm!

GM | If the player characters killed Ragnaw, Rotten Polly Ringworm will mock the player characters for being so easily deceived and doing her dirty work.

"Ha! It is done! The natural order is preserved. There shall be no goodly green dragon roaming Moonshadow Wood now, or ever, thanks to you fools," the woodcutter cackles!

The form of the woodcutter morphs, revealing a hideous, green-skinned figure dressed in a filthy brown robe laden with pouches and bone trinkets. Long, matted, white hair frames her gaunt, malevolent face.

If the player characters were promised the bag of mushrooms, Rotten Polly pulls out the pouch from under her robes and throws it at the nearest one. Regardless of how the player characters react, she will use her action to cast *invisible passage* and flee, letting the player characters know this isn't the last they'll see of Rotten Polly Ringworm. You've now got a recurring villain with which to torment the player characters in future adventures!

REWARDS

Orc: 100 XP each

Ogre: 450 XP

Harpy: 200 XP each

Dryad: 200 XP

Green dragon wyrmling: 450 XP

Swarm of rats: 50 XP

Brown bear: 200 XP

Green hag: 700 XP

Consider giving half XP rewards for the harpies and the green hag if the monsters escaped. ⬡

NEW MAGIC ITEMS

ROD OF THE EANT
Rare (requires attunement by a spellcaster)

The *rod of the eant* has five charges. While holding it, you can use an action to cast one of the following spells: *entangle* (expends one charge) or *locate animals or plants* (expends two charges). The *rod* regains 1d4 +1 charges daily at dawn. If you expend the *rod's* last charge, roll a d20. On a one, the *rod* withers and is destroyed.

A TALE OF TWO GNOMES

**WRITTEN BY SHARANG BISWAS AND HADEEL AL-MASSARI,
ILLUSTRATED BY JONATHAN HILL**

A 5E Adventure for Levels 4–6 | You will need a copy of the 5E core rulebooks to fully utilize this adventure. You should also familiarize yourself with the map and spells used by the foes prior to playing the adventure.

Glossary | PC: Playable Characters | GM: Game Master | DC: Difficulty Class
HP: Hit Points | NPC: Non-Player Character

Adventure Scaling | This adventure is designed to be highly challenging for a group of 3rd- to 5th-level players, though it can easily be challenging for a larger group or a group of upper 2nd-tier characters by giving all the foes maximum hit points and adding +2 to the DC of tests and saves.

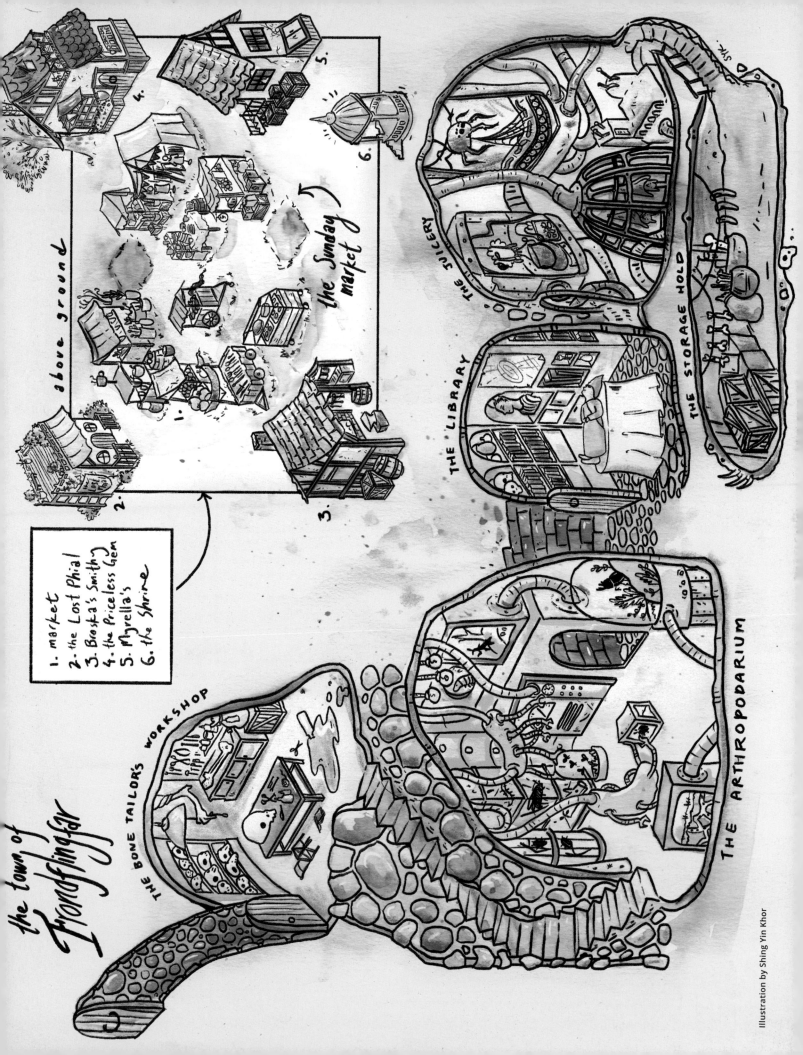

the town of Frondflingar

1. market
2. the Lost Phial
3. Brosfa's Smithy
4. the Priceless Gem
5. Myrella's
6. the Shrine

above ground

the Sunday market

THE BONE TAILOR'S WORKSHOP

THE LIBRARY

THE JUICERY

THE STORAGE HOLD

THE ARTHROPODARIUM

Illustration by Shing Yin Khor

PLOT

A construct approaches the heroes with a cryptic warning that its inventor is in danger. The heroes venture into the inventor's burrow and find their way to him (dealing with his zany experiments and traps along the way) only to discover his rival instead, who makes a compelling argument against the very gnome they were trying to rescue.

BACKGROUND

Master Frazie is a brilliant inventor. There's no question about that. He's also friendly, helpful...qualities that might make him a real pillar of the community. Except that his crafting interests are a little...unusual. The gnome's research and practice focus on fusing the mechanical and the organic, creating clockwork and steam-powered devices out of alchemically treated materials such as horn, skin, shell, and even bone. His proclivity for that last ingredient has earned him the title of "Bone Tailor," and not always in a complimentary fashion. Yes, his Augmented Limb Implant *might* enhance a gnome's strength three-fold, but would *you* want a gnoll-femur actuator implanted in your arm? In particular, his skeletal automatons are handy. But many worry they're not too many steps away from necromancy.

This type of controversial research has earned Master Frazie plenty of detractors, and none more vocal than Jettepo. Jettepo is a tinkerer of a more traditional bent. If brass and bronze were good enough for gnomes before, he believes they should be good enough for everyone! What Frazie does is obviously unethical and bordering on blasphemy (never mind that his Flexible Fascia Extensor beat Jettepo's Sonorous Tube at the Tinkerer Tournament last year, Jettepo would say.)

Early this morning, Jettepo stomped over to Master Frazie's burrow, with the goal of an angry confrontation. Jettepo suspected that the Bone Tailor has been stealing corpses in an attempt to turn them into a new kind of automaton, and he was right. Of course, Master Frazie is not known for his stellar social skills, and Jettepo is never one to deescalate a conflict.

The two got into a heated quarrel in Master Frazie's workshop, which escalated into a bout of clumsy fisticuffs. One of Master Frazie's automatons activated and set itself to emergency mode. It fled the burrow, hoping to find help for Master Frazie.

Locked in a fight, the two made their way through the burrow. As Jettepo was slowed down in the Arthropodarium, the Bone Tailor hid in the library with a heavy candlestick, and smashed it against his rival's skull as he entered. He then dragged the comatose body downstairs and dumped it into his Storage Hold to deal with later. The stress of the whole situation had been a little too much for the gnome, so he buried himself in feverish work.

STARTING THE ADVENTURE

GM | The gnome town of Frondflingfar is famous in the area for its Sunday Market and its high concentration of engineers and tinkerers. Adventurers might stop by on business with an inventor, en route to another location, or even as a spot to rest and recuperate after an adventure.

Heroes will arrive in Frondflingfar on or just before Sunday, with booths and stalls filling most of the town, and crowds of people haggling, chatting, and bustling about (or occasionally screaming, as a badly-made prototype explodes). Allow the heroes to explore the town and browse the stalls for a little while before introducing "The Lost Construct" plot hook.

THE TOWN OF FRONDFLINGFAR

GM | Frondflingfar is a small town of about 1,500 residents, consisting mainly of gnome burrows with a handful of public buildings and non-gnome houses scattered here and there. Due to this, much of the town appears to be open space or public gardens. These gardens are, in fact, tended by gnome families who make their homes in burrows beneath them, taking great pride in their individual gardens. The few buildings stick out strangely among the parks, with no real roads connecting anything.

THE TOWN'S ABOVEGROUND AMENITIES INCLUDE:

The Lost Phial: A shop that sells herbal teas, tinctures, medicines, and occasionally a magic potion or two. It is run by Lorla, a middle-aged gnome.

Broska's Smithy: The deaf dwarf Broska is known for her elaborate fern-like motifs in the arms and armor she crafts. No one knows how she lost her hearing.

The Priceless Gem: An inn run by Nathar, a young Brass Dragonborn, and his lover Amit, a spectacularly handsome human whose disdain for wearing shirts has not gone unnoticed.

Myrella's: A retired tinkerer and professor, the elderly human Myrella spends her days renting out space, selling parts, and helping with odd jobs.

The Shrine: A small aboveground shrine to a local deity or a gnome deity (GM's choice). Sister Whipfallow is a gnome nun who can provide a little healing. She thinks deeply about ethics, morality, and is a sounding board for Master Frazie's ethical dilemmas (he often poses "hypothetical" questions about ethics).

The Sunday Market: Every Sunday is Market Day, which attracts many visitors from out of town. Of particular interest are the various engineering and tinkering stalls that set up in the center of town. The Market is a chaotic collection of stalls, tents, and booths set up following a frazzled, messy sort of logic that outsiders can only hope to one day comprehend. Heroes that browse might find some of the following wares:

- A metal bracelet with a hidden pocket that can hold a slim roll of paper - 20 gp

- A silver ring that doubles as a loud, shrill whistle - 25 gp

- The prototype of a pair of boots made of various leather panels that can be repositioned to change the boots' size - 50 gp

- Earrings that deliver a mild, pleasant electric shock when tugged the right way - 200 gp

- A clockwork, flapping construct that can apparently be used to deliver letters. It can only travel 500 feet before it runs out of power - 30 gp

While exploring the town and market, feel free to introduce some of the following sights and sounds:

- A middle-aged and a youthful gnome playing chess, bickering about whether or not the Tailor's Hyper-Sensitive Tongue Replacement is "yucky."

- An old sheet torn from a pamphlet declaring Master Frazie's Flexible Fascia Extensor as the winner of the Tinkerer Tournament. A large "X" has been penciled onto his name.

- An elderly gnome saying kind things to a young human boy who's carrying her shopping.

- A pair of teenage elven boys stealing a surreptitious kiss behind a booth selling haberdashery.

- A stray cat with one eye that had been replaced with a dark stone. This is actually a product of Master Frazie's work. The stone eyeball allows the cat to see more colors, but it cannot move on its own.

RUMORS AROUND TOWN

GM | If the heroes decide to chat with any of the townsfolk, take the opportunity to sprinkle in some of the following rumors and information as you see fit:

- Some people have claimed that graverobbers have been stealing bodies and then carefully cleaning up and placing fresh dirt back in the grave. Reports are unconfirmed because no one wants to exhume the graves.

- Everyone's excited about the Tinkerer Tournament in the coming months! Inventors all over town are both hard at work and in a state of jealous paranoia (all in good fun, of course...right...?)

- Jettepo, a local inventor, recently asked Sister Whipfallow if he could address the town on the topic of the Undead during one of her sermons. His lack of deep knowledge, combined with the gnome townspeople's curious, probing questions resulted in much embarrassment for him.

- Master Frazie, another local inventor who many consider somewhat eccentric, has been visiting Lorla's shop a great deal recently. She's tight-lipped about what he's been buying.

THE LOST CONSTRUCT

While most of the town is full of stalls, tents, and booths, two conspicuously empty patches yawn vacantly in the middle of a row of stalls. The owner of a nearby pie stall informs you

TINK

KLINK

KLANK

that the two belong to Master Frazie, "The Bone Tailor," and Jettepo, two Master Tinkerers that live in town.

"It is unusual for them to miss a chance to show off their latest inventions on Market Day!" she says.

GM | A five-silver-piece purchase from the pie vendor, or a Charisma (Persuasion) DC 10 check will encourage them to reveal that the two tinkerers are rivals, and that some folks find Master Frazie's work to be a touch ghoulish.

Searching the empty area with a successful Intelligence (Investigation) DC 10 check reveals a crumpled slip of paper partially buried in the dirt. On it is a hasty sketch of an eyeball with strange lines emanating from it (anyone proficient with Tinkerer's Tools will recognize these as wires), a block of exotic calculations in an unfamiliar, difficult-to-decipher shorthand, and the following message in very precise writing, complete with italics:

"Animal models incompatible. Must try gnome sample. Unethical to use live gnomes (confirm with Sister Whipfallow?) Cemetery? Will that disturb neighbors? Disrespect the dead? Re-read *Philistinus et al*."

It is near these gaps in the rows of stalls where a glint of light catches your eyes. What appears to be a skeletal bird, about a foot in height, is aimlessly wandering the streets. Closer inspection reveals that it's actually an automaton of some sort: gears, pistons, and springs whir under the skeleton of a bird and tiny sparks glimmer under the eye sockets.

GM | A Wisdom (Perception) DC 10 check reveals that it is a little roughed up, with chipped bone, a slightly bent beak, and dental gears. An Intelligence (Arcana or Religion) DC 15 check might allow a player to glean that the construct is not powered by necromantic magic. An Intelligence (Nature or Medicine) DC 12 check reveals that the bones are, indeed, real. A critical success on the skill check further reveals that the bones come from multiple individuals of a single

species of local bird, a Muddy Lark (known for building particularly malodorous nests).

If undisturbed by the heroes, the automaton aimlessly bumps into one of them, and speaks in a voice punctuated by clicks and clangs.

"Alarm protocol activated! Master requires aid! Alarm protocol activated! Master requires aid!"

The automaton then clearly attempts to lead the party out of the Market and towards Master Frazie's burrow. If the party refuses to follow, it flaps about noisily and follows them, peppering silences with the same alarm phrase again and again.

The commotion might attract the attention of nearby locals, many of whom are unwilling to deal with The Bone Tailor's macabre constructs. However, they will quickly volunteer the information that the automaton clearly belongs to Master Frazie, and even provide directions to his burrow at the edge of town.

Further questions might reveal Master Frazie as a "generally kind sort of fellow," but with some odd notions of how to behave in society. Some find his inventions to be ingenious, but many are a little perturbed by them. A few gnomes will gingerly express worry about his wellbeing if what the automaton says is true and will encourage the heroes to go offer help.

THE BONE TAILOR'S WORKSHOP

GM | The entrance to Master Frazie's burrow is obstructed by a half-closed brass door with sharp edges. An Wisdom (Perception) DC 15 check allows a hero to spot a tiny mechanism that is supposed to allow the door to slide open, now clearly malfunctioning. Small heroes can squeeze through the gap in the door without too much trouble, but anyone of Medium size or larger will need to succeed on a Dexterity DC 15 check to avoid taking 3 (1d6) slashing damage. Alternatively, a hero can attempt to fiddle with the mechanism using Tinkerer's Tools (or Thieves' Tools with disadvantage) and making an Intelligence (Sleight of Hand) DC 20 check, causing the door to fully slide open. A muscular hero can instead attempt to bash the door open with a Strength DC 25 check. As a final resort, breaking down the door is an option. It has an AC of 18, and 15 hp.

The door opens into an inclined tunnel with smooth, rocky sides. There is no source of light except for the entrance. The tunnel slopes down towards a small, round workshop bored into the earth.

The gears, sheets of metal, and drawers full of different sized screws seem ordinary enough. But a moment's glance tells you that this workshop does not belong to an ordinary tinkerer.

A mummified human arm dangles from the ceiling, fingers clutching a lamp with a pull chain that ignites the wick within. Skulls of various animals, sorted by size and color, are arranged on the walls each with detailed drawings and calculations inked onto them. A polished wooden shelf is attached to a wall by a strange ropey material (GM: An Intelligence (Medicine) DC 15 check reveals them to be dried intestine) *and is covered with dozens of precisely perforated beetle wings. The workshop is filled with creature parts and tools to manipulate them, displayed unabashedly alongside the more mundane tinkerer's equipment.*

Adding to the strangeness of the workshop are the evident signs of a struggle. Tools and components, once neatly tucked, hung or stacked away, are chaotically strewn about. Oil and other viscous liquids form puddles on the floor, and an entire set of shelves has been knocked onto its side, spilling its contents of shells, antlers, and butterfly wings onto the floor.

GM | A small, sparsely furnished sleeping chamber adjoins the workshop, with a simple bed, nightstand, and cupboard full of neatly folded work clothes. The room is tidy. An en suite lavatory is clean and well-maintained, with a small potted mushroom placed on the sink. A Wisdom (Insight) DC 12 check tells a hero that Master Frazie clearly does not spend a lot of time in this room.

Two sets of oily shoe prints, both sets small enough to belong to a gnome or halfling, retreat from the workshop towards an open wooden door, down a set of stairs and into darkness. A faint light can be perceived at the bottom.

As soon as the party enters the workshop, the automaton will begin to try and lead them down these stairs, occasionally repeating, "Master requires aid!" until the heroes follow it into the darkness.

Searching the room will require an Intelligence (Investigation) DC 15 check. A success will reveal *The Bone Tailor's Tools* (see the "New Magic Items" section), a tiny iron key, and a small, battered, leather-bound book with a strange, coppery smell about it and text handwritten in a red-brown ink. Sewn into the cover is a title: *Reflections on the Inverse of Living Condition*. The book's internal headings and graphic illustrations, all hand-sketched, clearly mark it as a necromantic text. There is no author listed. A wizard or anyone succeeding on an Intelligence (Arcana) DC 15 check knows that the work is a beginner's text, more theoretical than practical in nature; however, the book appears to be a first edition volume, and might be valuable to certain people.

A critical success in the search will also reveal that two gnome-sized people probably scuffled in this room. A failure by five or more on the ability check means a hero trips on a fallen object, and bashes into a shelf, taking 2 (1d4) bludgeoning damage. If the hero is carrying a torch, candle, or lamp, a critical failure might ignite a puddle of oil, dealing an additional 3 (1d6) fire damage, and resulting in a small fire that the party needs to put out.

The Arthropodarium

The staircase is well cut, with smooth walls similar to the entrance tunnel. As you descend, the dozens of chittering, chirping, hissing, and rustling noises begin to assert themselves. When you reach a large chamber dimly lit by a few sputtering lamps dangling from a chandelier, the insectoid noises are almost overpowering.

The room is filled with boxes and cases of various sizes and shapes, each containing a colony of many-limbed, crawling critters of some sort. Mud-colored butterflies flutter inside fine mesh cages; spiders the size of a gnome palm armed with oversized mandibles crawl in glass cases; a swarm of scorpions with bioluminescent legs clack their tails against glass walls; an earthen termite mound shivers inside a wood and glass box; a transparent bucket seethes with angry, shocking-pink maggots. If you can imagine a creepy bug of some sort, it is likely present in this room.

GM | The ceiling of the room is also fitted with a set of rails, from which thick, jointed copper cables descend to a trio of insectoid servitor-automatons. Each is about the size of a large dog, possesses six arms, and appears to be made of hundreds of pieces of shiny insect exoskeleton, fitted together into a ghoulish mosaic. The servitor-automatons are preoccupied with picking up various tools and small containers, and arranging them around the room, before returning to the same objects and placing them elsewhere. They make rhythmic tick-tock noises as they move, and cause the cables that attach them to the roof to undulate almost hypnotically. They do not stray from this task. On one wall of the room is what appears to be a control panel made of beaten bronze, also attached to the ceiling with cabling, and covered with buttons and knobs made of differently colored coral. At the far end of the room is a door.

Observing the servitors for a while makes it quite clear that they do not deviate from the routine. An Intelligence (Insight) DC 10 check (made with advantage by anyone proficient with Tinkerer's Tools) will tip the player characters off to the fact that they are controlled using the panel, and are unlikely to even notice the heroes should they walk in.

As the heroes enter this room, the bird-construct suddenly changes its message. "Warning. Servitor construct Malfunction. Beware Repellent Atomization." It says this three times before trying to draw the party towards the door.

A Wisdom (Perception) DC 15 check allows the heroes to notice some broken glass on the floor. A giant wasp and a swarm of insects (wasps) had escaped when Master Frazie and Jettepo scuffled and fumbled through this room, and are currently flying near the ceiling, hidden in shadow. Unless their buzzing is noticed by a Wisdom (Perception) DC 15 check, they will swoop down onto the heroes as they step into the center of the room and attack with a surprise round.

A NUMBER OF INTERESTING THINGS CAN HAPPEN DURING COMBAT:

- At the start of every round, randomly select a hero and roll 1d6 on the hero's turn. On a one, a servitor will attempt to move past them. Failing on a Dexterity save DC 12 tangles the hero in the servitor's cabling. Unless a hero spends their action making a Strength (Athletics) DC 10 check, they count as having the Restrained condition, and will take 2 (1d4) bludgeoning damage at the end of their turn, until they are free of the cables.

- On a critical miss with an attack, the GM can determine that a servitor was hit instead. If so, the servitor explodes, releasing a noxious spray of sickly sweet Insect Repellent. Any hero standing within 10 feet of it takes 4 (1d8) poison damage, while the giant wasp or the swarm will take 7 (2d6) acid damage. If heroes want to hit the servitors directly, treat them as objects with an AC of 13 and 6 hp. Even a single point of damage, however, can cause one to explode.

- On the first missed attack of any round, roll a 1d4. On a one, a glass terrarium is hit, releasing the bugs within. Inflict 2 (1d4) piercing damage to the attacker from the bites and stings of the bugs as they escape.

- A hero can attempt to fiddle with the control panel. A quick, close glance reveals that it's a little damaged and tinkering with it may lead to unexpected consequences. Additionally, the button array was designed by Master Frazie and was made to be used only by him. So, attempting to figure out the controls are almost impossible. If a hero tries to press buttons randomly, roll a 1d4:

  1. The servitors stop moving (meaning heroes no longer get caught in the cables) or start up again.

  2. All three servitors explode simultaneously. See above for effects.

  3. The servitors each release a puff of sweet-smelling Insect Repellent. For the rest of combat, both the giant wasp and the swarm make all attacks at a disadvantage.

  4. The panel explodes, dealing 3 (1d6) fire damage and 3 (1d6) piercing damage to anyone next to it.

- **Loot:** An Intelligence (Investigation) DC 15 check in the room unearths a scroll of *Speak with Animals*, and a finely carved porcelain jug filled with rotting ground meat worth 10 gp (once emptied).

The door at the far end of the room is heavy, unlocked, and swings shut on its own accord when opened.

The Library

Past the Arthropodarium, you find yourselves in a spacious library. Well-built wood and ivory shelves line the walls,

filled with various manuals and texts. Each shelf is labeled with a topic on a white card in Master Frazie's precise handwriting, and is alphabetically sorted by author.

The walls of the library are adorned with hand-drawn blueprints and technical diagrams for all sorts of devices. A bust of a distinguished-looking gnome wearing a monocle with its hair in a tight bun sits on one of the bookshelves. It's fashioned from what appears to be a yellow-brown clay.

In the center of the room sits a round table covered with a white cloth. A gnome in a dressing gown lies on it, completely still.

GM | An Intelligence (Medicine) DC 15 check (made with advantage by gnome heroes) reveals the bust to be made of gnome earwax. Additionally, any gnome will recognize that bust to be one of Pilliana Micklemuffin, a renowned natural philosopher, famous for donating all of her wealth to support homeless and orphaned gnomes and halflings in big cities.

Most of the books on the shelves are on the topics of engineering, architecture, natural lore, and medicine. Taking a few moments to browse the shelves reveals that many of the titles are concerned with ethics, theology (emphasizing deities of nature and deities of law and justice), and a few biographies of famous gnome tinkerers.

At first, the gnome in the middle of the room might appear asleep. Barring further probing, a Wisdom (Perception) DC 10 check tells the heroes that the gnome isn't breathing. A Wisdom (Medicine) DC 12 check reveals that the gnome has no pulse and is clearly dead but is somehow preserved. Casting *detect magic* will tell the players that the preservation is alchemical in nature, and not caused by a spell such as *gentle repose*. If the heroes loosen the dressing gown, they will see that large portions of the body have been replaced by clockwork. However, instead of metal, the mechanisms are made of wood, ivory, and what looks to be chitinous giant wasp shell (heroes will instantly recognize this material from the Arthropodarium).

The library has no visible exit apart from the door through which the party just entered. The bird-automaton will begin to run around the room in circles, occasionally emoting loudly with a cry of "Master Requires Aid!"

If the party wishes to investigate the room, have each hero make an Intelligence (Investigation) DC 10 check. Reveal the following based on the number of successes, counting any roll of 15 or higher as two successes. If the heroes inform you that they are investigating the parts of the library where the features below are found, grant them Advantage on the roll.

- **Zero successes:** Simply attempting to investigate the room allows them to notice a semi-circular skid mark on the floor, as though one of the shelves can swing outwards. They also notice that there are four prominent gaps in the books on the shelves, and exactly four books piled onto a little side table near one wall.

- **At least one success:** A dented candlestick has rolled under the table. It is heavy and has a trace of fresh blood on it. The blood is Jettepo's.

- **At least two successes:** Of the drawings on the walls, the heroes recognize two: the bird automaton that they've been following, and the servitor-automatons from the Arthropodarium. Additionally, two illustrations stand out: a detailed drawing of an enlarged cockroach labeled "Hissing Cockroach," and a watercolor of a slimy puddle labelled "Gray Ooze."

- **At least three successes:** Hidden behind a set of false books is a locked iron safe. Opening it requires either the iron key from Master Frazie's workshop, or a Dexterity (Sleight of Hand) DC 15 check. A failure by 8 or more results in the release of an envenomed fang which deals 3 (1d6) poison damage and adds one level of exhaustion that lasts until the next short or long rest. Inside the safe lie a vial of *oil of preservation* and a sheaf of technical papers titled *Tournament Entry #17: "The Cadavatron": A Hybrid Automaton Utilizing a Flesh-Chassis to House Nervous Control Components to Actuate Bioclockwork Mechanisms*.

- **At least four successes:** Every so often, a few, seemingly random books on different shelves seem to shiver ever so slightly. A *detect magic* spell reveals a strong aura of Transmutation magic on those books. Reading

or otherwise touching those books does nothing special, except that an occasional shiver might again be felt.

- **At least five successes:** There are a large number of volumes on necromancy present, but most are theoretical treatises, with little practical instruction. Many are discussions on the ethics of that particular branch of magic.

One of the bookshelves is actually a secret door that swings outwards. The four gaps in the bookshelves are cunningly concealed pressure-plates that require a specific weight to be placed on them in order to open the door. The gaps are in the following shelves:

- III: Statics, Dynamics, & Mechanics
- VI: Natural History References
- X: Philosophy (General)
- XI: Philosophy (Ethics)

The simplest way to open the door is to place the four books that are on the side table into the gaps in their own shelves in a specific order, based on the titles of the works spelling out the word OPEN.

The books, the sections they belong in, and the order they must be placed are as follows:

1. **O**n Weights and Counterweights: A Balanced Perspective (Shelf III)

2. **P**hilistinus' Discourses on the Morality of Experimentation on the Living Body (Shelf XI)

3. **E**nchoridia's Precise Illustrations of a Diverse Set of Insects (Shelf VI)

4. **N**ew Frontiers of Philosophy: Unifying the Divine and the Profane (Shelf X)

If the heroes are struggling, allow them a Wisdom or Intelligence (Insight) DC 10 check to realize that the titles of the books are significant, and that gnome humor often involves hiding messages within words. You can also offer a hint about which shelves the books belong to. Rolling a 15 or higher alerts them that the first words are important, and could they spell out something else? Rolling a 20 should unravel the entire puzzle for them.

If the heroes put the books into the shelves in the wrong order (anything other than O -> P -> E -> N) or on the

wrong shelves, the books that previously seemed to shiver animate and attack (one book per hero).

Alternatively, a hero with Tinkerer's Tools can attempt to fiddle with the secret bookshelf's mechanism with a DC 20 Dexterity (Sleight of Hand) check (Thieves' Tools also allow a check, but at a disadvantage). Failure by 5 or more activates the animated books. Finally, the party can simply attempt to break down the shelf (AC: 15 hp: 4), though after the first blow, the books immediately animate.

As the party slides the last book into place, there's a low groan and the bookcase slowly slides open, uncovering a low, gnome-sized tunnel that slopes downwards. The bird automaton grows agitated and excited, and rushes through the tunnel.

Any small member of the party can walk through the tunnel with no difficulties. Larger party members will need to squeeze through the opening and crawl on all fours.

THE JUICERY

The walls of this tunnel are slick, moist, and warmer than you would expect. Beads of condensation drip onto your lips. They taste salty.

The enormous cavern you emerge in burps, gurgles, and sloshes with activity. It's probably one of the most bizarre, chaotic scenes you've ever witnessed. Pipes and tubes festoon the room, some copper, some made of a fleshy, translucent material. The pipes connect pods of activity, each more surreal than the next. Here, a sheep is suspended over a simmering cauldron, a mechanical piston gently milking her udders, the piston itself powered by a wheel inside which a colony of beetles continuously scuttles. There, an enormous spider swings back and forth on a leather strap like a pendulum, periodically depositing strands of webbing on a living conveyor belt of caterpillars. Further on, a disk covered in guano hums gently in rotation, shedding measured amounts into the waiting mouths of tubes below, a cluster of bats snoozing in a cage above. And in the middle of it all on a raised platform, a frenzied, little gnome in a leather apron feverishly tinkers with the complex system surrounding it.

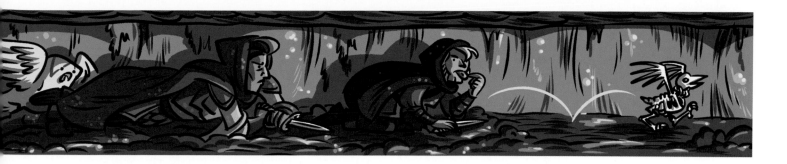

GM | The gnome is none other than Master Frazie, the Bone Tailor (see stat blocks). As soon as the heroes enter, he looks up, eyes teary and ablaze with mania, and bawls, "No! No one else will harm my work!" He then quickly activates a number of mechanisms, curls into a ball, and begins to cry.

At this point, the bird automaton collapses out of exhaustion (and loss of clockwork) but continues to squeal its message from time to time. Heroes can carry it but will need to use one hand to do so. You may hint that the gnome tinkerer might take comfort in seeing it returned.

Master Frazie has activated traps and mechanisms in the Juicery, which will continue to plague the players until he is drawn out of his funk, allowing him to switch off the remaining devices. He is currently in an almost catatonic state, sobbing and consumed by emotion. Simply calling out to him from afar will have little effect. Roll initiative and use that to determine the order in which the heroes attempt to approach Master Frazie. Keep track of the distance they have moved. They will have to reach him while overcoming the obstacles in their way, as well as contend with the mechanisms the Bone Tailor has activated.

Master Frazie is on a platform 60 feet away from the entrance. The area between the platform and the entrance is a maze of pipes, devices, and pods of activity, and is considered difficult terrain. The platform is 10 feet tall, with a retracted rope ladder next to Master Frazie. The platform is made of a rough rock that can be scaled with a Strength (Athletics) DC 10 check.

Each time a hero moves towards Master Frazie, choose one of the obstacles that they must get past from below (the precise route they take can be generalized). They can also go around the obstacle, but that requires another 15 feet of movement in difficult terrain that doesn't add to progress made towards reaching the platform.

- A translucent pane of a glassy material is in their way, along the surface of which light pink liquid flows. Ask the hero to describe how they easily get past this obstacle, with minimal effort.

- A swarm of bees coalescing around an artificial hive, from which honey dribbles down. Walking through the swarm inflicts 2 (1d4) piercing damage (no check or save).

- A puddle of spilled, milky liquid with a slick, rainbow sheen. Stepping into it causes a hero to slip, fall prone, and end their turn unless they succeed on a Dexterity save. This effect can only happen once per hero in this puddle.

- A vertical, slowly turning wheel about 6 feet tall, attached to a snarl of gears and blades that are crushing a vat of fruit into pulp. A hero can attempt to jump through the spokes with a Strength (Athletics) DC 12 check. Failure means the hero is violently pushed into the vat and ends their turn. The hero must make a Strength (Athletics) DC 15 check on their next turn to climb out of the vat (and consuming 10 feet of movement) or fall back in and take 3 (1d6) bludgeoning damage from the wheel.

- A set of vents in the ground from which emerges a

silvery vapor. The gas is cloying and soporific and will add a level of exhaustion to anyone whose eyes, ears, nose, or mouth makes contact with it. If a hero runs through it with eyes and mouth squeezed shut, fabric shielding their nose, and hands clamped around the ears, they can ignore this effect, but will have a 50% chance of running in the wrong direction.

- A trio of cauldrons connected with U-shaped pipes, each holding a bubbling liquid of a different color, lies in the hero's way. Ask them how they smoothly get past this obstacle.

- A plague of toads hopping between a set of ivory poles of different heights, each with a button on top. The toads are poisonous to the touch, and a hero must make a Dexterity save DC 12 or gain the Poisoned condition for the next 15 minutes.

As a consequence of Master Frazie's mechanisms, one of the following events occur at initiative 20 of each round, until the gnome is mollified:

- **Round 1:** The walls of a small maze near one hero spring apart and a swarm of rats pours out. The swarm follows that hero across the room, placing itself in initiative right after the hero.

- **Round 2:** A hose near a hero detaches itself and begins to writhe, spraying a random hero each turn with boiling digestive juices on initiative count 19, dealing 5 (1d6 + 2) acid damage. Treat the pipe as an object with AC 14 and 12 hp.

- **Round 3:** A jar full of cockroaches near a hero begins to hiss discordantly in unison, producing a strange noise whose frequencies disrupt any speech attempted by the heroes. Until the cockroaches are stopped or the jar is broken, the heroes cannot speak to anyone, and all spells with verbal components have a 50% chance of fizzling out.

- **Round 4:** A gray ooze splashes onto a hero from some pipe overhead and immediately activates. It will blindly

follow that hero through the Juicery. Master Frazie has a special elixir to dissolve it once he's calmed.

Once a hero reaches the Bone Tailor, a Wisdom (Insight) DC 15 check reveals that the gnome is emotionally over-whelmed by something other than the heroes, and that he was lashing out unthinkingly. A hero needs to succeed on a Charisma (Persuasion) DC 17 to calm the gnome (attempt-ing to do so is an action, and can be repeated), whereupon he will then turn off his devices and constructs, calm the beasts using a jingly device at his belt, and neutralize the Gray Ooze with an alchemical concoction of his own devising. If the bird automaton is brought to Master Frazie, subsequent Charisma checks are made with advantage.

Master Frazie is very distraught and apologizes for the whole "misunderstanding." He explains that his rival Jettepo entered his burrow and started destroying his work. Master Frazie says that he had to subdue Jettepo, and he's kept the uncon-scious body in the Storage Hold. A Wisdom (Insight) DC 10 check confirms that he's telling the truth (colored by his own perspective, of course). He admits he got a "little hotheaded" and asks the heroes to help him wake his rival in the Storage Hold. They came all the way here to help, after all? He will hand them a reward from his storage for all their trouble.

He also hands the heroes a vial of *potion of healing* as recom-pense for setting his mechanisms and creatures on them.

A wide trapdoor in the stone platform leads to the Storage Hold. Master Frazie can provide a light, if the party needs it.

THE STORAGE HOLD

A metal ladder set into a long shaft leads down to the Storage Hold, a dark cavern devoid of furniture but piled with all sorts of junk. As you might have come to expect in Master Frazie's burrow, the junk includes machine parts of glass and metal, but also large bones, dried animal hides, ropes of teeth strung together, and even what appears to be a set of long, dried tongues tied together.

GM | Master Frazie immediately begins muttering to himself and searching through his piles of junk. The party may wish to help locate Jettepo's unconscious body. Almost immediately though, a clamor of noise erupts from the other end of the room.

Out of a huge mound of braided human hair and metal tubing, Jettepo arises, seated on the back of an enormous construct. Jettepo looks the worse for wear: his clothes are torn, dried blood cakes the side of his face, and a lump the size of a small egg sits on his scalp, a visual reminder of where Master Frazie hit him. His eyes are mad with fury.

GM | (See stat blocks for a full description of Jettepo).

However, it's his mount that really draws your eye. Jepetto rides a bizarre amalgamation of discarded and damaged machine parts, tools, and junk, crudely lashed together.

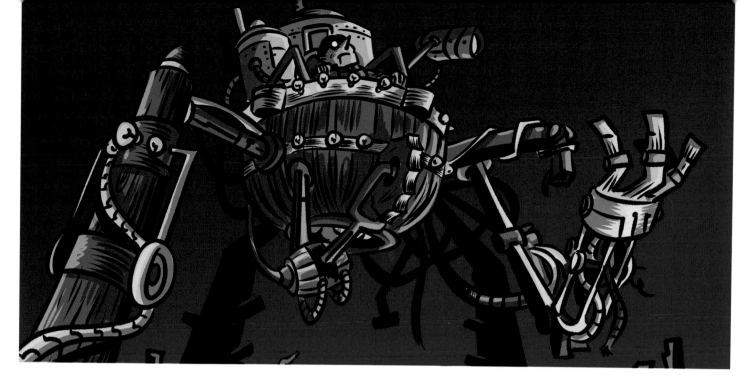

Blue lights glow all over its frame, and unlike what you've seen in Master Frazie's burrow, there is a distinct lack of bone, chitin, or other organic material. The whole thing lurches with a shambling gait, grinding and groaning along. Master Frazie's rival has been busy, it seems.

"SEE, FRAZIE?" the gnome shrieks hoarsely. "THIS IS WHAT REAL GNOME-CRAFT LOOKS LIKE! NOT LIKE YOUR ABOMINATIONS! I'LL TEACH YOU WHAT HAPPENS WHEN YOU MESS WITH A TRUE GNOME!"

GM | Jettepo and the jury-rigged construct attack Master Frazie. He will pointedly ignore the heroes unless they get in his way.

A Wisdom (Perception) DC 10 check tells the party that Jettepo isn't secured to his creation in any way. An Intelligence (Insight) DC 15 check allows the players to realize that bludgeoning damage will be extra effective at knocking parts off the construct.

If Jettepo is thrown off the construct, it continues to fight, but with disadvantage. Jettepo will burst into tears and cower in a corner.

A TALE OF TWO GNOMES

TURNING IN FRAZIE'S RIVAL

GM | Once the construct is defeated, the party can question Jettepo. Jettepo will reveal that Master Frazie knocked him out with a candlestick and threw him into the Storage Hold "to rot, for all I care!"

He will also readily reveal that he came in over to berate Master Frazie for his grave robbing and "abominable" constructs that make use of skeletons and animal parts. He insists that Master Frazie is no true gnome and his

unethical, disgusting research must stop.

Master Frazie will counter the claim by saying that everything is perfectly legal and ethical, according to the extensive bioethics research he's been doing. He believes that Gnomedom needs to progress forward and embrace radical, new methods of tinkering and engineering. And really, do dead animals and gnomes need their bodies anymore?

The heroes will have to decide what to do. It's unclear who started the fight, and the heroes will have to make a decision: is Master Frazie right about gnome progress and science, or does his grave robbing render his arguments moot? Is grave robbing even a serious enough crime? Or was Jeteppo right in confronting the Bone Tailor? Did he go too far? Should either (or both) of them be sent to the Town Watch? Heroes can pick a side but reconciling the two rivals will be all but impossible.

If the heroes side with Master Frazie, he rewards them with a pair of *goggles of night*. If the heroes side with Jettepo, he gives them a small bag containing *dust of dryness*. If they send both to prison, they are rewarded with two Tiger's Eye gems worth 10 gp each.

REWARDS

In addition to the XP from any monsters defeated, award the party the following XP:

- 25 bonus XP per player if both gnomes survived

- 100 bonus XP per player if the party solved the library puzzle

- 25 discretionary XP to any heroes who did something especially clever, daring, or interesting during the adventure ⬡

MONSTROSITY CONSTRUCT

Large Construct, unaligned

Armor Class 8
Hit Points 85 (9d10 + 36)
Speed 30 ft.

STR	DEX	CON	INT	WIS	CHA
19 (+4)	6 (-2)	18 (+4)	1 (–5)	5 (–3)	1 (–5)

Saving Throws Dex +0

Damage Immunities poison, psychic

Damage Vulnerabilities bludgeoning

Condition Immunities exhaustion, blinded, charmed, deafened, frightened, paralyzed, petrified, poisoned

Senses blindsense 60 ft. (blind beyond this point), passive Perception 7

Languages -

Challenge 2 (450 XP)

Magic Resistance. The Automaton has advantage on saving throws against spells and other magical effects.

ACTIONS

Multiattack. The Monstrosity Construct makes two bash attacks or one bash attack and one Acid Spew Breath Weapon Attack.

Bash. *Melee Weapon Attack:* +6 to hit, reach 5 ft., one target. *Hit:* 13 (2d8 + 4) bludgeoning damage.

Acid Spew Breath Weapon (Recharge 5-6). *Ranged Attack:* +6 to hit, range 100 ft., one target. *Hit:* 13 (3d8) acid damage. Acid jettisons out from the mouth of one of the corpses.

NEW MAGIC ITEMS

THE BONE TAILOR'S TOOLS

Wondrous Item, Uncommon

Master Frazie's research and engineering of both the mechanical and the organic demands a specialized set of tools. In addition to (very well crafted) pliers, wrenches, screwdrivers, and sundry that you might expect in an ordinary set of Tinkerer's Tools, this set includes some medical equipment such as a bone saw, needle and thread, and scalpel, as well some rather exotic looking tools whose use is probably best left to the imagination.

This set of tools counts as both a set of Tinkerer's Tools and a Healer's Kit. When the 10 uses of the Healer's Kit are used up, a hero can replenish the kit at half the cost of a regular Healer's Kit. While using these tools, proficiency in one counts as proficiency in the other, and all ability checks involving those skills are made with advantage.

OIL OF PRESERVATION

Potion, Uncommon

This cloudy, off-white *oil* smells pungent and bitter. Applying it to a corpse is the equivalent of casting the *gentle repose* spell on it, except that the effects last for one week.

Applying it onto a living creature grants it resistance to acid and poison damage for one hour, but the creature also suffers disadvantage on all Constitution checks and saves for the same duration.

NPCS IN THE CORE BOOKS

- Giant Wasp
- Swarm of Insects (wasps)
- Swarm of Rats
- Gray Ooze

ITEMS IN THE CORE BOOKS

- *Potion of Healing*
- *Goggles of Night*
- *Dust of Dryness*

ALONE TIME

WRITTEN BY KAT KRUGER, ILLUSTRATED BY AMELIA ALLORE

A 5E Adventure for Levels 4–6 | You will need a copy of the 5E core rulebooks to fully utilize this adventure. You should also familiarize yourself with the map and spells used by the foes prior to playing the adventure.

Glossary | PC: Playable Characters | GM: Game Master | DC: Difficulty Class
HP: Hit Points | NPC: Non-Player Character

Adventure Scaling | This adventure is designed to be highly challenging for a group of 3rd- to 5th-level players, though it can easily be challenging for a larger group or a group of upper 2nd-tier characters by giving all the foes maximum hit points and adding +2 to the DC of tests and saves.

Illustration by Kyle Latino

the ONION CAVES

PLOT

The adventuring party accepts a quest from an old, female dwarf named Hilda Twilightforge, who explains that her clan was run out of the Onion Caves by an ettin named "One-Armed" Tommass. She offers a handsome reward to retrieve a family heirloom in a hidden chest, buried in the farthest reaches of the caves. The cache contains numerous treasure items that she is willing to part with in exchange for their services. She explains that the chest that contains the heirloom has the Twilightforge crest on it: an anvil with a semi-circle of stars above.

Although the ettin who destroyed the settlement still lives in the neighboring cave, they only roam at night. As long as the characters are able to obtain the item before nightfall, the job should be an easy one. After giving assurances to the characters that the cave is long abandoned, Hilda provides an old map and a day's worth of provisions. In fact, she knows the caves have been resettled by an orc clan that raids on a certain day of the week, which is why she insists that the job be done by nightfall.

The characters arrive to find that the caves are indeed abandoned. Or so it seems. Moving throughout the winding tunnels becomes increasingly perilous as the adventuring party faces one trap after another. After some time exploring, they realize the cave has a lone occupant, Kevin Orckin, a young orc left behind to keep the war hearth fire burning while his clan is out on a raid.

Eventually, the wily orc leads the adventuring party to the neighboring cave where the characters are forced to face off with the ettin and, in doing so, discover that they have been led to burgle an orc lair.

BACKGROUND

The Onion Caves, named so for the bulb-shaped caverns that wind deep within the Tronjheim Mountains, are rumored to hold many hidden treasures left by dwarves after an ettin destroyed their settlement. Since then, locals have tended to steer clear of the area on account of the ettin, known as "One-Armed" Tommass. As a result, an orc clan has taken up residences in the abandoned caves.

RULES

GMs should familiarize themselves with the following from the core rulebooks:

- Difficult Terrain
- Passive Checks
- Traps

STARTING THE ADVENTURE

GM | The adventuring party sets off at dawn after accepting the job from Hilda Twilightforge. When they wake, they discover a storm has blown through the area and heavy winds have caused damage around the mountainside. Despite fallen trees and icy conditions making some of the already overgrown path difficult terrain, they arrive at the Onion Caves early in the morning.

Your path ends at the Tronjheim Mountains. Its spires reach into the clouds, unseen by your eyes. Thankfully, the entrance to the Onion Caves is just ahead of you.

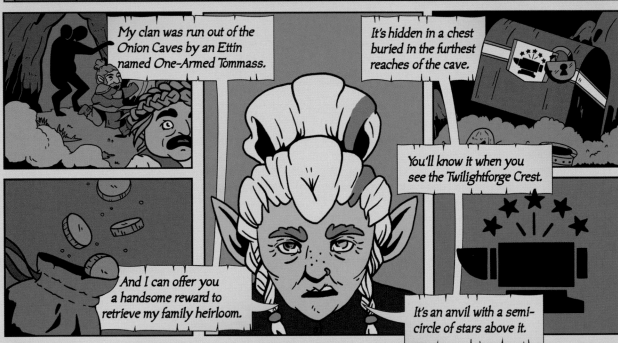

Illustrated by Kaylee Pinecone | Lettered by Haley Rose-Lyon

Well... I assure you, the Onion Caves are long abandoned during the day.

Here's some provisions for your journey.

Thank you. We won't let you down.

Though One-Armed Tommass still lives in the neighboring cave, he only roams it at night.

So as long as you are able to retrieve the heirloom by nightfall...

...the job should be an easy one.

THE ONION CAVES

The characters can easily find the entrance to the Onion Caves with the map provided by Hilda Twilightforge.

The entry to the cave is recessed into the mountainside, providing a modicum of shelter from the chill in the air. Before you stands a heavy stone door, engraved with dwarven runes.

GM | The adventuring party finds the archway sealed off. Any character who can read Dwarvish understands the following: "Private property. Area is protected by powerful magic. Trespassers are in for a shock."

- **Threat:** *Glyph of warding* (see spells in core rulebooks for details)

With a successful DC 15 Intelligence (Arcana or Investigation) check, any character determines the entrance is protected by a *glyph of warding*. A character who knows this spell makes the check with advantage, and can further note the type (explosive runes). The trap is triggered when a creature approaches within 10 feet of the door, causing explosive runes to erupt with magical energy in a 20-foot-radius sphere centered on the glyph. The sphere spreads around corners. Each creature in the area must make a DC 13 Dexterity saving throw. A creature takes 5d8 lightning damage on a failed save, or half as much damage on a successful one.

In order to disable the trap, a character must dispel the magic or trigger it with a creature.

CARTOGRAPHY

Once past the entrance defense system, the adventuring party may proceed into the caves proper. As promised, the premises appear to be abandoned with no inhabitants in sight.

A tunnel branches off into three directions, the first two being deadends:

- **East:** Offal pit. The stench of rotting meat permeates the air.
- **Northeast:** Cave bears. The animals are hibernating and can be avoided. If disturbed, two brown bears attack in order to protect their three cubs (see core rulebooks for stats).
- **West:** War hearth. Unbeknownst to the characters, an orc clan has taken over the caves. They left on a regular raid earlier that morning. Any character who succeeds on a DC 15 Wisdom (Survival) check is able to determine orcs have made camp here.

This area is in shambles with many belongings left behind. As you move deeper into the caves, a chill fills the air. To the north is a slope that leads up to another passageway. To the far west is a shrine.

A SLIPPERY SLOPE

GM | The shrine has a blood-soaked sword hanging on the wall along with a pile of broken bones beneath it. Any character who succeeds on a DC 10 Wisdom (Survival) check determines the following:

- The embers in the hearth are still warm.
- At the shrine, the bones are broken dwarf femurs.
- The blood on the sword has long dried and is caked on.
- **Loot:** A primitive carved bone statuette (worth 25 gp), a pair of knucklebone dice each with a skull symbol on the side that would normally show six pips (worth 50 gp)

Any character with a passive Wisdom (Perception) score of 10 or higher eventually hears movement coming from the passage to the north.

- **Threat:** Icy slope

The slope to the north is covered in black ice, imperceptible to the naked eye. Any character who steps on the slope must make a DC 10 Dexterity (Acrobatics) check or take 2d6 bludgeoning damage, falling prone.

The area is considered difficult terrain. Additionally, the first character to reach the halfway point up the slope triggers the following:

A hooded figure briefly appears at the top of the slope. With a deft movement it pulls something from its cloak. In the next moment, a cream pie flies out in the air and lands in the middle of the slope where it magically (and unfortunately) transforms into a gush of water. Just as quickly as the figure appeared, it races off to the west.

GM | The figure is Kevin Orckin who is wearing a *cloak of mischief*. When the cream pie lands, it casts *create or destroy water* (see core rulebooks). Any character on the slope must make a DC 10 Dexterity (Acrobatics) check, or take 2d6 bludgeoning damage, falling prone.

At that point, Kevin heads down the tunnel to the west and escapes using a secret door. During the adventure, if the characters are able to catch up to the young orc, he has one cream pie that he can throw, which casts *entangle* (see core rulebooks). Upon impact on the ground, grasping weeds and vines sprout in a 20-foot square, turning the ground into difficult terrain.

Characters may attempt to converse with Kevin at any point during the adventure, but he will make every effort to conceal his identity as an eight-year-old child. He has in his possession a *"Teddy" Orckin toy*, which he has taught to say the following: "I'm gonna give you to the count of 10 to get your ugly mugs off my property before I blast you to smithereens!"

If he feels threatened, Kevin will have *Teddy* utter the threat then light a firecracker before fleeing. The firecracker can be thrown up to 60 feet away. It emits a cloud of smoke that creates a heavily obscured area in a 20-foot radius. The sparks from the firework sheds bright light in a 30-foot radius. Any creature in the area must succeed on a DC 15 Constitution saving throw or become blinded for 30 seconds. At the end of each of its turns, the target can make a Constitution saving throw. On a success, the blinded condition ends.

Characters make their way up the slope without further challenge.

The slope terminates at a passageway that leads east and west. The wet bandit who attacked you fled westward.

THE BEES' KNEES

GM | To the east, the adventuring party finds a sleeping area filled with old cots but nothing else of importance. To the west, a tripwire is strung across the middle of the passage.

- **Threat:** Bees' trap
- **Loot:** 1 apiarist's pot

Any character who succeeds on a DC 15 Wisdom (Perception) check notices the tripwire. A successful DC 10 Dexterity check allows a character to safely circumvent the tripwire or disable it with Thieves' Tools. Failing the check triggers the trap.

If the tripwire is broken, it causes an open apiarist's pot to spill over from a ledge in the ceiling, covering a 10-foot by 10-foot

area in honey. Any character fully within this area must succeed on a DC 10 Dexterity saving throw or be doused in the substance.

The honey causes five swarms of bees (swarm of insects, see core rulebooks) to attack. Each character covered in the substance attracts at least one swarm. Otherwise, the swarms attack indiscriminately.

After dealing with the bee trap, the adventuring party may proceed unaccosted to the west of the passage. Once safely on the other side of the tripwire, any character who searches the area can easily find the apiarist's pot on the ledge above. The pot has the Twilightforge crest painted on it.

The tunnel leads to a guard room with a large prisoner cell to the far west. There are no signs of life here. A skeleton rests in the corner of the cell.

SKELETON CREW

GM | The cell door is locked. A character proficient with Thieves' Tools can pick it with a successful DC 15 Dexterity check. On closer inspection, the stone prison wall is etched with innumerable tally marks. Any character who succeeds on a DC 10 Wisdom (Survival) check determines that the skeleton belongs to a dwarf.

If the adventuring party is able to pick the lock or otherwise enter the cell, they find the following on the skeleton:

LOOT: ROLL 1D10 TO DETERMINE A TRINKET

d10	TRINKETS
1	A small leather pouch of good luck charms.
2	A pendant of blue stone carved into the form of a rabbit.
3	A monstrous finger bone inscribed with the word "Undying."
4	A bronze amulet with a secret compartment.
5	An ancient book of dwarven lore and mythology.
6	A set of small, nesting doll adventurers.
7	A working, wooden miniature of a trebuchet.
8	A fancy, pewter snuffbox that contains mouse whiskers.
9	A dwarven pint tankard.
10	A small, glass bowl that conjures water and a goldfish every morning.

To the south of the guard room is a secret door through which Kevin made his escape.

Secret doors throughout the caves are unlocked and made of stone with iron hinges that swing open. Any character with a passive Wisdom (Perception) score of 15 or higher and who is within 10 feet of a secret door can detect it.

must make a DC 13 Dexterity saving throw, taking 4d6 fire damage on a failed save, or half as much damage on a successful one.

A successful DC 20 Wisdom (Perception) check reveals the pressure plate. A successful DC 20 Dexterity check using Thieves' Tools disables it, and a check with a total of 5 or lower triggers the trap.

Five swarms of bats (see core rulebooks) hang from the ceiling above. Unless provoked, they do not attack. Any character with a passive Wisdom (Perception) score of 10 or higher observes that the guano does not cover a 15-foot perimeter around the trap, as the bats avoid it.

Once the adventuring party has disabled or evaded the fire trap, they are able to easily discern a number of footprints in the guano. A successful DC 10 Wisdom (Survival) check allows a character to track fresh footsteps of a Small-size humanoid creature to another secret door to the south.

On the other side of the door, a passage leads west, with rooms to the north, before winding back down to the south. If the characters choose to investigate the rooms to the north, they discover:

More manure to tickle your noses! You have arrived in a food storage and livestock area replete with casks, kegs, and—you guessed it—live animals.

CALM BEFORE THE STORM

GM | The casks contain salted pork and apples, while the kegs hold strong ale. Additionally, sacks of animal feed are piled near a large pen where a dozen well-fed pigs root around in the mud.

At this point, the adventuring party may begin to realize the Onion Caves aren't quite as abandoned as Hilda Twilightforge suggested. The larder is brimming with

Otherwise, in order to find a secret door, a character must take the time to search the wall and succeed on a DC 15 Wisdom (Perception) check.

In this case, the stone has been heated through by a fire trap on the other side. Any character who pushes the door open with a bare hand must make a DC 10 Dexterity saving throw, taking 1d10 fire damage on a failed save, or half as much damage on a successful one.

When the characters proceed to the next area, they discover the following:

You arrive at an empty cavern within the vast tunnel network. There is no sign of the hooded figure, but your olfactory senses fill with the stench of guano.

DRAWING FIRE

GM | The orcs who live in the lair installed the fire trap. There is a pressure plate located 5 feet directly in front of the secret door to the north, from where the adventuring party entered the area.

- **Threat:** Fire trap

A creature that steps on the pressure plate triggers the trap, causing fire to erupt from it. A 15-foot cube of fire erupts, covering the pressure plate and the area around it (including the secret door). The target foodstocks, enough for more than a solitary inhabitant.

Any character with a passive Wisdom (Perception) score of 10 or higher eventually hears movement coming from the passage to the southwest. Following the sounds leads the adventuring party to the following:

You arrive at yet another tunnel leading east to west with a large stone archway in front of you. The dwarven masonry from the previous inhabitants retains its magnificent beauty. Carved stone reliefs depict a treasure chest on the keystone with painted coins and gems flowing on either side of the archway.

GM | Any character who succeeds on a DC 10 Wisdom (Perception) check notices that the keystone in the archway has two grooves, as though something has passed overhead enough times to wear down the stone. That something happens to be the ettin in the unmapped area to the south.

On the south-facing ledge of the archway are five cauldrons attached by ropes to a single pulley on the other side of the passageway. It is the cauldron trap from the section of the adventure entitled "This is Going to Hurt," detailed below. Characters must be on the southern side of the archway to notice it with a successful DC 15 Intelligence (Investigation) check.

When the characters make it to this junction, however, Kevin hurls another cream pie at the area to the west from a hiding spot behind the shrine to the east.

As you reach another crossroads in the Onion Caves, something flies just past you. A gruff child's voice taunts you with the directive, "Come and get me, ya filthy animals!"

Let Sleeping Dogs Lie

GM | The cream pie from Kevin's cloak has cast *silent image* in the room to the west. The adventuring party has now been made aware that they are dealing with a child, and may wish to ignore or attempt to reason with Kevin.

Characters who investigate the area to the west in order to reason with Kevin discover:

The room to the west can only be accessed through a small tunnel measuring about 2 feet in diameter and 5 feet long. On the other side, you make out a short, hooded figure, huddled into a little ball.

GM | The room beyond the narrow opening is, in fact, a wolf den. Fortunately for the adventuring party, the wolves are out on raid with the orc clan. However, Kevin has set up another trap.

- **Threat:** Crossbow trap

A tripwire is strung across the passageway at the halfway mark. A successful DC 15 Wisdom (Perception) check reveals the tripwire. A successful DC 15 Dexterity check using Thieves' Tools disables the tripwire, and a check with a total of 5 or lower triggers the trap.

The trap makes two attacks against the triggering creature. Each attack has a +8 attack bonus and deals 5 (1d10) piercing damage on a hit.

If the adventuring party chooses to ignore Kevin, the young orc is not easily dissuaded from protecting his lair, and will continue to antagonize the characters until they

leave the orc lair or are killed by the ettin who lives in the neighboring cave.

From behind a crude statue to the east, the hooded figure dashes toward the archway to the south. As he does so, he tosses a number of objects over his shoulder.

THIS IS GOING TO HURT

GM | Kevin has dropped a number of wooden toy carriages in the 5-foot area directly in front of the archway. These are treated as caltrops.

Any creature that enters the area must succeed on a DC 15 Dexterity saving throw, or stop moving this turn and take one piercing damage. Taking this damage reduces the creature's walking speed by 10 feet until the creature regains at least one hit point. A creature moving through the area at half speed doesn't need to make the save.

The makeshift caltrops are a diversion for the real trap.

- **Threat:** Cauldron trap

If the adventuring party decides to pursue Kevin to the south, the following occurs:

The figure turns briefly to pull down his hood and reveals the face of a smirking orc of about eight years in age. His straw colored hair is tousled as though he recently woke up. He calls out, "Hey, ya filthy animals! I hope you like the taste of iron!" Then he tugs on a rope suspended from the ceiling and flees further south.

GM | When the string is pulled, five heavy cauldrons on ropes swing down from the other side of the archway. The cauldrons are centered on the doorway. Any character fully within this area must succeed on a DC 15 Dexterity saving throw, or take 1d8 bludgeoning damage, get pushed 10 feet backwards, and be knocked prone.

Additionally, on impact the cauldron drops alchemist's fire on the prone creature. It makes a ranged weapon attack (+4 to hit, range 5/20 ft.). On a hit the target takes 2 (1d4) fire damage at the start of each of its turns. A creature can end this damage by using its action to make a DC 10 Dexterity check to extinguish the flames.

Kevin exits to the south in an attempt to lure the adventuring party into the neighboring cave where the murderous ettin lives. Should the characters wish to continue with their original objective of securing the treasure cache for Hilda

Twilightforge, they may opt to ignore Kevin and instead continue exploring the area in the "Child's Play" section of the adventure, which is detailed below.

Should the characters wish to find out more about Kevin and engage in conversation with him, see "Ending the Adventure" for notes on roleplaying the young orc. If any member of the adventuring party attempted to harm him at any point, any skill check made to interact with Kevin is made with disadvantage.

A CAVE OF ONE'S OWN

GM | Should the characters choose to follow Kevin, they take a winding passage to the den of "One-Armed" Tommass:

You make your way down the twists and turns of the tunnel until you are spit out into the mouth of a large cavern. Here, the air is pungent with the stench of rotting meat and body odor. The entire area is in no danger of winning an award from **Good Cave Keeping** *magazine.*

The ettin den is littered with broken crates, animal carcasses, and piles of dirty rags that can provide half-cover to any creature fighting or hiding behind them. The area measures 100 feet in diameter with a ceiling of 60 feet.

Kevin is occupied with getting the attention of "One-Armed" Tommass. He does so by hurling rocks with his sling from a distance of 30 feet. Characters who succeed on a DC 14 Dexterity (Stealth) check are able to sneak into the cave undetected. On a failed save, Tommass cries out, "Stranger danger!" This alerts Kevin to the presence of the adventuring party.

See "Ending the Adventure" for notes on roleplaying the NPCs and how to resolve the final scenario.

CHILD'S PLAY

GM | If the characters head to the east instead of following Kevin south to the ettin's den, the young orc eventually lures "One-Armed" Tommass to this area. Allow some time for the adventuring party to explore before the ettin arrives.

To the east is the area on the map provided by Hilda Twilightforge where an "X" marks the location of the

hidden treasure cache. Just outside the archway to this cave is a shrine featuring a crude stone effigy.

GM | Any character who succeeds on a DC 15 Intelligence (Religion) check recalls that orcs believe a one-eyed god created their kind. The deity represents conquest, strength, and survival. His shrine is surrounded by bloody offerings.

Beyond the shrine is the orc war chief's quarters. Kevin is his youngest son and resides in this area, as evidenced by some of the possessions detailed below.

This large room shows clear signs of being lived in. It features a throne-line chair made of bones and sinews near a fire that burns in the center. Gruesome war trophies are piled on either side of the chair. Beyond, on the easternmost wall, cots are arranged in clusters.

GM | The trophies include skulls and bones, cave bear paws, dwarf beards, dire wolf hides, and a chipped glass eye. None of these items are in a condition to be of any monetary value.

The hot coals in the central firepit deal 1 fire damage to any creature that enters the firepit, or 1d6 fire damage to any creature that falls prone there.

In order to find the hidden chest, characters must dig beneath the cots. When they do so, they discover a wooden box under one of the cots. It is inscribed with rudimentary

runes on the side. Although orcs derive their written language from Dwarvish, they are rarely literate and instead use symbols to communicate basic concepts. Any character who reads orc runes understands the words to mean, "Kevin's stuff! Hands off!" Alternatively, any character who reads Dwarvish and succeeds on a DC 15 Intelligence check can decipher the runes. Inside this box is a collection of toys—miniature figures of warriors and wooden weapons of orcish make and a few dwarven dolls.

Before the adventuring party is able to unearth the treasure cache, Kevin arrives with "One-Armed" Tommass.

See "Ending the Adventure" for notes on roleplaying the NPCs and how to resolve the final scenario.

ENDING THE ADVENTURE

The characters have several options to resolve the situation. A fight with "One-Armed" Tommass is deadly, and requires strategic planning to defeat them.

"One-Armed" Tommass, like all ettins, is divided in personalities. It is possible for the characters to negotiate with the more intellectual head of the giant or to trick the more dim-witted head.

Likewise, Kevin is a child who believes the adventuring party is a band of thieves—rightfully so. The young orc is aware of the hidden treasure that was left behind by the former residents of the Onion Caves, as it is how he obtained the *cloak of mischief* and the *apiarist's pot*. Both items have the Twilightforge crest.

ROLEPLAYING "ONE-ARMED" TOMMASS

An ettin is a brutish, two-headed giant that is treated as a distant cousin by orcs. The giant shares one body and, although this particular body has two arms, the heads consider themselves to have

one arm each—thus the name "One-Armed" Tommass. The right head is named Tom, while the left head is named Mass. Tom claims their names are actually Tomm and Ass much to the latter's annoyance.

They share an aversion to water, as evidenced by the thick crust of dirt on their skin, greasy hair, yellowed, crooked teeth and tusks, and the half-rotting hides that hang from their shared body. Tom is the dim-witted one of the two, while Mass fancies himself an intellectual.

For their part, Tommass keeps to themselves in their area of the Onion Caves. The orcs from Kevin's clan bring large game and other creatures to appease the ettin. In exchange, Tommass ensures intruders are met with murderous rage.

ROLEPLAYING KEVIN

The precocious orc is the youngest son of the war chief. His clan went out on a raid earlier that morning, leaving him behind to keep the war hearth fire burning. Unfortunately, he overslept and the hearth burned out. He was on his way to check on the flames when he heard intruders in the cave.

Having been left in the cave alone, he is simply protecting himself from the adventuring party who he perceives to be burglars. He tells the characters, "This is my lair; I have to defend it."

Kevin is terrified of Tommass. Kevin's older brother, Ruhk, has told him that Tommass was rumored to have murdered the dwarves who

once inhabited the caves with a mining axe, and ate them because their appetite was insatiable. And their favorite food is children.

As Kevin is so frightened of the ettin, the adventuring party has an opportunity to glean information about the giant from the child. Any character who succeeds on a DC 11 Charisma (Persuasion) check can gain the following knowledge about Tommass:

- They have an aversion to water.

- Their breath weapon reaches a 15-foot cone.

- The two heads rarely agree on anything.

- They murdered a bunch of dwarves a long time ago and can probably do the same to a low-tier adventuring party.

- It's possible they feast on small children like candy.

SUCCESS

If Kevin and Tommass are defeated in combat, the adventuring party accomplishes their job for Hilda Twilightforge. When they inform her that the caves are now occupied by orcs, she feigns ignorance and is profusely apologetic. She offers the adventuring party whatever magic items they found with the Twilightforge crest, only taking a small trinket from the cache for herself.

Having laid low an eight-year-old child and his hideous cousin, you certainly must feel good about yourselves. You are able to make off with the treasure cache that Hilda Twilightforge promised, feeling a sense of accomplishment mixed with a bit of shame. In the retelling of the story, you all agree to change some of the details to say you defeated an ettin and the son of an orc war chief.

SUCCESS

If the adventuring party negotiates with Kevin and Tommass, they are able to convince them that the hidden cache belongs to one of the former occupants. The young orc reluctantly turns over the magic items with the Twilightforge crest.

Kevin Orckin sees you off by way of a secret exit. He waves enthusiastically while saying, "I don't want to see you again for the rest of my whole life." Before you can turn around and wend your way down the mountainside, you hear an angry howl from inside the cave followed by a deep male voice screaming, "Kevin! Why is the war hearth fire not burning anymore?" The young orc responds with hands on either side of his surprised face.

FAILURE

If the adventuring party is killed by "One-Armed" Tommass, they fail in their mission to retrieve Hilda Twilightforge's treasure cache.

The stinking fumes of ettin breath blanket you in your untimely death. As you struggle to retain consciousness, you notice some of the rotting carcasses in the area are humanoid and chewed on. There aren't much worse ways to die than as ettin dinner.

FAILURE

If the characters are run out of the Onion Caves, they are unable to accomplish the job for Hilda Twilightforge. Whether they return to her or not, she tells anyone who will listen of their great failure.

You quickly learn that Hilda Twilightforge is not only very cross with your disappointing performance, but she also happens to be the village gossip. Her tale of your incompetence spreads far and wide, well beyond her little village. So much so that you are unable to find work in the region and are laughed out of most taverns. You do, however, take a little comfort in the fact that she wasn't aware that your failure was at the hands of an eight-year-old child.

REWARDS

- 100 XP for disarming the *glyph of warding*

- 400 XP for defeating the brown bears

- 100 XP for disarming or evading the bees' trap

- 500 XP for defeating the swarm of bees

- 100 XP for disarming or evading the fire trap

- 100 XP for disarming or evading the crossbow trap

- 250 XP for disarming or evading the cauldron trap

- 1100 XP for defeating or negotiating with "One-Armed" Tommass

- 25 XP for defeating Kevin Orckin or 200 XP negotiating with him

- 50 XP for unearthing Hilda Twilightforge's treasure cache

LOOT FROM THE TREASURE CACHE

2200 cp, 800 sp, 40 gp, box of perfumed candles (25 gp), feathered ribbon (25 gp), feathered talisman (25 gp), pair of iron dice (25 gp), leather vest (25 gp), iron brazier (25 gp), iron tiara (25 gp), carved wooden goblet (25 gp).

KEVIN ORCKIN

Small humanoid (orc), chaotic evil

Armor Class 11
Hit Points 9 (2d6 + 2)
Speed 30 ft.

STR	DEX	CON	INT	WIS	CHA
13 (+1)	12 (+1)	12 (+1)	10 (+0)	11 (+0)	10 (+0)

Senses darkvision 60 ft., passive Perception 10

Languages Common, Orc

Challenge 1/8 (25 XP)

Aggressive. As a bonus action, the orc can move up to its speed toward a hostile creature that it can see.

Plucky. Kevin Orckin gains a +2 bonus to all Charisma skills, saving throws, and ability checks.

ACTIONS

Dagger. *Melee Weapon Attack:* +3 to hit, reach 5 ft., one target. *Hit:* 3 (1d4 + 1) piercing damage.

Sling. *Ranged Weapon Attack:* +3 to hit, range 30/120 ft., one target. *Hit:* 3 (1d4 + 1) bludgeoning damage.

"ONE-ARMED" TOMMASS

Large giant, chaotic evil

Armor Class 12 (natural armor)
Hit Points 85 (10d10 + 30)
Speed 40 ft.

STR	DEX	CON	INT	WIS	CHA
21 (+5)	8 (−1)	17 (+3)	6 (−2)	10 (+0)	8 (−1)

Skills Perception +4

Senses darkvision 60 ft., passive Perception 14

Languages Giant, Orc

Challenge 4 (1,100 XP)

Two Heads. The ettin has advantage on Wisdom (Perception) checks and on saving throws against being blinded, charmed, deafened, frightened, stunned, and knocked unconscious.

Wakeful. When one of the ettin's heads is asleep, its other head is awake.

ACTIONS

Multiattack. The ettin makes two attacks: one with its battleaxe and one with its morningstar.

Battleaxe. *Melee Weapon Attack:* +7 to hit, reach 5 ft., one target. *Hit:* 14 (2d8 + 5) slashing damage.

Morningstar. *Melee Weapon Attack:* +7 to hit, reach 5 ft., one target. *Hit:* 14 (2d8 + 5) piercing damage.

Breath Weapon. (Recharge 5–6). The ettin uses the following breath weapon:

Stink Breath. The ettin exhales noxious fumes in a 15-foot cone. Each creature in that area must succeed on a DC 13 Constitution saving throw or fall unconscious for one minute. This effect ends for a creature if the creature takes damage or someone uses an action to wake it.

New Magic Items

CLOAK OF MISCHIEF
Wondrous item, uncommon

This ordinary cloth, made from tan wool, has one internal pocket that appears empty. Reaching inside the pocket, however, reveals the presence of a cream pie. The *cloak* weighs 1/2 pound.

You can use an action to pull the cream pie from the pocket and throw it up to 20 feet. When the object lands, it casts a spell determined by rolling a d8 and consulting the table that corresponds to the bag's color. See the spell descriptions in core rulebooks for details on the effects of casting.

Once three cream pies have been pulled from the pocket, the *cloak* becomes a regular item of clothing and its magical properties can't be used again until the next dawn.

d8	SPELL
1	*Create or destroy water*
2	*Entangle*
3	*Faerie fire*
4	*Fog cloud*
5	*Grease*
6	*Hideous laughter*
7	*Silent image*
8	*Sleep*

"TEDDY" ORCKIN TOY
Wondrous item, common (requires attunement)

This *toy* is an enchanted, stuffed teddy bear with tusks like an orc. While the *toy* is within 5 feet of you, you can spend a short rest teaching it to say up to 25 words. You must also set a condition that occurs within 5 feet of the *toy* to trigger the *toy* to speak. During a short rest, old phrases can be replaced with new ones.

APIARIST'S POT
Wondrous item, uncommon

This ceramic pot appears to be able to hold a gallon of liquid and weighs 12 pounds, whether full or empty.

You can use an action to cause the jug to produce honey by uttering the words, "More honey with bee." Afterward, you can uncork the jug as an action and pour that liquid out, a quarter gallon per minute, up to one gallon.

SHIP OF THE DEAD

WRITTEN BY COMFORT LOVE & ADAM WITHERS,
ILLUSTRATED BY MARTIE ABDURRASHEED

A 5E Adventure for Levels 4–6 | You will need a copy of the 5E core rulebooks to fully utilize this adventure. You should also familiarize yourself with the map and spells used by the foes prior to playing the adventure.

Glossary | PC: Playable Characters | GM: Game Master | DC: Difficulty Class
HP: Hit Points | NPC: Non-Player Character

Adventure Scaling | This adventure is designed to be highly challenging for a group of 3rd- to 5th-level players, though it can easily be made challenging for a larger group or a group of upper 2nd-tier characters by giving all the foes maximum hit points and adding +2 to the DC of tests and saves.

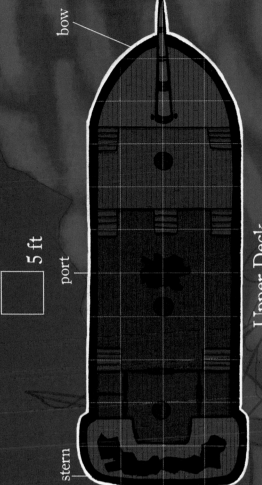

bow

5 ft

port

stern

Upper Deck

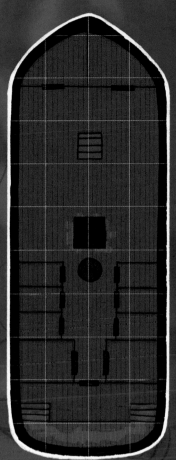

Lower Deck

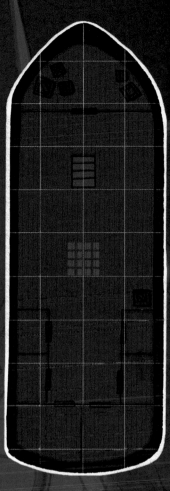

Cargo Deck

the FAIR MAIDEN

Exterior

Illustration by Melanie Kim

PLOT

A great evil guards a sunken treasure. The PCs are hired by a surly old captain to aid in finding a sunken ship's bounty. To do so, they will have to survive a terrible storm, an attack by a giant sea monster, and a confrontation with a cruel hag and her undead minions. If they succeed, they may not only gain a rich reward, but free the trapped souls of a crew of good men.

BACKGROUND

It has been nearly 50 years since the last voyage of the *Fair Maiden*. In her time, she was a fine, swift trade vessel that crossed several seas and saw a multitude of foreign shores. Her captain, Rhys Halsted, was a man both brave and bold, who was both explorer and noble broker of commerce. Such was his reputation that his ship was often filled with vast treasures for international trade. He held a stellar operating record, never losing a shipment—until one final voyage.

The *Fair Maiden* set sail from a port, full to bursting with gold, from a completed transaction with a great lord. She sailed off to return the profits to her patron, but tragedy struck at sea.

Beneath the waves, there lived a cruel, twisted sea hag, Urswyk. Polluting the waters around her aquatic home with her evil and hatred, Urswyk had once enjoyed drawing unwary seamen to her and offering dark deals that always led to total corruption and despair.

But Urswyk was growing older and more embittered toward the beautiful topsiders, and her joy in these games waned. She grew to prefer using her precious baby—an enormous, horrific sea monster—to drag their ships down to the briny deep to die.

Urswyk's baby caught the *Fair Maiden* that night, and though she put up a mighty fight, she was ruined and sunk. Such a fine ship was she that Urswyk made the vessel into her new lair, using her magic to trap Rhys Halsted and his crew between life and death as her undying playthings.

No man escaped to tell the tale, and nobody ever learned what happened to the ship. Rumors spread, however, and the popular belief was that Halsted had betrayed his employer and taken off with the gold, setting himself up on some distant shore. The Halsted name was ruined, his family left destitute.

To this day, each month when the moon is full, you might see the ghostly spirit of the *Fair Maiden* and her spectral crew sailing the sea—trapped forever, their souls condemned to relive their last voyage for all time as their bodies serve a sea hag's dark whims.

RULES

Since a fair portion of this adventure will happen on or under the sea, it would be wise to familiarize yourself with the rules for underwater combat.

YOU'VE HEARD OF THE FAIR MAIDEN? SHE WAS AN IMPRESSIVE CRAFT, BELLY BURSTING WITH GOLD. GOLD THAT WAS NEVER DELIVERED.

SHE SUNK DOWN DOWN DOWN...

SOME SAY THE OLD CAPTAIN MADE OFF WITH THE BOUNTY.

BUT OL' HALSTEAD KNOWS BETTER.

KNOWS WHERE SHE LAY, I DOES.

I'VE GOT EVERYTHING READY. ALL I NEEDS IS A CREW.

YOU LOOK A BRAVE BUNCH.

BUT WILL YOU RISK IT FOR A PRETTY PINCH OF GOLD?

WELL... WHAT DO YOU SAY?

CLAP

SOUNDS INTERESTING. LET'S TALK.

STARTING THE ADVENTURE

GETTING THE PCS INVOLVED

The adventure begins with the PCs being approached by Captain Gregor Halsted to join his crew to retrieve the cargo of the *Fair Maiden*. There are a number of ways this can be set up: The PCs could hear talk around town about the crazy old captain hiring men for his doomed quest. They could encounter his ship at the docks and be told about the journey by other crewmen or the Captain himself. Or they could simply be approached directly at some point. The PCs likely appear to be the adventuring sort, and that's exactly who Halsted has been trying to recruit for a dangerous mission such as this.

However you arrange it, there will be a meeting with Captain Halsted to discuss the details.

CAPTAIN HALSTED AND THE LAST CHANCE

Even as he approaches, you can tell a lot about this grizzled older man. He is unquestionably a man of the sea, with his heavy and weather-worn leather coat, equally rough and leathery skin tanned a deep umber, and the acidic tang of salt in the air around him. He has a week's worth of stubble on his jaw, creases at his mouth denoting a ready frown, and a pair of long, jagged scars arcing from the back of his head down the side of his face. Heavy bags sag under eyes that, while sunken-in darkened pools, nevertheless burn a brilliant sea-green as he looks at each of you in turn. You can almost feel him taking your measure, then he nods to himself as if satisfied.

"Name's Halsted. Captain Gregor Halsted of the exploration vessel the **Last Chance**. *And you might be just what I need…"*

Captain Halsted will explain the situation to the PCs in as much detail as they require. He is taking on a new crew for a voyage to exhume a sunken ship, the *Fair Maiden*. She is a large trading vessel, and her belly's full to bursting with gold that never made it to her destination. Nobody has ever found her final resting place—most assume the old captain made off with the bounty himself—but Captain Halsted knows better. He knows where she sank, knows how to find her, and has secured equipment both mechanical and magical to allow a small team to swim to the bottom safely and retrieve the treasure. He just needs men brave enough to try.

While running the captain in this first meeting, remember that he wants the PCs to join the expedition and feels the best way to accomplish that is honesty, both about the dangers ahead and the rewards they could reap. He will freely tell them that a great, terrible beast of the deep roams the area.

"It's all tentacles and teeth," he might say, "Able to swallow men in one bite, and more than capable of dragging even the sturdiest vessels under."

"That's why I need fighters," he explains. He'll tell them he's tried this voyage twice before with no success. Once, he barely escaped with his life (thus the scars). "But the beast can bleed, and if it bleeds, it can die."

If the PCs question why it's worth confronting such a monster, Halsted will explain the value of the bounty. The *Fair Maiden* was sailing for a royal patron, trading with a wealthy and powerful baron around these parts. "She was returning home with enough gold and jewels to make great lords sleep easy before she was sunk. That kind of wealth…she only comes so often in a man's life, and never easy."

As a final important note, the captain isn't keeping any treasure for himself save one item: a single enchanted chest. "Its contents are mine alone," Halsted explains, "The rest of the treasure is for the crew to divide."

GM | Halsted's plan is to sail to an area of the sea by moonrise, where he knows the spectral *Fair Maiden* will appear, continuing its old route. They will follow the ghost ship to where it sank, revealing the exact location to dive. He has a set of enchanted *bubble harnesses* (see "Magic Items") to allow underwater breathing and a ship built to raise underwater cargo.

While Halsted knows about the sea monster and that the *Fair Maiden* sails under the full moon as a ghost ship, he doesn't know anything about Urswyk the hag. He'll share all he knows about the sea monster, but won't want to talk about the ghost ship for fear that the idea of following such a vessel would spook a superstitious sailing crew.

THE HALSTED FAMILY PRIDE

While running Captain Halsted as an NPC, it's important to remember how personal this mission is for him. The captain of the *Fair Maiden* was his grandfather, and when rumor spread that he stole the treasure, it ruined his family. His father, Mikah, died trying to restore their good name. Halsted himself has spent his whole life in pursuit of the truth, and will risk anything—including his own life—to prove his grandfather wasn't a criminal. That's why he needs that single enchanted chest; it protects the manifests and documents within, showing that Rhys Halsted did his best to complete the voyage. If he returns this evidence to the nobility his grandfather worked for, they could clear his family's name. This mission is about securing a future for Halsted's own children and grandchildren, and he will go to any ends to make that happen. Feel free as GM to have the captain share this background with PCs who are curious or spend time getting to know him.

4-5	**Wave Strike:** A huge wave crashes on the deck. Make a DC 10 Strength saving throw to prevent being swept overboard. Each time this result is rolled, the deck becomes flooded. Until the flooding is mitigated by some means, all players above deck are at disadvantage on Strength and Dexterity checks.
6-9	**Turbulent Waters:** The ship is rocked hard, making movement difficult and the deck unstable. All players are at disadvantage on their next check made this encounter.
10	**Lightning Strike:** A random character is targeted by lightning. Roll 1d4: on an even result, a PC is struck. On an odd result, an NPC crewmember is struck. Lightning attacks with a +5 bonus, dealing 9 (2d6 + 2) lightning damage on a hit.

After the storm has passed, determine the state of the ship based on the number of failures accumulated during the challenge:

- 1 Failure: -50 hp, -1 AC, -5 Damage Threshold (DT)
- 2 Failures: -100 hp, -3 AC, -10 DT
- 3 Failures: -200 hp, -5 AC, -15 DT

Additionally, if the heroes did not pass the skill challenge, the ship's masts are broken, and it cannot move until 20 hp worth of repairs have been made. This will make the fight against the sea monster much more difficult (see the "Terror of the Deep" section below for details).

SINKING THE *LAST CHANCE*

The premise of this adventure is that the ship has to survive to carry the players to and from their destination. However, if you like more extreme consequences for failure, a bigger challenge for the players, or just like when absolutely everything goes wrong in an adventure, you may consider allowing the *Last Chance* to be destroyed.

There are two likely points for this to occur; the first is during the storm. If the players fail the skill challenge, you can simply rule that the ship takes too much damage and will sink. The crew will rush to lifeboats, with Captain Halsted ensuring all the gear needed for the dive to the *Fair Maiden* is secured. Players will have to decide if they still wish to continue the expedition, possibly facing a horrible sea monster with little more than dinghies and their own strength of arms.

The second point at which the ship could be sunk is while fighting the sea monster. The sinking ship could manage

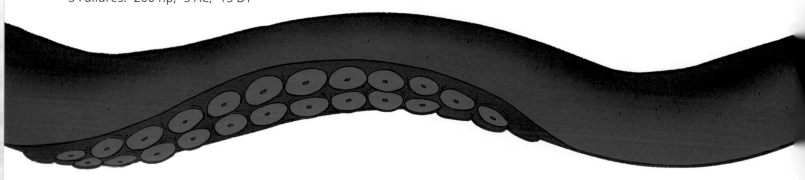

to bring the monster down with it, or it could provide a distraction that allows the players to sneak around it to the *Fair Maiden* below. In any case, the captain will make sure all necessary equipment is safe and secure to complete the adventure.

Without the *Last Chance*, players will be in a difficult situation. They'll have lifeboats (or maybe just large, floating debris) and little else, facing a long return voyage. Securing a vast treasure on such small boats would be difficult, but clever PCs may find solutions. However it happens, the direction of the entire adventure could radically shift without a large, sturdy ship to rely on.

REPAIRING THE *LAST CHANCE*

GM | After the storm, depending on the PCs' performance, the *Last Chance* is going to need repairs. Fortunately, Captain Halsted was prepared for this possibility.

Stowed aboard the ship is a large supply of repair materials—wooden planks, iron sheets, and more designed to allow for repairing damage to the ship while still at sea. However, supplies are limited:

TABLE 4

AVAILABLE REPAIR SUPPLIES	
Damage Dealt	**Maximum Repairs**
HP Damage	Up to 150 hp restored
AC Damage	Up to 3 AC restored
DT Damage	Up to 10 DT restored

Because the available supplies were prepared specifically to fix damage to the *Last Chance*, and because she's such a ramshackle, piecemeal vessel to begin with, repairs can be made far more quickly than would otherwise be possible: 1 hp per hour (up to 12 hp per day) and one AC and 2 DT per day.

THE BARNACLE BEAST

While working on the repairs of the ship, taking a moment to wipe sweat and salt from your brow, one of the crew rushes up to the captain. "Uh, Cap'n, sir...? We've got us a mite bit of a problem belowdecks." Captain Halsted responds with a questioning glare, and the nervous seaman takes his hat and wrings it in his hands before stammering, "S-somethin's been...that is, there's these wee holes sproutin' in the hold..."

GM | Halsted orders the PCs to deal with it while he continues supervision of the rest of the repair work. They'll discover several small, circular holes bored into the hold, each about the diameter of a man's arm. The ship is taking on water, and something has to be done.

While repairing the holes, players notice a hard, sharp rapping on the hull. Shortly thereafter, a long, needle-shaped and bone-like beak will burst through the wall near the ground, snap up a rat, and retreat, leaving a new hole behind.

This is the Barnacle Beast—a scavenger that usually lives closer to shore, but was washed out to sea by the storm. It latched onto the ship's hull and is feeding on what's inside with a woodpecker-like beak. In order to prevent taking on more water, the players will have to figure out a way to remove the beast.

There are several possible options, here. First, it is conceivable that they could find a way to trap the beak inside the ship when it pokes in for a rat. If it can't withdraw its beak, it can't poke more holes.

Secondly, while its hook-like legs are good at latching into wood, it could be detached using a number of methods. Any kind of fire, magical or otherwise, will immediately cause it to let go of the hull and drop away (though PCs would have to lure it higher on the hull and out of the water to use nonmagical fire on it). They could use some kind of pry-bar to force it off, or even try to tempt it away with tastier prey dangled further out in the water.

Of course, they could also just kill the thing. Use the Barnacle Beast stat block at the end of this adventure. This isn't a difficult monster to fight; though nearly 20 feet long with a very tough and protective shell, it has few methods of attack. The bigger problem will be that this creature is a heavy bleeder, and all that blood will attract 1d4 hunter sharks. Because of all the blood in the water, the sharks begin combat with Blood Frenzy active, granting them advantage on melee attack rolls.

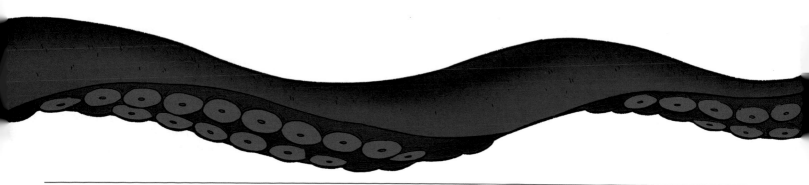

The beast is smart enough to realize the cannons are dangerous, and will make efforts to avoid them by keeping its head and grabbing tentacles at the bow or stern of the ship. It is therefore a good idea for players to find ways to draw the beast to the port or starboard sides so the cannons can make their attacks.

REDISCOVERING THE *FAIR MAIDEN*

GM | When the monster is slain and all is calm, PCs can finally begin their dive. The party will descend into the sea with the following additional crewmen:

- Flint
- Jossika
- "Half-Mast"
- Hemmick *
- "Bilge Rat" *

- Burnzie *

   * These crewmen will not be present if the PCs failed to convince the nervous crewmembers to stay (see "The Ghost Ship" section).

Use the Ship's Mate stat block at the end of the adventure as a base for these crewmen.

The *Last Chance* has an elaborate hauling mechanism to pull chests and crates to the surface. In addition, PCs are provided the following equipment:

- **Bubble Harness** *Wondrous Item, common* When you wear this set of shoulder straps, the attached thick brass ring around the neck creates a bubble of oxygen around the character's head, which allows them to breathe underwater. This air bubble does not filter out toxins, and does not protect against poisons, gasses, or other inhaled hazards. Each member of the team receives one *bubble harness*.

- **(2) *Wands of Light*** *Wand, common* Generates light as per the *light* spell. They have 10 charges each, and regenerate 1d4 charges per hour spent in full sunlight.

- **(6) 100 ft. lengths of rope with clamps** for dragging treasure chests, barrels, etc. from the sunken ship.

- **(5) *Potions of Healing***

The dive down is blissfully uneventful. Searching for the last resting place of the *Fair Maiden* requires a successful DC 20 Wisdom (Perception) check. When they discover the ship, read the following:

You find the Fair Maiden *perched precariously at the edge of a great ravine. Fully half the ship hangs over the abyss, held in place by a delicate balance of seabed growth and detritus. Looking at her now and remembering the vision of what she used to be, approaching the* Fair Maiden *feels like walking on someone's grave. This feeling turns into a worrying chill that runs down your spine like bony fingers and settles in your gut. The closer you get, the more disturbing it all feels—and the more wrong the ship appears. Though clearly the vessel you're looking for, something in its decades of rest has twisted and changed it. Corrupted it. You have a very bad feeling about what awaits you within.*

GM | Being that this ship is now the lair of an evil sea hag, it has indeed been corrupted over the years. What was once a beautiful, majestic galleon is now a dark, rotting, Lovecraftian thing. From the moment the party sets foot on the deck of the ship, they are in Urswyk's domain.

LAIR OF THE SEA HAG

GM | Moving through the ship should be a deeply unnerving experience. The walls, floors, and decoration have all twisted and warped into a grotesque, darkly disturbing parody of themselves. Players will see visions at their periphery, turning to find nothing there. Hallways will seem to loop around on themselves, causing the players to walk in circles. The journey to the heart of the ship will take much longer than it would seem for a vessel of this size. Urswyk is funneling them to the center of her lair, the heart of her power, and she wants them disoriented when they arrive.

A DARK BARGAIN

In the grand hag tradition, Urswyk used to strike bargains with her victims, offering them their heart's desire and twisting the deal into a torment. For GMs so inclined, she may make such a bargain with the PCs. Rather than bringing the entire party to the heart of her lair, you may choose to bring only a player or two who you know have great ambitions, or who are just generally susceptible to temptation. Sequester these players and let them meet the hag separately from the rest of the group, so she can appear to them as a less overtly evil (but no less ugly) old woman and offer a dark bargain. In return, she demands that which the players value most. It may not be something she takes immediately, as she prefers to complete the deal at an unspecified time and place down the line. If the bargain is struck, you can skip the Confrontation with Urswyk section entirely (though she still pushes the *Fair Maiden* into the abyss). If the bargain is rejected, she is furious and begins her attack while the rest of the party is still elsewhere in the ship. The players, while taking the moral high ground, have put themselves in a very difficult spot...

When the party meets the hag, read the following:

You enter into what was once the captain's cabin, but has become something much darker. The walls, windows, and floor are overgrown with sickly fauna. Skeletal remains adorn the walls, along with trinkets from the surface. Hanging from the ceiling, what you first thought to be weeds are in fact faces—dozens upon dozens of severed faces hanging like grisly tapestries from above. At the center of it all stands a black iron cauldron, bubbling green, and a hideous monster of a woman. Hair like spindly weeds hangs in clumps from her skull. Her pale skin is translucent and iridescent like a fish, with patches of scales broken here and there by a sort of withering rot. A leather necklace dangles a flame-shaped charm at her chest. Eyes stare out of sunken black pits like smoldering pearls that freeze your hearts.

GM | Urswyk won't wait long before attacking, targeting the weakest party members first.

Threat: (1) Urswyk Spirit-Binder (see stat block section)

Tactics: Urswyk will use her Water Form ability and Ink Burst lair action to disorient the party and make herself hard to hit. She will Summon Minions whenever she can to bolster her numbers. She will try to wear one party member down at a time so she can raise them with her Undead Minions ability. If Urswyk's hit points are reduced to 10 or fewer, she will attempt to flee.

The encounter ends in one of two ways. First, if the party manages to slay Urswyk, she releases a shockwave that deals 1d8 necrotic energy to all creatures in the area. Upon her death, all her undead minions drop to the floor and the faces hung from the ceiling begin to glow. Their ghosts (the crew of the *Fair Maiden*, and her captain) can be seen briefly, giving thanks for their freedom before dissipating and passing on.

If Urswyk escapes, she will flee through the windows at the back of the room and throw the fire pendant from her necklace behind her. It explodes as a *fireball* spell. Players may pursue her if they wish, but may have more pressing concerns.

THE SINKING SHIP

Urswyk's final blast will shake the *Fair Maiden* loose from the delicate balance that held her in place on the cliff's edge. The ship is soon to fall into a deep abyss from which nothing can be salvaged. There is enough time to try and retrieve some of the treasure, but it is likely that several of the party are injured, possibly on death's door. The PCs can attempt to prevent the ship from going over the edge, focusing on trying to save the crewmembers that came with them while

BEAST HEAD *Huge monstrosity, neutral evil*

Armor Class 13 (Natural Armor) | **Hit Points** 114 (12d12 + 36) | **Speed** 30 ft., swim 40 ft.

STR	DEX	CON	INT	WIS	CHA
19 (+4)	14 (+2)	16 (+3)	2 (-4)	7 (-2)	5 (-3)

Skills Intimidation +1, Stealth +4

Damage Vulnerabilities fire

Condition Immunities charmed, frightened

Senses blindsight 60 ft., passive Perception 8

Languages -

Challenge 3 (200 XP)

Body Part. The beast head is part of a larger body. It controls the grabbing tentacles. If the head dies, the tentacle dies immediately.

Aversion to Fire. If the beast head takes fire damage, it has disadvantage on attack rolls and ability checks until the end of its next turn.

ACTIONS

Bite. Melee Weapon Attack; +6 to hit, reach 5 ft., one target. *Hit*: 21 (4d8 + 4) piercing damage.

Swallow. The beast head makes one bite attack against a Large or smaller creature that a grabbing tentacle has grappled. If the attack hits, the target takes the bite's damage, the target is swallowed, and the grapple ends. While swallowed, the creature is blinded and restrained. It has total cover against attacks and other effects outside the beast head, and it takes 14 (4d6) acid damage at the start of each of the beast head's turns.

If the beast head takes 20 damage or more on a single turn from a creature inside it, the beast head must succeed on a DC 20 Constitution saving throw at the end of that turn or regurgitate all swallowed creatures, which fall prone in a space within 10 feet of the beast head. If the beast head dies, a swallowed creature is no longer restrained by it and can escape from the corpse by using 30 feet of movement, exiting prone.

BARNACLE BEAST *Large monstrosity, unaligned*

Armor Class 14 (Natural Armor) | **Hit Points** 19 (3d10 + 3) | **Speed** 20 ft., swim 30 ft.

STR	DEX	CON	INT	WIS	CHA
14 (+2)	9 (-1)	14 (+2)	2 (-4)	10 (+0)	5 (-3)

Damage Resistances bludgeoning from nonmagical weapons

Damage Vulnerabilities fire

Senses darkvision 60 ft.; passive Perception 10

Languages -

Challenge ¼ (50 XP)

ACTIONS

Beak. Melee Weapon Attack; +4 to hit, reach 10 ft., one target. *Hit*: 6 (1d8 + 2) piercing damage.

SHIP'S MATE *Medium humanoid, any alignment*

Armor Class 12 (Leather Armor) | **Hit Points** 19 (3d8 + 6) | **Speed** 30 ft.

STR	DEX	CON	INT	WIS	CHA
14 (+2)	12 (+1)	14 (+2)	10 (-)	12 (+1)	9 (-1)

Skills Perception +3, Survival +3

Senses passive Perception 13

Languages Any one language (usually Common)

Challenge ½ (100 XP)

Defensive Formation. The ship's mate gains a +2 bonus to its AC if at least one of the mate's allies with a weapon is within 5 feet of the mate and the ally isn't incapacitated.

ACTIONS

Sabre. *Melee Weapon Attack*; +4 to hit, reach 5 ft., one target. *Hit*: 6 (1d8 + 2) slashing damage, or 7 (1d10 + 2) slashing damage if used with two hands to make a melee attack.

Shortbow. *Ranged Weapon Attack*: +2 to hit, range 80/320 ft., one creature. *Hit*: 5 (1d6 + 2) piercing damage.

GHOSTLY CREWMAN *Medium undead, any alignment*

Armor Class 10 | **Hit Points** 9 (2d8) | **Speed** 30 ft., fly 25 ft.

STR	DEX	CON	INT	WIS	CHA
7 (-2)	11 (+0)	10 (+0)	6 (-2)	13 (+1)	14 (+2)

Damage Vulnerabilities psychic, radiant

Damage Resistances bludgeoning, piercing, and slashing from nonmagical attacks

Damage Immunities poison

Condition Immunities exhaustion, paralyzed, petrified, poisoned, prone

Senses darkvision 60 ft., passive Perception 11

Languages Any languages it knew in life

Challenge ¼ (50 XP)

Ethereal Sight. The ghost can see 60 feet into the Ethereal Plane when it is on the Material Plane, and vice versa.

Incorporeal Movement. The ghost can move through other creatures and objects as if they were difficult terrain. It takes 5 (1d10) force damage if it ends its turn inside an object.

ACTIONS

Spectral Weapon. *Melee Weapon Attack*: +4 to hit, reach 5 ft., one target. *Hit*: 5 (1d6 + 2) necrotic damage.

Etherealness. The ghost enters the Ethereal Plane from the Material Plane, or vice versa. It is visible on the Material Plane while it is in the Border Ethereal, and vice versa, yet it can't affect or be affected by anything on the other plane.

CAPTAIN GREGOR HALSTED *Medium humanoid (human), neutral good*

Armor Class 13 (leather armor) | **Hit Points** 75 (10d8 + 30) | **Speed** 30 ft.

STR	DEX	CON	INT	WIS	CHA
13 (+1)	14 (+2)	16 (+3)	14 (+2)	14 (+2)	14 (+2)

Saving Throws Dex +4, Con +4, Wis +4

Skills Athletics +3, History +4, Intimidate +4, Nature +4, Persuasion +4, Survival +4

Senses passive Perception 12

Languages Common, Dwarvish, Elvish

Dauntless. Captain Halsted can choose to reroll any single attack roll, ability check, or saving throw. He must use the result of the new roll. He can use this ability three times per long rest.

Commanding Figure. As a bonus action, Captain Halsted can grant one ally within 120 feet (that can see and or hear him) advantage, as if he was using the Help action.

ACTIONS

Multiattack. The captain makes three melee attacks: two with his scimitar, and one with his dagger. Or the captain makes two ranged attacks with daggers.

Scimitar. Melee Weapon Attack: +4 to hit, reach 5 ft., one target. *Hit:* 5 (1d6 + 2) slashing damage.

Dagger. Melee or Ranged Weapon Attack: +4 to hit, reach 5 ft., or range 20/60 ft. *Hit:* 4 (1d4 + 2) piercing damage.

REACTIONS

Parry. The captain adds 2 to his AC against one melee attack that would hit. To use this ability, the captain must see the attacker and be wielding a melee weapon.

ROLEPLAYING INFORMATION

Captain Halsted is a hard and weather-worn fellow. His leathery skin and many scars speaks of a hard life at sea, while the look in his piercing sea green eyes speaks fully of his grim, determined purpose.

Ideal: "In life, one must be as relentless as the seas themselves to ensure one's success."

Bond: "Not even death will keep me from clearing my family's reputation!"

Flaw: "There is, indeed, no sacrifice too high to achieve my goals."

THE SECRETS OF THE PLAGUE SPIDERS

WRITTEN BY FINLAY LOGAN, ILLUSTRATED BY KATIE GREEN

A 5E Adventure for Levels 3 | You will need a copy of the 5E core rulebooks to fully utilize this adventure. You should also familiarize yourself with the map and spells used by the foes prior to playing the adventure.

Glossary | PC: Playable Characters | GM: Game Master | DC: Difficulty Class
HP: Hit Points | NPC: Non-Player Character

Adventure Scaling | This adventure is intended for four 3rd-level characters. If the party is stronger or weaker (more/fewer members or higher/lower level), you can modify the difficulty of combat encounters by adjusting the hit points, damage, or number of monsters. For a weaker party, lower the average damage of monsters by two and their hit points by five. For a stronger party, increase the number of foes, or replace one plague spider with one plague spider hunter.

THE HOUSE ON GREEN WILLOW LANE

1D—BELLY OF THE SPIDER QUEEN
2D—DUNGEON
3D—ALTAR OF ANCIENT VENOM
4D—EGG SAC CHAMBER

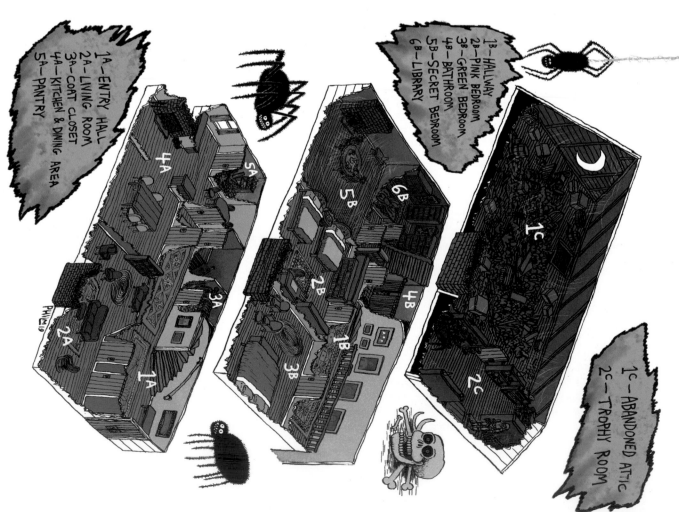

1A—ENTRY HALL
2A—LIVING ROOM
3A—COAT CLOSET
4A—KITCHEN & DINING AREA
5A—PANTRY

1B—HALLWAY
2B—PINK BEDROOM
3B—GREEN BEDROOM
4B—BATHROOM
5B—SECRET BEDROOM
6B—LIBRARY

1C—ABANDONED ATTIC
2C—TROPHY ROOM

PLOT

It's been fifty years since the local hero, Stella Luminita, helped put an end to the Spiderplague, and neither she nor the spiders have been seen since. But now the plague spiders are back, and no one in town is safe. It's up to the party to find the source of the evil and put it to rest once and for all.

BACKGROUND

The legend of Stella Luminita and the Spiderplague is well known in town. Player characters can discover this information by asking questions of the locals in the market square or the temple.

- Fifty years ago, the town was overrun by a plague of mutant spiders. This event, known as the Spiderplague, nearly wiped out the town. The Spiderplague was stopped by a local hero, a paladin named Stella Luminita.

- Stella wore golden armor and carried a glowing long-sword. Her face was always covered, but people agreed that she had long hair that was so bright it looked white.

- Stella got her powers from her deity, the Lord of the Living Light, the same one that the town's temple is dedicated to.

- The spiders that attacked the town during the Spiderplague were a rare variety. They were deep purple with a skull-shaped mark on their abdomen. Their painful bites caused weakness and paralysis. Some were said to hunt in packs like wolves.

- Rumors swirled that the Spiderplague was brought on by dark elves performing clandestine rituals to bring the wrath of their deities upon the town. At the time, dark elves were rare and mistrusted; only one family lived in the area, in an old house on Green Willow Lane at the edge of town.

- A brigade of townsfolk led by the local clerics from the Temple of the Golden Light got together to drive the dark elves out and hopefully stop the Spiderplague. In the chaos, the parents were grievously wounded and the son killed. They had a daughter, but no one is sure what happened to her.

- Soon after the Spiderplague, Stella disappeared from town and was never heard from again. Since then, the town faced its share of struggles, but Stella never came back to help, and the town learned to carry on without her.

- Most of the people who remember the Spiderplague have died or moved to other places, and the event has faded into local legend; more myth than fact. Vanna Hawthorn, the local priest, is one of the few people in the village who remembers. A teen at the time, his experiences inspired him to become a priest.

- Today, the old house on Green Willow Lane is inhabited by a quiet older woman. From what the villagers can figure out, her name is Melanie Noctophel and she's a widow with no children. She keeps a spare room in her house for travelers who don't have a place to stay in town.

- The village gets a fair amount of travelers coming to visit the beautiful temple. Some return, and some say they will but never do.

- There are concerns that the plague spiders weren't completely eradicated. Five years ago, youngsters playing down by the Big Rock River discovered a cave filled with plague spider cocoons and eggs. Recently, people claim to have seen small purple spiders in the woods east of town. And just last year, Red Harry, the fishmonger's son, turned up dead after a summer festival, covered in webbing and swollen bite marks.

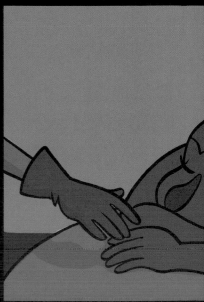

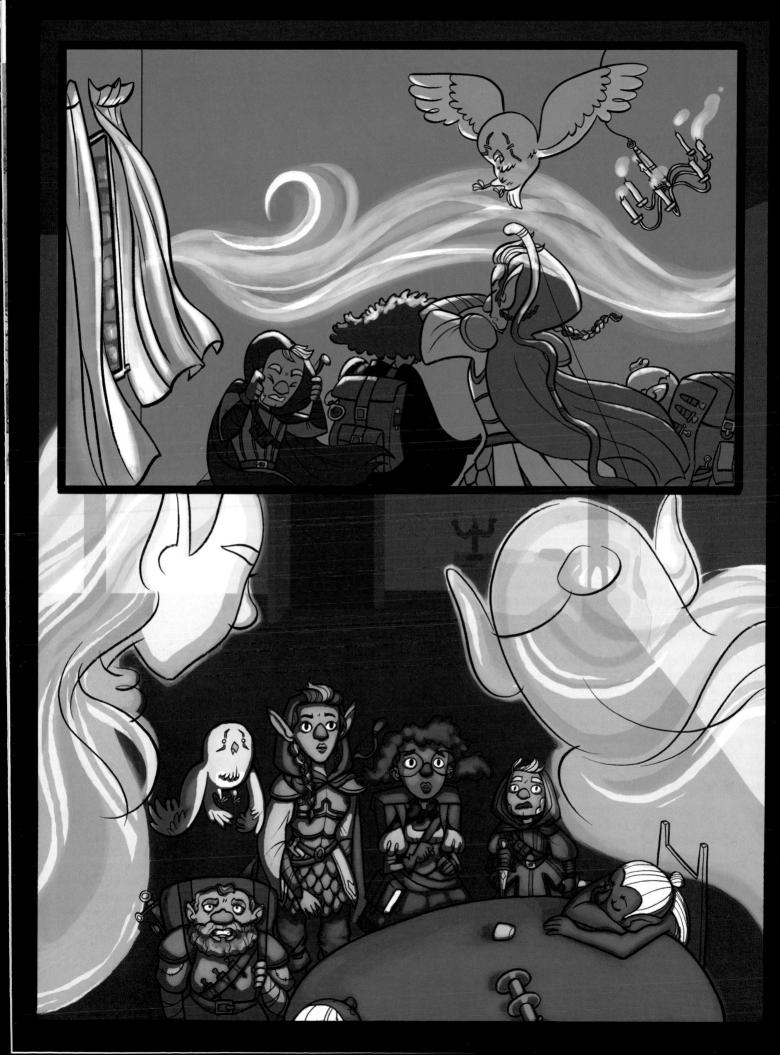

Dexterity (Acrobatics) or Strength (Athletics) check to leap or balance across on the few remaining safe boards. A character who fails their check falls to the hallway below, taking 1d6 bludgeoning damage.

Once the characters have crossed safely, they can clear the debris away from the door. The door is made of plain oak banded with iron, with an imposing lock decorated with a spiderweb pattern. The lock can be picked with a DC 18 Dexterity check using Thieves' Tools, or opened using the iron key found in the kitchen.

- **Loot:** Rummaging in the debris with an Intelligence (Investigation) DC 10 turns up 15 cp, a glass figurine of a dog worth 2 gp, and a tarnished silver baby rattle worth 10 gp.

TROPHY ROOM

This small, dimly-lit room contains trophies and relics from the past. Shelves display statues and old books bound in fine leather. On the wall above the table, two longswords chased with gold are mounted, one of them glowing faintly, illuminating the room. On the left side of the room, a suit of golden armor gleams brightly, as if freshly polished. On the right, an enormous purple spider looms out of the shadows, its mandibles open, ready to bite!

GM | After first glance, it becomes clear that the spider is a taxidermized monster and poses no threat. It is larger than any spider the characters have seen before. A character who succeeds on a DC 15 Intelligence (History or Nature) check recognizes that this must be one of the monstrosities that attacked the village during the Spiderplague.

The golden armor was worn by Stella Luminita in her youth and bears the signs of many battles fought. The books and statues are prayer books and devotional statues dedicated to the Lord of Living Light.

Suit of Armor: A character who succeeds on a DC 15 Wisdom (Perception) check notices that suit of armor is

actually hinged. The front of the suit swings forward to reveal a secret staircase leading to the basement.

Trapped Staircase: The staircase hidden inside the suit of armor is trapped, and will turn into a slide if anyone puts weight on the trapped stair. Characters checking for traps who succeed on a DC 12 Wisdom (Perception) check notice that starting from the eighth step from the top, the stairs are not completely attached to the wall. Players can jump over the trapped step using a DC 12 Dexterity (Acrobatics) or Strength (Athletics) check. A DC 12 Dexterity check with Thieves' Tools is needed to disarm the mechanism that triggers the rest of the stairs, or a character could attempt to jam it using an appropriate tool. These checks are made with disadvantage if the characters are moving quickly.

- **Loot:** The room contains a +1 longsword (see core rulebooks) decorated with shooting stars and Stella's motto, "Her light shines bright." In addition, the room contains two ivory statuettes worth 100 gp each, and a prayer book with a rose quartz inlaid in its cover, worth 50 gp.

LOWER FLOOR

GM | Beyond the ordinary-looking basement lies the subterranean complex where Melanie traps her victims and performs dark rites to her new patron, the Queen of Darkness.

BASEMENT

The smell of musty air hits you as you descend the creaky wooden stairs to the basement. Decaying shelves and household refuse litter the room. A heap of old clothes lies in one corner, and mold covers the low ceiling.

GM | A pressure plate concealed beneath the old clothes releases a section of floor that slides backwards to reveal a hole leading down to darkness. The seam in the floor

indicating the portion of the floor that moves can be spotted with a DC 15 Wisdom (Perception) or Intelligence (Investigation) check. The drop is 20 feet straight down. As soon as the pressure plate is released, the sliding door closes again. Investigating the shelves (DC 15, roll with advantage if the characters have already located the trapdoor) reveals that one of the cans near the pressure plate is attached to the shelf with a hinge, and functions as a lever. The hinge is rusty, requiring a DC 12 Strength check to operate. Pulling it locks the door in place (open or closed).

A staircase below leads to one of the subterranean passages in Melanie's secret lair.

SUBTERRANEAN PASSAGES

These underground passages have been carved from the rock. The weight of the earth above you has an oppressive feeling as you make your way down the corridor.

GM | Eight passages lead off from the main chamber, forming an image of a giant spider. One houses the dungeon, one conceals the staircase leading to the basement, and one is home to a pair of gricks that have made their nest in a pile of rubble. These gricks can be used to challenge players who poke around the other tunnels too long (see core rulebook for stats). The remaining passages are empty except for spiderwebs, crunchy husks of dead insects, and bad vibes.

DUNGEON

This long narrow room is lined with white cocoons, each about 8 feet tall. Behind them, manacles bolted to the stone walls are barely visible, hidden by the soft white wisps forming halos around the cocoons. The floor is littered with what appear to be shrunken and withered bodies.

GM | Melanie uses this dungeon to imprison her victims, where they become food for her spiders while awaiting a place in her dark rituals. The party may enter from the Belly of the Spider Queen, or they may enter through the trap in the living room (deliberately or otherwise). If the characters are quiet (DC 13 Dexterity [Stealth]) and leave this area without disturbing anything, they may avoid alerting any nearby creatures. However, falling through the trapdoor or disturbing a cocoon will cause nearby giant plague spiders to scuttle from their hiding places near the ceiling and attack.

- **Threats:** 3 giant plague spiders, 1 plague spider hunter (see stat block section)

- **Loot:** The victims in the cocoons carried a variety of valuables on them. Searching the room and succeeding on a DC 12 Intelligence (Investigation) check reveals 35 gp, 130 sp, a necklace set with three moonstones valued at 150 gp, a *potion of poison resistance*, and a *potion of greater healing* (see core rulebooks).

BELLY OF THE SPIDER QUEEN

The light in this massive, ten-sided chamber reflects

dizzyingly off flecks of mica in the columns and rock walls. The whole of the enormous room seems to shimmer and sparkle. Webs stretch across the open spaces, dotted with white where unsuspecting creatures collided with the sticky strands. Tall, arched doorways lead out from eight of the walls to the east and west, while on the northern wall you can see green light coruscating from a chamber high above. You hear echoing sounds of other creatures: the scuttling of arachnids, and the distant flapping of wings.

GM | If the characters enter from one of the hallways (not the stairs from the attic), add:

An opening on the southern wall leads to a staircase that ascends into darkness.

The secret staircase in the attic leads to this area. The cavernous room is home to a nest of stirges that feed on the small prey that escapes the spiders' notice. If the party makes no effort to be stealthy (by failing a DC 10 Dexterity [Stealth] check or making excessive noise in the area), they will attract the attention of five stirges, which fly down from the ceiling and attack.

- **Threats:** 5 stirges (see core rulebooks)

NYMGAR AND T'RISS *Medium undead, neutral*

Armor Class 11
Hit Points 22 (5d8)
Speed 0 ft., fly 40 ft.

STR	DEX	CON	INT	WIS	CHA
1 (−5)	13 (+1)	10 (+0)	10 (+0)	12 (+1)	17 (+3)

Damage Resistances acid, fire, lightning, thunder; bludgeoning, piercing, and slashing from nonmagical attacks

Damage Immunities cold, necrotic, poison

Condition Immunities charmed, exhaustion, frightened, grappled, paralyzed, petrified, poisoned, prone, restrained

Senses darkvision 60 ft., passive Perception 11

Languages Common, Elvish, Undercommon

Challenge 2 (450 XP)

Ethereal Sight. The ghost can see 60 feet into the Ethereal Plane when it is on the Material Plane, and vice versa.

Incorporeal Movement. The ghost can move through other creatures and objects as if they were difficult terrain. It takes 5 (1d10) force damage if it ends its turn inside an object.

ACTIONS

Withering Touch. Melee Weapon Attack: +5 to hit, reach 5 ft., one target. Hit: 10 (2d6 + 3) necrotic damage.

Etherealness. The ghost enters the Ethereal Plane from the Material Plane, or vice versa. It is visible on the Material Plane while it is in the Border Ethereal, and vice versa, yet it can't affect or be affected by anything on the other plane.

Horrifying Visage. Each not undead creature within 60 feet of the ghost that can see it must succeed on a DC 13 Wisdom saving throw or be frightened for one minute. If the save fails by five or more, the target also ages 1d4 × 10 years. A frightened target can repeat the saving throw at the end of each of its turns, ending the frightened condition on itself on a success. If a target's saving throw is successful, or the effect ends for it, the target is immune to this ghost's Horrifying Visage for the next 24 hours. The aging effect can be reversed with a *greater restoration* spell, but only within 24 hours of it occurring.

Corrupting Emotion (Recharge 5–6). The ghost releases a torrent of pain and anger. All living creatures with 30 feet must succeed on a DC 13 Charisma saving throw. On a failure, a living creature suffers 10 (3d6) psychic damage.

REGINALD'S CLOSET

WRITTEN BY TELINE GUERRA, ILLUSTRATED BY HARI CONNER

A 5E Low-Tier Adventure | You will need a copy of the 5E core rulebooks to fully utilize this adventure. You need to familiarize yourself with the adventure and the map to fully enjoy this adventure. It is intended for low-tier characters (level 3).

Glossary | PC: Playable Characters | GM: Game Master | DC: Difficulty Class
HP: Hit Points | NPC: Non-Player Character

PLOT

The party is traveling a wooded road when they come across a halfling merchant, Reginald Bythehill. Reginald is attacked by marauders who want something he has. After the party defends him, he takes them to his house to show them a powerful magic item. Instead, the party is dropped into a room with no way out. The party must decipher a message written in code on the wall in order to uncover the item, *Gilda's Ring of Resurrection*, and leave.

BACKGROUND

The pantheon of gods worshipped by halflings isn't very well known to outsiders. They are pragmatic, unpretentious gods that never get caught up in the battles of other deities.

RULES

Before you begin, be sure to make note of the characters' passive perception.

Familiarize yourself with the rules for swimming, surprise, and investigation.

STARTING THE ADVENTURE

"Adventurers! Adventurers! Wait! I have here the very products, the very things you need. Even if you don't know you need them yet!" The halfling runs out into the road in front of you. A horse rears.

He is balding, plump, and wears a vest and a long coat. He carries a large trunk of peculiar design. He shakes it, and legs come out of the bottom, the sides snap open to make a table, and he pulls back the top to reveal his wares neatly presented: daggers, a short sword, a couple of vials.

"Reginald Bythehill, purveyor of weapons, preferred seller for dungeon explorers, at your service. Now you look like someone who appreciates a good blade. This dagger is made of dwarven steel, good steel. Try it for yourselves."

GM | Reginald doesn't have much, but he does have two *potions of healing* (valued at 50g) that he is willing to sell for ten percent above market price, considering how far they are from civilization. Besides a few daggers and one shortsword, he also has arrows and crossbow bolts. The daggers are indeed dwarven steel, and have the imprint of the maker, Kyutco, on the hilt. Dwarven steel does not have special stats in 5e, nor are there bonuses for well-made weapons.

As Reginald sells his wares to the party, any player with passive perception of 12 or higher will notice a number of ravens that seem to be watching from the treetops. Any player with a passive perception of 15 or higher will get a feeling of being watched or see something move in the trees.

If anyone performs a Perception check, a DC 15 sees something is moving in the trees and prevents being surprised.

DC 18 or higher, the player spots the glint of armor. This will give the perceiver a chance to get a surprise round on the attackers, if they so desire.

Once the party is done shopping, Reginald closes the case and urges the party to come see him again.

If the party has not perceived the threat, then they will continue up the road a bit before they hear Reginald cry out for help as he is attacked.

THE MARAUDERS

The attackers are a mixed group of mercenaries.

If the party did not see them coming, they will return to find the attackers picking up Reginald as he struggles, and one of them attempting to open the case. If the party did see them coming, they can attack them in the trees before the marauders reach Reginald.

Reginald does not fight. He will run towards party members, trying to put the party between himself and the attackers. He is carrying his case, and always uses his action for double movement, so during each round, he moves 40 feet (see stat block for more info).

The marauders seem to have no real strategy except to reach Reginald. If they do reach him, they will take his case, pick him up, and run away. If two or more of their number are killed, the rest will cut their losses and run away, each in a different direction.

If any of them are captured, a DC 10 Persuasion check will lead them to reveal that they were hired by a wizard to capture Reginald and his belongings. None of them know or care why they were sent. They don't know where they were instructed to take him (they didn't think to ask) or who hired them. They seem like adventurers that are down on their luck, looking for an easy score.

- **Threats**: D4 orcs (see core rulebooks) with spiked battle clubs;

  D6 human fighters (see "Thug" stat block in core rulebooks; armed with longswords instead of mace as in stat block – Long sword. *Melee Weapon Attack*: +4 to hit, reach 5 ft., one creature. *Hit*: 6 [1d8 + 2] slashing damage or wielded two handed – *Hit*: 7 [1d10 + 2] slashing damage);

  D4+2 drow archers (see "Scout" stat block in core rulebooks) in the trees, firing from cover.

- **Loot**: d8 copper pieces, 1 day's rations, and a flask of rotgut each
- **Fighting off marauders**: 100 XP

REGINALD IS SAVED!

Reginald checks himself over, relieved. "Oh, I knew when I saw you, you were good eggs! Good eggs, indeed. You worship good gods, then, eh? I've slept through my share of sermons, but I'll be giving an extra offering, I tell you. Thanks for keeping my body and soul together. It may not be much of a body, but I'm quite attached to it."

GM | Reginald will gather up the case, or what's left of it, and head home. If the party offers to accompany him, he will gladly accept. If not, he will wonder aloud how far the attackers have gone, and when they will be back.

He knows the marauders will return. If the party killed them all, he knows that whoever sent them will send more next time. He is pathetic and weak.

If the party does not volunteer to accompany him, he will promise them a reward for their help if they come with him to his house. He will offer all the money he has on him, which is 18 gold (plus whatever the party paid for any items they bought), and he has a 600 more carefully hidden.

He leads the party off the road, down a deer path, to a tidy little house built among the roots of a giant tree. There's a neat garden off to one side and a separate door to a work room. He leads the party in the front door.

If anyone asks Reginald why he lives in so isolated a place, he will say that he likes the solitude. With a Persuasion check of DC 15, Reginald will reveal, with great embarrassment, that he found the house unoccupied a few months ago, and didn't see the point in letting a perfectly good house go to waste.

Passive perception of 14 or higher notices that as the party travels, a raven follows them.

The house has a low roof and tiny, halfling-sized furniture. Upon entering the house, anyone taller than a halfling will need to do a DC 10 Dexterity check to avoid hitting their head on the rafters.

INSIDE THE HOUSE

Once you are inside, Reginald closes the door and turns to you, his face serious. "They aren't the first what's attacked me, and they won't be the last. I'm afraid I've bitten off more than I can chew. You are good folk. I could tell as soon as I saw you. I can trust you."

He pulls the curtains shut, looks up the chimney, then whispers. "I recently made a discovery. I think it might be quite important. At first, I thought it was a great honor. But since then, I can barely leave my house. It has been terrible for business. It's the entrance to a vault. And from what I can tell, there must be something valuable inside."

GM | Reginald leads them to a closet, and asks them to go in. The closet is 5-foot by 5-foot and has the same low ceiling. The party will need to do whatever it takes to cram in together. Reginald is paranoid about being spied on and assures them that the closet is the only place they can't be overheard. He promises to tell them how to find the vault if they come with him into the closet.

There are coats and clothes hung on hooks, a broken chair, a broom, and other things. A dusty old rug covers the floor, but it is too large and bunches up against the walls.

Once everyone in

the party has crammed into the closet and the door is shut, the closet is pitch dark, but anyone with darkvision can see. Reginald lights a candle. He has climbed onto the top of a trunk. "I do like you folks," he says, and then pulls back the rug and pries up a floorboard. Under the floorboard, sigils and runes have been etched into the earth.

If the party is willing, Reginald will say the activation phrase, and the party will teleport.

A successful *detect magic* spell will reveal the Teleportation Circle, which is the only way to enter the vault. The circle is directed at a particular location with teleportation runes etched around it. All that is required to use this Teleportation Circle is a willingness to be teleported and the activation words. It does not require the casting of any spells by Reginald or the party.

If confronted, Reginald will reveal that he doesn't completely understand what this circle is. He did, however, find a lovely note with the activation words written on it. He shows it to the party. It is written in Halfling.

If anyone reads Halfling, they can read the note. It says, "A great treasure is nearby. Under the floor is the gate. Say, 'greli-ac, greli-corn, greli-deor' to get in. Also, here is a recipe for excellent cheese bread. It goes well with tea."

Reginald does not want to go into the vault with you. He is a merchant, not an adventurer. If the party asks him to go with them, he will attempt an opposed Persuasion check to avoid going.

If the party forces him to go, he will. He will continue to act with great caution, choosing to hide rather than fight.

THE VAULT

You find yourself transported onto a crystal platform, high above a pool of water, with stairs that wind down.

The platform cracks underneath you. It was never meant to bear so much weight. Below you is a pool of water. You hope the water is warm as the platform shatters.

GM | The party drops 30 feet into the pool of warm, salty water. The platform was built to hold the weight of one halfling.

A successful Swim check of DC 15 will get players to the edge of the pool. Players wearing heavy armor will have disadvantage on their Swim check. If a player on land throws a rope or in some other way assists a swimmer, the swimmer can have advantage on their roll.

A Perception check underwater of DC 10 shows that the pool is 200 feet deep, and widens considerably at the bottom. Shadows move in the depths.

When the last player emerges from the pool, the players see two separate dorsal fins rise out of the water and start

to circle slowly. These fins are from a pair of magically summoned hunter sharks (see core rulebooks) that are summoned once every 24 hours when the water of the pool is disturbed, in this case when the PCs fell into it.

The PCs find themselves in a round room, 60 feet in diameter. The walls and floors are made of cut stone, expertly constructed. In the center of the round room is the round pool of water that is 50 feet in diameter, leaving a walkway area that goes all the way around the room. There are two doorways on opposite sides of the room, east and west, each one raised above the floor by 5 feet. These doorways have no doors but are instead covered with fabric veils. Players can enter either door whenever they wish. The ceiling is a smooth dome. Everything looks extremely well made, with no sign of rot or crumbling.

The room is filled with light, though it is impossible to see where it is coming from.

THE PUZZLE

The walls of the main room are embossed with carvings of sea creatures—every creature you can imagine. Fish, dolphins, sharks, mer-people, squid, and so on. They all appear to be looking at a place on the wall to the north,

where a frame surrounds the following message:

KULX XKNOOLJQ QGDGC BNOOJEX

KULX EJQP VJGX QJK QGLBU

ALQV KUG XKGGV PJW ZNQQJK CLVG

KJ OGNV PJW JQ PJWC FNP

The message is not in any known language and cannot be read with *comprehend languages*.

On the ground are dozens of round stones, shaped like soup cans. Each stone has a letter embossed identically on both flat sides. If the party checks the stones, they find every letter of the alphabet represented, and many versions of each letter.

Each letter in the message on the wall is set on its own round stone. Each letter stone that the party finds on the ground is a slightly different length, but the stones with the same letters are the same length.

The way the wall puzzle works is that the letter stones on the ground can be pressed over the letters in the wall, pushing the former letter back, and replacing it in the message so that the decoded message is revealed.

If they put in a letter, all the corresponding letters will change. If they put an "A" in for a "G," for example, all the "G's" will turn

to "A's." They can put the wrong letter into the wall.

In each of the two rooms, the players will find purple stones that represent hints.

With a Perception or Investigation check of DC 12, they can hear mechanical noises when a stone is pushed in, but they are very subtle, made by extremely skilled hands. The puzzle works as a giant, complicated key, but to what end is unclear.

GM | Players who are familiar with this kind of puzzle might be able to solve it on their own, while players who haven't seen this kind of puzzle before will need help.

Use your discretion. The puzzle should take some time to solve, but not be frustrating or overwhelming.

Based on your party's needs, you can approach the puzzle in one of three ways.

FOR PLAYERS WHO ENJOY DIFFICULT PUZZLES

When they plug the purple stones into a letter slot on the wall, reveal to them what the decoded letter for that slot is.

So if they put the purple stone into a slot for "K," a "T" appears on the purple stone. Each purple clue stone can only be used once.

For each Knowledge or Investigation check of DC 15, reveal one of the following hints:

The most common three letter words in the English language are "you," "and," "the," or "but."

"TH" is a very common letter combination.

Very few two letter words end in "o." The most common is "to."

FOR PLAYERS WHO PREFER EASY PUZZLES

When they plug the purple stones into a letter slot on the wall, reveal to them what the decoded word for that slot is.

So if they put the purple stone into a slot for "K" in "KULX," "THIS" appears. Be clear that all the corresponding letters in the puzzle also change. Purple hint stones work only once.

If they plug in the wrong letter, the wall spits it back out immediately. This is not to encourage random letter placement, but to keep players from going down the wrong track. If players resort to random letter placing, it will take twenty minutes to solve the puzzle, no check needed. Go on to "For players who don't want to do the puzzle."

Give the hints to help solve the puzzle for every Intelligence or Wisdom ability checks of DC 10 the PCs can make, if needed.

FOR PLAYERS WHO DON'T WANT TO DO THE PUZZLE

If you have players who prefer to fight and other players who want to do the puzzle, you can add an optional conflict here: a magically summoned giant octopus or the two hunter sharks.

A **Giant octopus** (see stats in core rulebook) dwells in the pool, and while the players are occupied with the wall, it reaches a tentacle out and tries to grab a player character and pull them into the pool.

Once a player is in the water, they will be attacked by two hunter sharks (see stats in core rulebook).

- **Threats**: Giant octopus and 2 hunter sharks

THE ANSWER TO THE PUZZLE IS:

THIS STALLION NEVER GALLOPS,

THIS PONY DOES NOT NEIGH

FIND THE STEED YOU CANNOT RIDE

TO LEAD YOU ON YOUR WAY.

THE EASTERN ROOM

An easy climb up five feet puts the party in front of a doorway covered by a veil. Up close, the party sees that the veil is decorated with birds and snakes of all kinds. It is as though someone were listing species here.

The veil moves aside easily, silently. Beyond it is darkness. The only light is what comes through the doorway.

The first thing you notice inside the room is the sound, a rustling of thousands of small, hard things. The second thing you notice is the shape in the center of the room. The shape is still, though the edges seem to vibrate. Its skin catches the light in a pattern like glitter.

The shape stands. The rustling grows louder as it moves. It is humanoid, though it has no eyes, no mouth, no distinct features at all.

Something round and glowing is embedded in its forehead.

GM | This round, domed room is 20 feet in diameter. There is no light source in this room. Players are immediately attacked.

This is a bug golem, made of cockroaches, scorpions, and centipedes, all writhing together in the shape of a man.

The insects are alive, trying to break free of the monstrosity, and they will grab on to whatever touches the bug golem and crawl away.

When the bug golem is hit, a chunk of insects goes flying off, forming a swarm of insects that then attack the party (see stat block).

When the golem is killed, the insects that make up the body are freed, and the ones still living scatter around the room. All that remains is the purple stone, a cylinder like the letter stones in the main room. It is not required for the adventure that players fight the golem. They find the remains of other adventurers.

- **Threat**: Bug Golem-1800 XP
- **Loot**: 3d6 gold pieces and a purple hint stone

THE WESTERN ROOM

An easy climb up five feet puts the party in front of a doorway covered by a veil. Up close, the party sees that the veil is decorated with bugs and insects of all kinds. It is as though someone were listing species here.

The veil moves aside easily, silently. A breeze stirs the veil.

This room is filled with randomly placed pillars, some of which have toppled. In the center of the room is a giant spider web. In the center of the web is a round stone, glowing purple.

GM | In this room, but not in the web, two phase spiders (see stats in core rulebook) await. A Wisdom (Perception) DC 16 check reveals the beasts. As soon as players enter the room, they will attack.

The spiders do not have to be killed. If party members get the stone and leave the room without disturbing the spiders (if the players choose a stealth approach or some other kind of clever solution to avoid confronting the spiders), they will not follow.

NEW MONSTER STAT BLOCK

BUG GOLEM *Medium construct, neutral*

Armor Class 9 | **Hit Points** 93 (11d8 + 44) | **Speed** 30 ft.

STR	DEX	CON	INT	WIS	CHA
19 (+4)	9 (-1)	18 (+4)	6 (-2)	10 (+0)	5 (-3)

Skills Stealth +2

Damage Immunities lightning, poison, bludgeoning, piercing, and slashing from nonmagical weapons not constructed of adamantine

Condition Immunities charmed, exhaustion, frightened, paralyzed, petrified, poisoned

Senses darkvision 60 ft., passive Perception 10

Languages Halfling, but can't speak

Challenge 5 (1800 XP)

Berserk. Whenever the golem starts its turn with 40 hit points or fewer, roll a d6. On a 6, the golem goes berserk. On each of its turns while berserk, the golem attacks the nearest creature it can see. If no creature is near enough to move to and attack, the golem attacks an object, with preference for an object smaller than itself. Once the golem goes berserk, it continues to do so until it is destroyed or regains all its hit points.

Aversion of Fire. If the golem takes fire damage, it has disadvantage on attack rolls and ability checks until the end of its next turn.

Immutable Form. The golem is immune to any spell or effect that would alter its form.

Lightning Absorption. Whenever the golem is subjected to lightning damage, it takes no damage and instead regains a number of hit points equal to the lightning damage dealt.

Magic Resistance. The golem has advantage on saving throws against spells and other magical effects.

Magic Weapons. The golem's weapon attacks are magical.

ACTIONS

Multiattack. The bug golem makes two melee attacks.

Slam. *Melee Weapon Attack:* +7 to hit, reach 5 ft., one target. *Hit:* 13 (2d8 + 4) bludgeoning damage.

REACTIONS

Insect Swarm. When the bug golem takes less than 20 hp of damage in a single hit, it releases an insect swarm from its body. Each swarm is identical to the insect swarm stat block found in the core rulebook.

FOREST OF DELUSION

WRITTEN BY GEOFFREY GOLDEN, ILLUSTRATED BY ANNA LIISA JONES

This is a self-contained gamebook adventure. You don't need any rulebooks or even other gamers to play it—just a pencil and two dice.

PLOT

Vesska Moonwynd is an elf ranger lost in a strange and sinister forest where no one can be trusted. In this game-book adventure, navigate Vesska through the treacherous woods, battle monsters, and make it to your cousin's wedding on time! (Or your mother will kill you!)

RULES

Ready for an adventure? You can play this one right now! All you need is a pencil, the Character Sheet on page 122, and two dice: a d6 and a d20.

NAVIGATION

To make decisions, go to the corresponding Passage Number. (For example, if you want to milk the cow, go to 91. If you want to fight the cow to the death, go to 66.) It might be helpful to make a map to keep track of where you've been.

ITEMS

Found an item on your journey? Keep track of it in your Character Sheet's "Inventory" section. Remember, you only have five arrows in your quiver—whenever you use one, subtract it from your total.

PERCEPTION

Think a character you encounter might be hiding something? When prompted, you can roll a d20 to do a Perception check (once per section). Roll a 16 or above and you'll get more info—or summon your owl familiar, Flake, to automatically pass the check (once per game).

COMBAT

There are monsters in these here woods. When you encounter an enemy, here's what to do...

1. Roll a d20. If the number is equal to or greater than the enemy's Defense number, you hit them! (Yay!) Otherwise, they hit you. (Boo!)

    a. You Hit Them! Roll a d6 to determine how much damage you inflicted. Add +5 for your dagger and +7 for your arrows. You choose which weapon to use, but you only have five arrows. If you rolled a 20 on step one, multiply the total damage inflicted by 2. Subtract the damage from the enemy's hit points.

    b. They Hit You! Enemies attack differently. The story will tell you how to determine their damage as you encounter them. Subtract the damage they cause from your hit points on your Character Sheet.

2. Repeat until either you or your enemy is at zero hit points.

DEATH

If you get to zero hit points, reset your Character Sheet and start again at Passage Number 1.

It'll take quick wits and a bit of luck to make it through the adventure. Can you get all three endings? Happy questing!

INTRODUCTION

You are Vesska Moonwynd: noble elf, gifted archer, pub lightweight.

You rub your eyes, waking in a bed of straw. Your head is pounding. This isn't the Fanfare Inn Express. It's an abandoned shack in some forest. You must've had too much evermead at the inn and decided to go exploring.

You're traveling to Elven Court for your cousin's wedding. Mother will be there. She wanted you to be a noble, like her. Instead, you're a ranger with a hangover. You remember her advice for you:

"If you're going to live in the woods like a filthy animal, be careful who you trust. It's kill or be killed out there."

You get to your feet, stretch, and wipe a few bits of straw off your butt. You rummage through a small shelf of junk—torn-up spell books, a box of broken wands—then grab something useful.

ADD *POTION OF HEALING* TO YOUR INVENTORY

Drink at any time, even during battle. When you do, restore all your hit points.

- **Continue to the next Passage.**

1

You gather your things and leave the shack. You look at the sun between the forest treetops. You're running late to the wedding. Shit.

And then you notice the giant spider a few feet from where you're standing! It's the size of the shack and baring its huge fangs.

"Oh great," you think, "Now I'm going to be even later."

GIANT SPIDER

Hit Points: 14 | Defense: 7 | Bite Attack: Roll a d6.

- **If you survive, go to 12.**

- **If you die in battle, start over from the Introduction.**

MIDDLE of the WOODS

CHARACTER SHEET

NAME • Vesska Moonwynd

CLASS • Ranger

RACE • Wood elf

BACKGROUND • Noble

HIT POINTS • 12

DAGGER • 1d6 + 5 damage

LONGBOW • 1d6 + 7 damage

UNIQUE ABILITY
Summon Flake the Owl
Automatically pass one Perception check per game

INVENTORY:
Start with 5 Arrows

ARROW COUNTER

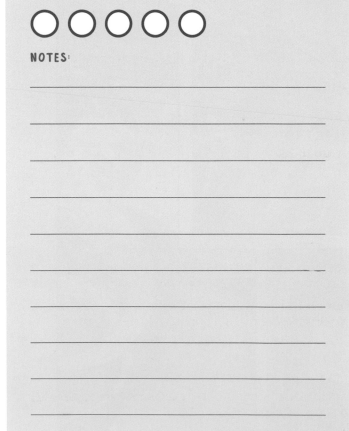

NOTES:

_____

_____

_____

_____

_____

_____

_____

_____

_____

2

There are scribbles on the inside of the canoe. She's written the word "EVEN" in big, bold letters.

Figure out the box combination, then go to that Passage Number.

- **To go back and take the north path, like the elf warrior suggested, go to 5.**

3

You walk westward on the trail. Drops of green liquid fall off the blue leaves, pooling into bubbling hot puddles on the ground. This is a very strange place.

Off the path, you notice a wild elf in tattered brown rags with long, stringy brown hair, practicing her archery. She turns her head to you.

"You must leave this place at once," she commands.

"I'd love to," you respond. "Which way do I go?"

"The cave tunnel. No-Elves Wail at Night."

"We don't? That's news to me."

And with that, she vanishes into the forest. The trail splits off in two directions.

- **To walk northeast, go to 23.**
- **To walk northwest, go to 8.**
- **If you do a successful Perception check, go to 19.**

4

You squint as the elf warrior scratches his head. Tiny sparkles fall from his hair like dandruff. Hmmm.

- **To take the north path, go to 5.**
- **To continue east, go to 20.**

5

As you travel north, you notice these trees grow no leaves.

The path takes you to a dead end. You hear flapping wings behind you. Leaves and branches on the ground blow away.

You turn around. Scaly green skin, cat-like yellow eyes, a puff of toxic smoke escapes its mouth of sharp teeth: you are face-to-face with a dragon wyrmling!

"I'll...make her...p-p-p-proud," the young dragon stutters.

You've been tricked, and now you have no choice but to fight this beast.

GREEN DRAGON WYRMLING

Hit Points: 22 | Defense: 10 | Claw Attack: Roll a d6 twice. Add both numbers together.

- **If you survive, go to 14.**

6

You take the silver bracelet out of your Explorer's Pack and present it to your mother.

"Can you put this on the gift table for me?" you ask.

"It's beautiful," she states, surprised. "I'm impressed. I always imagine you wrestling in the mud all day with giant boars and gelatinous cubes. How did you get the money for a gift like this?"

"Me, the boars, and the cubes all chipped in," you smile, then make your way to your seat. The ceremony is about to begin.

Your mother looks dumbfounded. Maybe this won't be such a bad trip home after all.

- **THE END**

7

You walk along the north path. Many of the plants along this route are black, dead, or dying.

You see a dark cave up ahead. Suddenly, you're struck with deep-seated terror...you forgot to get the couple a wedding gift!

- **Go to 25.**

8

As you walk, you no longer hear any birds. Strange.

You hear rustling. A green dragon wyrmling emerges from the trees! It screeches and flares its wings!

"I will prove I'm the deadliest dragon in my family," the wyrmling shouts.

"We'll see," you coolly reply.

GREEN DRAGON WYRMLING

Hit Points: 22 | Defense: 10 | Claw Attack: Roll a d6 twice. Add both numbers together.

- **If you survive, go to 24.**

9

You notice something strange about the boy's claw marks. There is dried blood, but it's dark brownish-red, like a human wound. Elf blood is clear.

- **To take the north path, go to 7.**
- **To take the skybridge, go to 13.**

10

You walk a few paces into this new part of the forest. The bark on the trees morph from purple to green and back again within minutes.

The forest trail leads north. Along the way is a giant tree with what looks like a door. A young elf boy leans against it.

- **To walk north, go to 7.**
- **To talk to the boy, go to 21.**

11

"You missed the rehearsal dinner! Your clothes are caked in mud! Where have you been?" asks your noble elf mother, marching towards you.

You arrive at the ancient ruins of Elven Court for what's sure to be a quiet, peaceful wedding.

"Hi, Mom," you state wearily. "I got lost."

"A ranger who gets lost?" she chides. "I don't see a gift. Please tell me you didn't forget to bring the couple a gift."

- **If you have no gift, go to 17.**
- **If you have a dragon tooth, go to 27.**
- **If you have a bracelet, go to 6.**

12

The giant spider collapses onto the shack, destroying it! Perhaps you missed your true calling as an exterminator.

You walk down the muddy path. Grime gets on your leather boots, and you just got them cleaned professionally.

After a while, you arrive at a fork in the trail.

- **To walk west, go to 3.**
- **To walk east, go to 15.**

13

You open the door inside the large tree and discover a winding, wooden staircase. You walk up many stories, until you reach an opening.

The opening leads to a series of wooden bridges 300 feet in the air, connecting the trees together.

You take the canopy walkway as far as it goes. You exit another staircase tree and look around at the forest floor.

- **Go to 23.**

14

Badly injured, the young dragon lunges at you!

You leap out of the way just in time. The dragon knocks into the trees behind you. A few of the trees fall like dominoes from the impact, and a bit of light is revealed in the distance.

As you climb over the dead body of the wyrmling, you pick up one of its teeth from the ground. You kind of have a thing for teeth.

ADD WYRMLING TOOTH TO YOUR INVENTORY

You weave through the trees and make your way to the clearing up ahead.

- **Go to 10.**

15

You take a right. The leaves above you glitter like gold. There must be magic in these woods.

You're stopped by a tall elf warrior. His dirty green hair is slicked back into a ponytail.

"Who goes there?" he demands.

"Vesska Moonwynd," you reply, "on my way to Elven Court for a wedding."

"Moonwynd?" his eyes light up. "I know your family..."

"Who doesn't?" you sigh.

"The path splits up ahead. Go north. There's a cave tunnel that leads out of the forest."

"What's east?"

"Nothing, unless you like mud."

- **To take the north path, go to 5.**
- **To continue east, go to 20.**
- **If you do a successful Perception check, go to 4.**

16

"Welcome to the middle of the forest!" reads a hand painted sign. How helpful.

The trail splits. You can go north or head west.

- **To travel north, go to 22.**
- **To travel west, go to 8.**

17

"I had to travel hundreds of miles on foot," you tell your mother. "I survived tough terrain and battled wild beasts just to be here today!"

"I take it that's a no?" your mother chides.

"I'll gather a basket of fruits for them tonight," you sigh.

The ceremony is about to begin. As you look for your seat, you realize the most harrowing part of your journey has just begun.

- **THE END**

18

The dragon mother collapses. A cloud of poison escapes her mouth, foul and potent.

You pick up one of her teeth off the ground. Polish it up and it would make a lovely wedding gift.

ADD DRAGON TOOTH TO YOUR INVENTORY

You continue exploring the cave, following the lit torches. It takes a while, but you finally see light. This has got to be it: the end of the forest!

- **Go to 16.**

19

Deep in the distance, you see a tree with a compass painted on it. North, East, West, South.

- **To walk northeast, go to 23.**
- **To walk northwest, go to 8.**

20

The trail leads to a white river. Sharp rocks jut from the water like knives. A short, barefoot elf patches a hole in her

THE MATCHMAKERS

WRITTEN BY CRYSTAL FRASIER, ILLUSTRATED BY ALANE GRACE

A low-tier 5E adventure | You will need a copy of the 5E core rulebooks to fully utilize this adventure. You need to familiarize yourself with the adventure and the map to fully enjoy the adventure.

Glossary | PC: Playable Characters | GM: Game Master | DC: Difficulty Class
HP: Hit Points | NPC: Non-Player Character

Adventure Scaling | This adventure is intended for players levels 2-4. To challenge higher level players, increase all DCs by +2 per tier over low. Increase to hits and average damage of foes by +1 per tier above low. While 1st-level PCs may find some of the adventure challenging, this can be remedied by lowering all average damage by 3 (minimum 1) and capping all DCs at 15.

PLOT

After a series of brilliant alchemical discoveries, the once-humble gnomish alchemists Millendi and Eisenmin Metriculous have become local celebrities in the small gnomish community of Pattelon. With their stars still on the rise, the couple would like to marry their son, Marmor, into a respectable gnome family in their community. With no one in the family especially gifted in the social graces, they're prepared to pay 300 gp to any respectable adventurers who help Marmor become a husband.

BACKGROUND

Millendi and Eisenmin have operated the Metriculous Alchemical Wares and Wonders shop—a specialty store mostly catering to adventurers—in Pattelon for almost a hundred years. The Metriculouses were never wealthy or well-known until Millendi's recent invention of self-applying axel grease, which has brought the family a measure of wealth and local fame.

Several prominent local families have now made overtures, offering to marry their adult children to Marmor Metriculous, the couple's son, but the mothers worry their politically savvy neighbors may be using Marmor as a pawn to win ownership of their alchemical formulas.

PATTELON

Pattelon mostly consists of a long, winding street marked by, and named for, a large waterwheel at one end. In your home campaign, it may be the gnomish district in a larger settlement, or a freestanding gnomish community. While many gnome settlements are subterranean, Pattelon is built into the side of a hill, and only half of any given structure's first floor rests below ground. Several buildings stand two or three stories tall as boastful examples of gnomish engineering. The community hosts a population of 450 gnomes—roughly three-quarters rock gnome—and a smattering of halflings. Most of the architecture is built to accommodate residents standing four feet or shorter, but nicer homes and businesses are built with a "tall room" to accommodate visitors of embarrassingly excessive size.

The local economy revolves around the waterwheel and attached mill—owned by the Stemillen family—which provides rotational force to power many of the street's businesses and winds highly-potent clockwork batteries—developed and built by the Zunar family—that more distant families rely on for automation and tinkering. Other economic drivers include orchards and greenhouses growing exotic plants, several distilleries, scribes, and a playhouse showcasing various avant garde productions. While adventurers purchasing various supplies bring in much-needed funding, they are generally distrusted after a visiting band burned the community to the ground fifty-seven years ago (never mind that the gnomes have accidentally burned their own community to the ground three times since then). The

Metriculous family's reliance on adventurers has largely sunk their standing in the local community until now.

In addition to Metriculous Alchemical Wares and Wonders, other local businesses that may attract adventurers to Pattelon include Fandabulous Books (run by a gnomish acolyte who also sells low-level spells); Viscum Album which sells homeopathic curatives and druidic spell components; and Gogan's, a famed (or infamous) high-end restaurant that combines alchemical techniques with food preparation to create meals of unusual color, shape, or texture.

RULES

GMs should be generally familiar with the 5e rules, especially the rules for ability tests.

Running "The Date" encounter requires the PCs to succeed several times for a positive outcome, so be prepared to track the total number of successful skill checks they accumulate during this event.

STARTING THE ADVENTURE

Whether the PCs are summoned by the gnome couple or simply drop by Metriculous Alchemical Wares and Wonders to shop between adventures, begin the adventure by reading the following:

"You're exactly the sort of respectable adventurers we need," the gnome proprietor announces when you walk into the shop. She shakes your hands vigorously. "Eisenmin Metriculous, and this is my wife Millendi!" A more subdued gnome behind her begins pouring cups of what looks like tea, but smells like cake.

"Millendi and I have enjoyed a bit of professional success. The Metriculous family is moving up in the community! But it's not all good news. Now that we're suddenly somebodies of note, all the other families who were already somebody want a piece of that, er... body? We've had eight different marriage offers from prominent families for our dear little boy, Marmor! But Marmor's a bit, wellll..."

"He's shy," her wife chimes in quietly.

"Shy. Yes. That's a word." Eisenmin jingles a purse full of coins. "Milli and I aren't well-versed in the social graces, and we want to make sure our boy winds up with someone who loves and supports him, not just a family that wants to inherit Milli's alchemical discoveries. If you're willing to ask around, find someone Marmor likes and likes him back, and help guide them through to early stages of courtship, we'd be happy to compensate you for your time. Say 300 gold and a batch of my famous carrot cookies?"

I RECEIVED ANOTHER OFFER FOR MARMOR'S HAND THIS MORNING.

OH DEAR...

THAT MAKES EIGHT IN TOTAL DOESN'T IT?

DO YOU SUPPOSE WE SHOULD SEND OUT AN INQUIRY THEN, EISENMIN?

...

THEY HAVEN'T EVEN BEEN ON A PROPER DATE WITH OUR BOY, MILLI! I'D LIKE TO INTERVIEW THEM MYSELF, THAT WAY I COULD BE SURE OF THEIR INTENTIONS.

OH DARLING, DON'T YOU THINK MARMOR WANTS TO START ON THE *RIGHT* FOOT WITH HIS BETHROTHED TO BE? NOT WITH HIS MOTHER SPOUTING INTIMIDATIONS AT THEM?

I SUPPOSE YOU'RE RIGHT...

IT'S BEST WE WATCH FROM AFAR.

Hiring ADVENTURERS with matchmaking spirit
300 gp

WELL THAT SETTLES IT. WE'LL FIND SOME LOVELY FOLKS TO DO SOME MATCHMAKING DETECTIVE WORK FOR US!

"Just get him out on a date or two," Millendi clarifies. *"And try to make sure it goes well."*

"So, what do you say?"

GM | Eisenmin and Millendi have been married almost fifty years and are solidly middle-age. Eisemin—a retired adventurer—is short, even by gnomish standards, with sturdy hips and short, curly hair. Her skin is dark, freckled, and she likes to dress comfortably and retire in the evenings with a good pipe as she handles the shop's books and any physical repairs. Millendi is pale and tall, with pink streaks beginning to develop in her otherwise gray hair. She's the actual alchemist of the store but prefers to let her wife handle customers unless they want to talk shop—she knows alchemy and very little else. They're both friendly and good-natured, but awkward and in over their heads. While they love Marmor, both admit they haven't understood him particularly well since he hit puberty.

Their shop sells potions, alchemist's fire, acid, oil, alchemist's and brewer's supplies, various industrial lubricants, and wind instruments—which the local gnomish guilds have officially classified as a form of alchemy. While the PCs are working for them, the couple offers them a 10% discount on all goods.

THE SUITORS

A total of eight families have made offers to marry their own children to Marmor, but of those, five don't especially like or respect the Metriculous family and only want to gain access to the family's alchemical knowledge. Millendi's self-lubricating axel grease has proven indispensible for Pattelon's mill and for many devices the gnomes build, and this new wealth is bringing out the worst in some of Pattelon's upper crust. Eisenmin provides a list of the families. The PCs can learn more about each with a successful DC 12 Skill test. The proficiency for each family, and what the PCs can learn, are listed below; PCs may use a DC 15 Investigation check in place of the listed skill, if they prefer.

- **Bixbivan (Intelligence–History):** The Bixbivans make their fortunes as adventurers, and so are much more accepting of the Metriculous family than most of Pattelon's gnomes. The family patriarch, Bing, is aware of Eisenmin's own history as an adventurer and hopes Marmor and his daughter Majority will give him adventurous grandchildren.

- **Cartoblatelbon (Charisma–Persuasion):** The Cartoblatelbon's are old-money, and loathe the Metriculouses, but their finances are direr than they'll admit, and they want Marmor's newfound wealth.

- **Kettlehops (Charisma–Deception):** The Kettlehops operate Pattelon's first and most prestigious distillery and are their own family of alchemists. They claim

they want to unite Pattelon's greatest alchemists into a dynasty, but in reality, the family matriarch simply wants to take over the Metriculous's shop and eliminate their only rivals.

- **Pleasance (Intelligence–Nature):** The Pleasance family operates the adjacent orchards and grows a variety of rare herbs for brewing. While middle-class, the Metriculouses are their steadiest clients, and rumors suggest their daughter Daranian had a childhood crush on Marmor.

- **Stemillen (Wisdom–Insight):** The Stemillen family own the waterwheel, making them the wealthiest and most influential family in town, and they want to marry Marmor to secure the only leverage anyone might have over them. However, their son Provini does seem genuinely kindhearted, operating Pattelon's charities using his family's money.

- **Thespomar (Charisma–Performance):** The Thespomars operate Pattelon's theater and have a longstanding feud with the Stemillen family. They want to marry Marmor to spite their rivals.

- **Wennelmuss (Wisdom–Medicine):** The Wennelmuss clan consists of biologists and scientists and have long looked down their noses at the "practical" science of alchemy and the Metriculous's shop. However, they want to expand their laboratory and would love to use Marmor's money to do it.

- **Zunar (Intelligence–Arcana):** The Zunar family manufactures the clockwork spring batteries much of

the community uses to power their inventions. They're an odd lot, but have sung Millendi Metriculous's praises for her ingenuity, and their anti-social child, Sarasota, has actually managed to say hello to Marmor in the market.

GM | Of the families listed, only the Bixbivan, Pleasance, and Zunar families actually like the Metriculouses or want what's best for Marmor. While the Stemillens hate the Metriculous family, their son, Provini, is a kinder soul than his parents and has long harbored a crush on Marmor, making him a viable fourth option.

Meeting Marmor

Marmor has a room upstairs from the shop but spends most of his time studying at the library. The PCs can interview him to learn more about his own desires and interests. He's a soft-spoken, gnomish lad of thirty-seven—reaching the age when most gnomes settle down and start a family—with his mother's thick, black hair and his other mother's fine bone structure. He's bookish and shy, but excitedly discusses alchemy if any of the PCs shows an interest.

Marmor wants to make his mothers happy, and so he doesn't want to discuss his own preferences as far as marriage goes. A successful DC 13 Charisma (Persuasion) or Wisdom (Insight) test encourages him to open up a bit and admit that he had crushes on several of his peers growing up—the outgoing Majority Bixbivan, the wistful Daranian Pleasance, and the elegant and kindhearted Provini Stemillen—but has been too shy to get to know any of them. If the PCs ask about Sarasota Zunar, Marmor admits that he admires their intellect, but isn't sure if they hate him or like him.

Meeting the Suitors

Marmor has four potential suitors that he likes and like him in return. The PCs must make a positive introduction before they can talk to the young people on the gnome's behalf, with the exact conditions listed for each suitor.

Following these introductions, each suitor also adds a special event the PCs will need to deal with during the Date encounter, as well as general preferences that will make all skill tests easier or more difficult if the PCs accidentally or deliberately incorporate them. While PCs should learn the skills they can use as they enter into events, each suitor's preferences should only be discoverable through use, roleplaying, or context clues.

MAJORITY BIXBIVAN

The only child of Ogelvie and Bing Bixbivan, Majority is a fearless soul and daring swashbuckler who has recently returned from a short adventuring career. She's excitable and easily distracted, with a big heart and a zeal for life. She admires Marmor's loyalty.

Introduction: Majority refuses to even consider marrying anyone who can't best her in a duel, but given her own childhood crush on Marmor, she is willing to let one or two of the PCs duel her in his place.

Threat: Use the "Spy" stat block (see core rulebooks) as Majority Bixbivan's statistics in the duel.

Preferences: Majority likes active dates, with hiking or dancing, and the PCs each gain inspiration if the date they arrange incorporates that. If the date is slow-paced or dull—a play, a poetry reading, most romantic locations—Majority is bored and the PCs gain disadvantage on all their rolls. Any PC attempts to describe or assist acts of derring-do for Marmor gain advantage.

Special Event: Let's Cut a Rug: During this event, Majority drags Marmor onto the dance floor (or into another action-oriented event appropriate to the date location), and the PCs must help the awkward gnome succeed while staying out of sight. PCs can try to lead Marmor (Charisma [Perform]* DC 13), discreetly puppet him (Dexterity [Sleight of Hand] DC 15), or convince the crowd that the young man's frantic flailing is a new dance craze from the big city (Charisma [Deception] DC 17). A successful check must be followed by a DC 10 Dexterity (Stealth) test or be lost.

DARANIAN PLEASANCE

"Dara" is flighty, always off in her own world, but a gentle and thoughtful soul whose gift with plants and animals makes her the perfect inheritor for Quady and Passma Pleasance's family orchards and homeopathy shop. She likes Marmor's gentle nature and extensive knowledge of plants.

Introduction: PCs must first *find* Daranian before they can speak to her. Tracking her through the Pleasance family orchards requires three successful DC 15 Survival checks, with each check taking 15 minutes. Once they locate her,

Dara is kind and accommodating, and they succeed automatically at introductions.

Preferences: Dara likes natural scenery, animals, and a laid-back pace, and the PCs each gain inspiration if the date they arrange incorporates these. If the date is especially urban or fast, Dara is left uncomfortable and the PCs gain disadvantage on all their rolls. Providing a vegetarian menu for Dara, or using a trained animal as a part of a check, provides advantage.

Special Event: Don't Let Them Hurt Him! A rat, pigeon, or other location-appropriate pest runs loose during the date, and the local proprietors try to kill it. Able to understand small animals, Daranian can hear the animal calling for help and wants Marmor—who can't understand small animals— to save it. PCs can intercede to calm the waiter (Charisma [Persuasion or Intimidate] DC 15), calm the pest (Wisdom [Animal Handling] DC 17), and/or nab the creature first (Strength [Athletics] DC 13), but a successful check must be followed by a DC 10 Charisma (Deception) or Dexterity (Sleight of Hand) test to attribute their success to Marmor or it is lost.

PROVINI STEMILLEN

The youngest son of the richest family in town, Provini has thoroughly absorbed the religious teachings his parents only pay lip service to, and he tries his best to provide comfort and charity to the community using the family wealth. A little vain and out of touch, he nonetheless is always willing to listen and learn, and he admires those same traits in Marmor.

Introduction: The Stemillens are more traditional than other gnomes, and the PCs must formally present themselves along with a gift from Marmor. This requires a successful DC 20 Charisma (Persuasion) check. PCs gain a +1 bonus on this check for every 15 gp in price their gift is worth, to a maximum of +5; double this bonus if the gift is associated with religion or art.

Preferences: Provini likes sophistication, good taste, and elegance, and the PCs each gain inspiration if the date they arrange incorporates these elements. If the date is homey or rustic, Provini is polite but awkward in the unfamiliar surroundings, and the PCs gain disadvantage on all their rolls. Provini's love of religion and charity means that any checks couched in these terms gain advantage.

Special Event: We Can't Just Leave Them Here! During the date, two reckless, gnomish children fall from a nearby balcony, stairway, or tree and injure themselves, howling in pain. If the PCs don't intercede, Provini ends the date to carry the children to a nearby temple to get them medical attention. The PCs can discreetly encourage Marmor to help (Charisma [Persuasion]* DC 13), locate the temple themselves (Intelligence [Religion] DC 15), and/or tend the children's injuries (Wisdom [Medicine] DC 17 or a cure wounds spell). At your discretion, this event may dramatically reshape how the rest of the Date events play out. If

the PCs do not succeed at at least one check, the date ends immediately.

SARASOTA ZUNAR

The eldest child of Shifrin and Wabbacot Zunar, Sarasota inherited their parents' love of academic study and mechanisms. They also live with severe agoraphobia and social anxiety. They don't get out much or interact with others, but once they get comfortable with a friend, they are inseparable and loyal. Sarasota has long harbored a crush on Marmor's keen mind and quirky laugh.

Introduction: Sarasota doesn't engage with strangers easily, limiting their responses to single syllables while they deliberately ignore the PCs to focus on a new puzzle box. If the PCs can help the gnome open the puzzle box (requiring a successful DC 12 Intelligence [Arcana] and a DC 15 Dexterity [Thieves' Tools] test), Sarasota feels more comfortable talking to them.

Preferences: Sarasota likes quiet dates in familiar places, especially if it involves reading or games, and the PCs each gain inspiration if the date they arrange incorporates that. If the date is loud or crowded, Sarasota is jumpy and has trouble focusing, and the PCs gain disadvantage on all their rolls. Any PC that attempts to make Marmor seem clever or well-read gain advantage.

Special Event: Panic Attack! Something—a loud noise, an old bully, or a bad memory—sets Sarasota's mind on edge and they begin to ramble and hyperventilate. The PCs can locate and eliminate the trigger themselves (Intelligence [Investigation] DC 15), recognize what's happening and coach Marmor through helping (Wisdom [Medicine]* DC 17), or tend to Sarasota directly (Wisdom [Insight] DC 13). If they do not succeed at at least one check, the date ends immediately.

GM | The PCs may interview as many or as few of their suitors as they like, but they must meet and interview a potential suitor before they can arrange a date between that individual and Marmor. Feel free to add as much or as little roleplaying to the actual interview as your players enjoy.

THE DATE

The creak and splash of the waterwheel sets a steady background rhythm to this lovely spring night. Romance is in the air!

Once the PCs have met at least one suitor, they can help plan a date and foster a burgeoning romance. The exact nature of the date is left up to the PCs, they should take into account Marmor's interests as well as those of the suitor; at the GM's discretion, especially inappropriate date locations or activities can impose disadvantage on some skill tests due to Marmor's own boredom or awkwardness.

Before the date, ask the PCs to decide on a time, meal, and appropriate evening entertainment for the young couple.

ENDING THE ADVENTURE

SUCCESS

If the PCs scored at least one result of "A Good Time Had by All," they complete their obligation to the Metriculous's satisfaction and receive their payment.

If the PCs manage to score at least one "A Night to Remember" result, they have succeeded with flying colors. The characters are rewarded as promised for assisting the Metriculous family and become friends for life. The gnomes extend their 10% shop discount indefinitely, letting the PCs buy alchemical supplies and potions at a discount for the foreseeable future.

Eisenmin wipes a tear from her eye as she listens to Marmor passionately recount the events of his date. "My little boy's all grown up and ready to start a family! And it's all thanks to you lot." She pushes a package wrapped in wax paper into your arms. "As promised: a baker's dozen of my famous carrot cookies!"

Millendi sighs in exasperation, staring expectantly at her wife for several moments before finally handing you a hefty bag of coins. "And your payment. Thank you again for helping our family."

FAILURE

If the PCs fail at all four dates, they fail to kindle any romance between Marmor and appropriate suitors, possibly leading the clueless gnomes into an unhappy arranged marriage in the coming months.

Eisenmin glowers at you as her wife tries to comfort their sobbing child. "I think you've done enough here. Please leave."

REWARDS

MEETING THE SUITORS

The suitors show their gratitude for arranging dates with small tokens of affection for the PCs.

- 50 XP for every suitor met

- 1 dose of *dust of dryness* for meeting Majority Bixbivan

- 2 herbal *potions of healing* for meeting Daranian Pleasance

- A rose-shaped gold and lacquer broach (250 gp) for meeting with Provini Stemillen

- A brass nightingale that sings when wound (100 gp) for meeting with Sarasota Zunar

THE DATE

- 600 XP for completing one successful date. 50 additional XP for every additional successful date the PCs shepherd with another suitor.

NEW MAGIC ITEMS

EISENMIN'S FAMOUS CARROT COOKIES

Wondrous item, common

These sweet, slightly bitter *cookies* are prepared with love (and her wife's various alchemical reagents) by Eisenmin Metriculous for special occasions. Eating a *cookie* grants a character darkvision to a range of 10 feet for one hour. If a character already has darkvision, eating a *cookie* instead increases the range of their darkvision by 5 feet. A character must take a long rest before they can benefit from eating another *cookie*. Eisenmin prepares 13 *cookies* for the PCs.

KEEPERS OF UROUGH'S FLAME

WRITTEN BY JOSHUA TRUJILLO, ILLUSTRATED BY MAX DLABICK

A low tier 5E adventure | You will need a copy of the 5E core rulebooks to fully utilize this adventure. You need to familiarize yourself with the adventure and the map to fully enjoy the adventure.

Glossary | PC: Playable Characters | GM: Game Master | DC: Difficulty Class
HP: Hit Points | NPC: Non-Player Character

Adventure Scaling | This adventure is intended for players levels 2-4. To challenge higher level players, increase all DCs by +2 per tier over low. Increase to hits and average damage of foes by +1 per tier above low. While 1st-level PCs may find some of the adventure challenging, this can be remedied by lowering all average damage by 3 (minimum 1) and capping all DCs at 15.

PLOT

Fortune awaits those who take the river through the Urough Sound, an infamous waterway home to orc legends both past and present. However, it is a dangerous path. Those not familiar with orc customs or the unpredictable tide may not live to survive the experience.

BACKGROUND

Urough was once a powerful and benevolent high priestess of the orcs in this land. Unlike her kin, Urough's calling was not battle, but rather community and constructing public works. The High Priestess ordered the construction of an orc-made river, the Urough Sound, to connect her choir's trade to that of others. It was a long, difficult engineering feat. Had she not the faith of her people, it never would have been completed.

But it was completed. And it was astounding.

The hand-carved waterway was unlike anything produced before, truly a wonder of its age. It was a tribute to the elements that Urough considered essential to her people: Flame, Sea, Stone, and Hearth. The Sound became vital to the fortunes of her orc choir.

Centuries passed, and Urough's contributions fell into legend and lore. Her descendants looked elsewhere for their survival, and the once-immaculate Sound became indistinguishable from the surrounding rivers and streams. Over time it fell into the domain of the goblins, who desecrated many symbols of what came before. However, those who desecrated the Sound found themselves cursed. It is said those spirits still haunt the Sound. Even still, it seems one cannot defy High Priestess Urough and expect to survive for very long.

Young adventurers still travel along this path, hoping for a blessing from the spirit of the High Priestess. To receive this reward, one must carry Urough's Flame through the Urough Sound. If you achieve this difficult task, you will be rewarded. Anything less may result in dire consequences.

RULES

UROUGH'S FLAME

At the beginning of the Urough Sound there is a flaming pedestal, ever-burning with Urough's Flame. It is a purple, magical flame. Contact with Urough's Flame on the Ceremonial Torches, Pedestal, or Altar deals 1d6 radiant damage.

It acts as a flame normally would (though if the flame sets something on fire, that new flame is nonmagical). Urough's Flame can be extinguished through any mundane or magical means.

Urough's Flame can only be passed between the sacred Pedestal, Altar, and Ceremonial Torches spread along this body of water. This is because they each contain the wondrous stones that the Urough Sound was carved from.

An Intelligence (Arcana or Religion) check of DC 13 reveals the magical, radiant nature of Urough's Flame from afar.

CEREMONIAL TORCHES

These distinct artifacts are made of some kind of mystical, purple stone, and feature beautiful, carved passages of Dwarvish text. However, only a player fluent in Orc can make sense of these writings, which praise High Priestess Urough.

They are attached to a wooden pike, about 5 feet tall. The Ceremonial Torches can hold a mundane flame as a normal torch would.

CANOES

There are some abandoned orc canoes at the entrance to the Sound, each seating up to two Small- or Medium-sized humanoids (a large humanoid requires their own canoe). A canoe's speed is 1½ mph.

The canoes have an AC of 10 and 40 hit points. Each has a built-in sconce (holder) containing a single Ceremonial Torch, and two wooden paddles. It is made of wood and tanned animal hides. It weighs 10 pounds.

At least one player will have to paddle each canoe as the pilot, while the second (if everyone is paired up) can be on lookout for hazards or obstacles. With a Help action, a second passenger may give advantage to the pilot of the canoe.

ROUGH WATER

Traveling over rough water requires a skill test (Vehicle Proficiency [Water]) or Strength check (Athletics) of DC 14. Either check can be made with advantage if the player is trained in Survival or Nature. A failed check results in the canoe taking (3) 1d6 crushing damage from the rocks beneath the water.

Failure by 5 or more requires all crew and passengers in the canoe to succeed at a Dexterity saving throw DC 13 (characters with Vehicle Proficiency [Water], or trained in Athletics, gain advantage to the saving throw). Any failure results in the canoe overturning, the crew and passengers being thrown from the vessel, and the Ceremonial Torch being extinguished. A player swimming over rough water must make an Athletics check DC 14, or take the same crushing damage from rocks. A player trained in Survival is also granted advantage to this check.

STARTING THE ADVENTURE

It is nearly sundown when your party arrives at the end of the road. Before you is a small river, which snakes around a

Illustration by Cara McGee

as well as the creation of the Urough Sound. She was known as a friend to all races and promoted trade and treaties to all. Legend tells of great fortunes for those who carry Urough's Flame to the Altar at the end of the Sound.

Flame: In the distance, just around the bend, you see a pedestal resting on a rock formation that is jutting out of the water. Burning brightly on that pedestal is a magnificent, purple flame unlike any you have seen before.

The Pedestal: About 60 feet from the canoes is the rock formation that Urough's Flame rests on. Players can easily dock their canoes and light their Ceremonial Torches with the flame.

The pedestal is made of hewn stone, and features etchings that have long been vandalized beyond recognition. There also appears to be the ruins of other jeweled statues and pedestals on these rocks.

Scattered near the Pedestal are several shiny stones that glisten in the sunset.

GM | The shiny stones are valued at 50 gp each, and weigh less than one pound on dry land. When the stones are wet, they take on the properties of a *sinking stone*.

Sea: After lighting your Ceremonial Torches, you can set them onto the canoes' sconces and continue your journey. The water is barely moving at all, which should make paddling easier.

Up about 90 feet ahead are some large statue pieces that you will need to navigate around. It seems like this area was once littered with majestic stone works that have since fallen into ruin.

GM | An Intelligence (Investigation) DC 14 check identifies that this entire waterway was hand-carved, with individual shovel and axe markings littering the cavernous walls on both sides. Advantage for this check is given to those proficient with mason's tools, or a dwarf with Stonecunning. It is truly a humbling sight.

Beneath the surface are five scattered patches of rough water. Four can be easily spotted with a Wisdom (Perception) DC 13 check. One patch can only be seen with success of DC 16 or more.

The Ruins: Your canoes approach a hodgepodge of stones and ruins, breaking up the river into smaller lanes. For some it is easy to recognize what was once there—a pair of outstretched orc hands, an ornate statue—while others

corner before leading into the unknown. This waterway cuts through enormous stone hills on either side.

Along the riverbed is an imposing stone statue of an orc priestess, easily a few hundred years old. The statue is holding a Ceremonial Torch in one hand, and a stone tablet in the other.

GM | The tablet is written in Dwarvish script but is only comprehensible to players fluent in Orc. Though it is an older dialect, anyone fluent in Orc is able to read it without difficulty.

The tablet translates roughly to the following:

"Here lies the spirit of Urough, fearless High Priestess and protector to this choir. Long ago, Urough and her followers built this river to celebrate the four spirits: Flame, Sea, Stone, and Hearth. These waters will test any who dare enter.

Those who carry Urough's Flame from the Pedestal to the Altar as tribute will be blessed on their journey ahead. Those who desecrate the Sound will find themselves doomed."

At the river's edge are a few worn-looking, two-seater orc canoes, each with an unlit Ceremonial Torch, a sconce, and two paddles of their own.

GM | An Intelligence check of DC 13 (History or Religion) takes special note of the statue's distinctive religious tattoos and decorative headdress. The tattoos on her body represent Flame, Sea, Stone, and Hearth: the four spirits worshipped by the legendary High Priestess Urough. It also features the symbol for peace, highly unusual for the warlike orcs! Clearly this is a likeness of Urough, the great leader and peacemaker.

Urough is remembered for her strength and benevolence,

have been completely decimated by both nature and the greed of human(oids). An overturned column looks like a good vantage point to survey the waters ahead, but it will require exiting the canoe. On the column is an unlit Ceremonial Torch.

Several canoes, similar to yours but battle damaged, are partially submerged along the edges of these stones. You are certainly not the first to travel these waters. It looks like some of the ships may still have cargo on them.

GM | Waiting for the adventuring party is a group of **goblin echoes**, hiding at various points along the water. Their goal is to attack anyone who passes, and they are focused first and foremost on the passengers of any canoes not wielding a Ceremonial Torch of Urough's Flame. If a PC is personally holding a lit Ceremonial Torch of Urough's Flame, the goblin echoes will not attack them (though they may attack the second PC in the canoe).

These goblin echoes are afraid of the water and will not try to board the canoes. Players can confront the goblin echoes in battle, either from the canoe or by climbing onto the nearby ruins, or players could try to bypass the ruins altogether. (This might be the wisest plan, as the goblin echoes will not enter the water and cannot travel more than 100 feet from where they originate due to their soul tether.)

Should a PC exit their canoe and walk up to the overturned column, they can make out very difficult waters ahead. They also find several discarded items in a ruined leather knapsack.

On the overturned column is an unlit Ceremonial Torch. This can be lit and accessed later, should players have their torches extinguished.

- **Threats:** Goblin echoes (3 +1 for each PC)
- **Loot:** 1 unusable, leather knapsack, 1 small waterskin pouch, 1 +1 sling, 1 cracked jar of dried kobold livers, a delicacy to living goblins. (They're still good to eat!)

Stone: The sun has set, and as you head down the Urough Sound, the only light source is coming from your torches. It is difficult to see much up ahead, and the sound of running water echoes throughout the Sound.

Even with your (potentially) limited vision, you can see a fork in the waters up ahead. A mammoth, crumbling stone wall divides the Sound in two.

Left: On the left, the water is narrower, but more still. You can see several small outcroppings of stone along the water, each containing broken stone and debris.

Right: The right path is wider, but the water looks rougher. Above, you see the stone walls on the right look damaged.

GM | The two paths are each different types of challenges.

LEFT

A Wisdom (Perception or Survival) or Intelligence (Investigation) check of DC 15 reveals submerged fishing traps just past the fork. Players with darkvision are given advantage. A canoe that comes into contact with these traps is immediately held in place by a fishing spear that deals 1d6 damage to the canoe while attaching to it. A spear can be removed from the canoe without sinking it as an action.

Hiding behind the stone outcroppings are (3 +1 per PC) hidden goblin echoes. To spot the goblin echoes, players must make a Wisdom (Perception) check of DC 14. Their primary strategy is not to attack the PCs directly, but rather to strike their canoes with a spear. Attached to the end of the spear is a rope that the goblin echoes will fasten to nearby rocks (a tethered canoe can still be overturned).

Like the previous band of goblin echoes, they will not attack a PC wielding Urough's Flame and will focus on canoes without it (if applicable).

If the players' canoes are damaged irreparably in this encounter, there is a replacement canoe nearby.

After defeating the goblin echoes, the canoes will pass by a huge mosaic mural from High Priestess Urough's lifetime...

With the flicker of your torches you can see it on the walls. It's a mosaic, a mural, at least several centuries old. The art style is primitive, comprised of small flecks of stone that tell a story when they're all seen together. It shows a group of orcs, carrying Urough's Flame from the pedestal you saw earlier.

However, the orc figures are without Urough's Flame when they arrive. What the drawings are greeted with is a horrifying, serpentine beast with a beak and several tendrils extending from its face.

An Intelligence (Nature) check of DC 13 identifies the beast as being some form of grick, a monstrous beast that can withstand heavy damage from nonmagical sources. A

successful check would also inform the player that gricks have the ability to camouflage themselves near stones.

- **Threats:** (3 +1 per player) goblin echoes
- **Loot:** 4 spears, 1 *oil of slipperiness*, 1 wooden shield

RIGHT

A Wisdom (Perception or Survival) DC 13 check reveals the location of four patches of rough water that could potentially damage or overturn the canoe. Two patches require a success of DC 16 or more.

Above, an Intelligence (Investigation or Nature) check of DC 13 spots burrowed holes in the rocky cliffs surrounding you. Something has been digging up there, making the rocks unsteady. They look like they can fall over at any moment.

As the players try to navigate these difficult waters, two mini-avalanches will occur at separate times. Small rocks tumble from the rocky cliffs on either side. Players must make a skill check (Vehicle Proficiency [Water]) or Strength check (Athletics) of DC 13 to avoid (7) 2d6 points of bludgeoning damage to the canoes. A failure by 5 or more by a player on a canoe causes each player on the vessel to make an additional Vehicle Proficiency (Water) or Strength (Athletics) check of DC 13, or they will overturn the canoe.

Past where the second set of rocks fell, an old orc canoe is washed up against some rocks. It is damaged (20 hp), but good enough to take PCs through the remainder of the Urough Sound, if necessary. In it is a small bag containing several items.

- **Loot:** 1 leather backpack, 1 bedroll, 1 horn, 50 feet of hemp rope, 1 shiny (sinking) stone

After making it through, the canoes will pass by a huge painting from High Priestess Urough's lifetime...

With the flicker of your torches, you can see it on the walls. It's a mosaic, a mural, at least several centuries old. The art style is primitive, comprised of small flecks of stone that tell a story when they're all seen together. It shows a group of orcs carrying Urough's Flame from the pedestal you saw earlier.

At the end of the mural you see Urough's Flame being delivered to the Altar by a warrior. The purple fire spreads over the orc harmlessly, and in the next image the orc's eyes glow brightly like Urough's Flame!

GM | The two paths along the river reconnect after passing the large stone wall. Up ahead is the Altar.

A Wisdom (Insight) or Intelligence (Religion) check of DC 13 (Religion) reveals to the players that lighting the fire pit with Urough's Flame will complete the ritual.

Hearth: Ahead in the distance is the same Altar you saw in the earlier stone mosaic, nestled along the side of the river on the shore. It rests on a large stone platform several steps up, adorned with carved symbols of the Orc symbol for Hearth.

The beach looks untouched, with no footprints to be seen. Several unlit Ceremonial Torches are on the platform, with a central fire pit at the top of the Altar.

GM | On the beach, players are being stalked by a fearsome basalt grick, who is camouflaged against the stone of the Altar. Players can spot it with an Intelligence (Perception) check of DC 20. The basalt grick prefers to strike an unsuspecting victim from the shadows, and is less likely to attack a player wielding Urough's Flame.

- **Threat:** 1 basalt grick

- **Loot:** 5d10 gp scattered around the Altar, 1 silvered dagger, 1 scroll of shatter (2nd level)

FOR PLAYERS WHO CARRIED UROUGH'S FLAME TO THE ALTAR:

As you light the surrounding purple torches with Urough's Flame, the symbols on the Altar begin to glow brightly.

You set your Ceremonial Torches onto the fire pit, and immediately a change occurs. At the center of the fire pit erupts a huge column of Urough's Flame! It glows brighter and brighter as it covers your body, but you are unharmed by the fire. When it washes over you, you feel restored. More so, you feel more alert, more connected to others.

You can faintly hear an unfamiliar voice. It is Urough, wishing you good fortune for the rest of your journey. You know with Urough's blessing, you will be able to help others like never before.

GM | Players who have successfully completed this trial gain access to the Urough's Grace (see below).

UROUGH'S GRACE (SPECIAL FEATURE)

As an action, you may target a single creature other than yourself within 30-foot line of sight with Urough's Grace. The target creature can add 1d4 to their next attack roll or saving throw. Once you have used this ability, you can't use it again until you finish a long rest.

FOR PLAYERS WHO DID NOT CARRY UROUGH'S FLAME TO THE ALTAR:

Covered in moss and tarnished carvings, the Altar seems a ruined artifact of a lost age. Having seen the wrecked ships

and hazards along the way, it would be natural to wonder if Urough is everything the legends say she was.

Just then, out of the corner of your eye, you notice a strange purple haze quickly drifting towards you. Before you can move, it completely envelopes you! You feel a warm, comforting presence. It is both familiar and foreign to you at the same time. It is Urough!

You feel restored and healed as the haze washes away. Perhaps next time you will be able to succeed in being a keeper of Urough's Flame.

GM | All players are cured of any blinded, deafened, paralyzed, and poisoned conditions they may be suffering from. They are also fully healed of full hit points.

ENDING THE ADVENTURE

Your party sets up camp, and after reflecting on your day, you lie down for a well-earned night's sleep. As you watch the stars, they begin to flicker, every so often changing to a familiar, welcoming purple.

Urough is watching over you...

REWARDS

For completing and surviving the adventure, players receive 70 XP apiece. ⬡

New Magic Items

SINKING STONES *Wondrous items, uncommon*

About the size of a plum, *sinking stones* appear to be mundane, lightweight, precious stones on dry land. However, when submerged in water, or wet with any liquid, they reveal their true nature.

A wet *stone* instantly increases in weight, to roughly 300 pounds apiece. They are often placed in hallowed grounds near bodies of water, damning unsuspecting thieves and adventurers to a watery grave. *Sinking stones* are not cursed and may be released at any time.

A person or beast that swallows a *sinking stone* will almost certainly expire, suffering 2d6 internal bludgeoning damage per round until the *stone* is removed.

NPCs Stats

GOBLIN ECHOES *Small undead, neutral evil*

Once raiders of sacred spaces, these restless creatures are forever bound to where they met their untimely end. Though their flesh continues to rot, their greed will never cease.

Armor Class 13 (natural) | **Hit Points** 7 (2d6)
Speed 30 ft.

STR	DEX	CON	INT	WIS	CHA
10 (+0)	14 (+2)	10 (+0)	9 (−1)	7 (−2)	8 (−1)

Skills Intimidation +1, Stealth +4

Senses darkvision 60 ft., passive Perception 8

Languages Common, Goblin (goblin echoes cannot speak)

Challenge 1/4 (50 XP)

Damage Immunities poison

Condition Immunities exhaustion, poisoned

Soul Tether. Goblin echoes cannot travel more than 100 feet from where they were slain. The souls of those slain by a goblin echo suffer a similar fate.

ACTIONS

Claw. Melee Weapon Attack: +2 to hit, reach 5 ft., one target. *Hit*: 3 (1d6) necrotic damage.

Soul Sling. Ranged Weapon Attack: +4 to hit, range 30/120 ft., one target. *Hit*: 4 (1d4 + 2) necrotic damage.

BASALT GRICK *Medium monstrosity, neutral evil*

Sprung from the deepest depths underground, basalt gricks are sturdier and more dangerous than their counterparts closer to the surface. Their name comes from the impervious, stone-like sheen on their scales.

Armor Class 15 (natural armor)
Hit Points 52 (8d8 + 16)
Speed 40 ft., climb 40 ft.

STR	DEX	CON	INT	WIS	CHA
17 (+3)	16 (+3)	14 (+2)	7 (−2)	12 (+1)	7 (−2)

Skills Stealth +5

Senses darkvision 60 ft., passive Perception 11

Challenge 3 (700 XP)

Damage Resistance bludgeoning, piercing, and slashing damage from nonmagical or nonsilvered weapons.

Stone Camouflage. The basalt grick has advantage on Dexterity (Stealth) checks made to hide in rocky terrain.

Weakness: Urough's Flame. Contact with Urough's Flame will force the basalt grick to make a Dexterity save (DC 15), or catch fire and take an additional (3) 1d6 fire damage at the end of each of its turns.

ACTIONS

Multiattack. The basalt grick makes one attack with its tentacles. If that attack hits, the grick can make one beak attack against the same target.

Tentacles. Melee Weapon Attack: +5 to hit, reach 5 ft., one target. *Hit*: 6 (1d6 + 3) slashing damage.

Beak. Melee Weapon Attack: +5 to hit, reach 5 ft., one target. *Hit*: 6 (1d6 + 3) piercing damage.

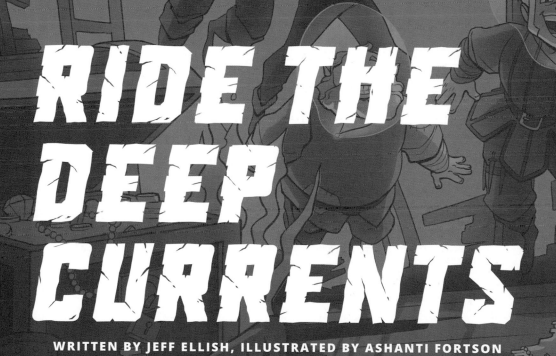

RIDE THE DEEP CURRENTS

WRITTEN BY JEFF ELLISH, ILLUSTRATED BY ASHANTI FORTSON

A Low-Tier 5E Adventure | You will need a copy of the 5E core rulebooks to fully utilize this adventure. You need to familiarize yourself with the adventure and the map to fully enjoy the adventure.

Glossary | PC: Playable Characters | GM: Game Master | DC: Difficulty Class
HP: Hit Points | NPC: Non-Player Character

Adventure Scaling | This adventure is intended for players levels 2-4. To challenge higher level players, increase all DCs by +2 per tier over low. Increase to hits and average damage of foes by +1 per tier above low. While 1st-level PCs may find some of the adventure challenging, this can be remedied by lowering all average damage by 3 (minimum 1) and capping all DCs at 15.

Illustration by Courtney Hahn

PLOT

Having just arrived in the undersea town of Long Haul Shallows, the players meet a young aquatic elf named Honorous Klemp, who is the newly appointed head of the Klemp Tuna & Other Living Stock Co. Klemp informs the party that he is looking for a few adventurous persons to escort a school of his finest tuna through the Forgotten Trench to the outskirts of the aquatic elf city of Deep Fortuna within the next three days, where he will be waiting with money in hand.

No one else in Long Haul Shallows is interested in the job, and for good reason: the Forgotten Trench belongs to the Hungry Depths Tuna Company. While driving the school of tuna from Long Haul Shallows to Deep Fortuna, the party is waylaid by sahuagin rustlers astride vicious sharks. Protecting the school won't be easy, as up from the depths of the trench comes a massive adolescent dragon turtle under the control of a sneering sahuagin boss.

If the party can survive the sahuagin attack and prevent them from making off with the school, they just might reach Deep Fortuna by their deadline. Honorous Klemp pays the party the promised sum—minus any fees for missing or damaged tuna—and shows a pointed interest in purchasing any adolescent dragon turtles they might have accrued during their journey.

At the GM's discretion, with input from the players, here are some options as to why the adventurers are in Long Haul Shallows and why they might want to help Honorous Klemp:

- Having made fools of themselves on the surface, the PCs are looking to establish new lives under the sea and Klemp can introduce them to some very important business people in Deep Fortuna.

- Cataloging unique wildlife in Fortuna County, the PCs are in search of an adolescent dragon turtle that they lost track of near the Forgotten Trench. Working with Klemp provides the PCs with funding and enough tuna to lure the dragon turtle out.

- Sahuagin raiders sank a ship transporting a powerful magical object, and the PCs have connected the attackers to the Hungry Depths Tuna Company. Working with Klemp is just a reason for the PCs to draw the sahuagin out of hiding and track down the missing object.

- You've never been under the sea, let alone on an authentic tuna drive! Klemp isn't paying you to escort his school to Deep Fortuna. You're paying him for the opportunity! What will everyone above water say when you tell them about your thrilling vacation?

BACKGROUND

Weeks ago, the head of the Klemp Tuna & Other Living Stock Co. died from a mysterious and sudden illness, immediately after which their son seized control of the company. Honorous Klemp is an aggressive up-and-comer who balks at any danger he doesn't have to directly participate in. While the Hungry Depths Tuna Company—a shady sahuagin joint operating out of the Forgotten Trench—has a reputation for merciless violence, Klemp doesn't care. Klemp isn't going to be driving a school of tuna through the Forgotten Trench to make an ambitious deadline that he promised to his buyers.

You are.

RULES

- Underwater Combat
- Mounted Combat

STARTING THE ADVENTURE

Whatever their reasons might be, the PCs meet with Honorous Klemp on the outskirts of Long Haul Shallows to have their first look at the school they'll be escorting. They have all secured regulation *jellycaps* from the border crossing at the shore.

THE DEMON OF QUEEN'S HAVEN

WRITTEN BY ADAM MA, ILLUSTRATED BY SAVANNA GANUCHEAU

A 5E Low-Tier Level-3 Adventure | You will need a copy of the 5E core rulebooks to fully utilize this adventure. You need to familiarize yourself with the adventure and the map to fully enjoy the adventure.

Glossary | PC: Playable Characters | GM: Game Master | DC: Difficulty Class
HP: Hit Points | NPC: Non-Player Character

Adventure Scaling | This adventure works best with a party of characters level 5, but could be modified to be more difficult for party of level-5 characters by increasing all enemies (or enthralled townsfolk) to their maximum hit points, and adding an additional cultist spy to each encounter.

QUEEN'S HAVEN THEATER

WHISTLE

SHIFF

TRAVELLERS, PLEASE, I MEAN NO HARM.

SOMETHING IS AMISS IN THE VILLAGE AHEAD, AND THE CAPTAIN OF THEIR GUARD WILL NOT HEED MY WARNINGS.

I KNOW THE WORD OF A STRANGER MAY NOT HAVE MUCH WEIGHT, BUT IF YOU CAN SPARE BUT A MOMENT I BELIEVE WE CAN SAVE MANY LIVES.

SHUFF

SH

MY NAME IS SOFIA.

AS I WAS ONCE A KNIGHT WITHIN THE ORDER OF THE WHITE ASH, I CAN TELL YOU WITH GREAT CERTAINTY THAT THERE IS A DEMON AMONG US.

AAA

I DON'T KNOW WHAT IT INTENDS TO DO HERE. I DON'T CARE.

ALL THAT MATTERS IS THAT IT MUST BE STOPPED, AND I CANNOT DO SO ON MY OWN.

PLOT

A famous bardic troupe has come to perform at a local village theater. As attendees gather to see the show, a retired paladin tries to warn those who will listen that not all seems right here. There's a demonic presence somewhere nearby. While she cannot say exactly where it's coming from, she's absolutely certain that someone involved with the musical performance must be responsible.

BACKGROUND

Queen's Haven isn't a true village by most rural standards. Most of its homes are owned by nobility. Inhabited irregularly, there are few farms and even fewer farmers. Heavy investments from foreign aristocrats ensure the village is well stocked, guarded, and maintained. As a seasonal playground for the rich, there are few places more comfortable than Queen's Haven—if you can afford to live there.

So naturally, when it was announced that the Jousting Notes would be performing an exclusive concert for the people of Queen's Haven, gossip spread like wildfire. Wealthy nobles scrambled to purchase seats for what was likely to be one of the most exclusive shows of the year.

It is an understatement to say the Jousting Notes are one of the most popular musical groups across the kingdom. Their performances have been described as a perfect showcase of natural talent and well-practiced showmanship. Notoriously harsh entertainment critic Jean Froun even provided them with a prestigious set of silver bells—an honor only given to musicians of the highest caliber.

All of Queen's Haven is brimming with anticipation for tonight's event, which is why anyone looking to stir up trouble is being treated with extra care. Unfortunately for the demon hunting Sofia Espada, it means being exiled outside of town for causing a stir.

RULES

GM | This adventure takes place over a single evening, as PCs explore the village of Queen's Haven in search for evidence of a demon lurking in their midst. Once players feel they have enough evidence against a particular NPC, they can accuse that NPC publicly for their crimes.

To help narrow down the list of suspects, players can hunt for clues that will reveal the demon's identity. These clues are scattered throughout Queen's Haven, and range from gossip to corrupted writings (see "Queen's Haven" for specific details).

A wrong guess will end their investigation and potentially get them removed from town, while revealing the identity of the demon will force it to lash out against its accusers. Worse yet, players must uncover the culprit before the concert ends, or else the ritual will complete, putting the entire village at risk.

STARTING THE ADVENTURE

Queen's Haven has always been an active community, but the village has certainly never been this busy in the past. A caravan of expensive and ornate looking carriages, stagecoaches, and wagons have been parked all along the main road leading to the village square. Some even have personal guards standing nearby—expensive-looking hired swords who give cold looks to anyone that gets too close.

It's a lot of fanfare, but you know the reason why. Love 'em or hate 'em, the Jousting Notes are one of the biggest names in bardic performances in town. Their concert has been highway gossip for weeks. If seats aren't already sold out, they will be soon.

As your group makes their way into town, you hear a sharp, distracting whistle. Standing off-road under the shade of a nearby tree is an older human woman, her body wrapped in an old, gray cloak. She extends a hand in warm greeting, and you notice the gleam of silver armor hidden away under the folds of her cloth.

"Travelers, please, I mean no harm. Something is amiss in the village ahead, and the captain of their guard will not heed my warnings. I know the word of a stranger may not have much weight, but if you can spare but a moment, I believe we can save many lives this evening."

She draws a small pendant from a pouch at her side—a silver star hanging in a vial filled with a cloudy liquid. You realize that the grey cloak hides more than her armor. This woman is missing her other arm.

"My name is Sofia. As I was once a knight within the Order of White Ash, I can tell you with great certainty that there is a demon among us. I don't know what it intends to do here. I don't care. All that matters is that it must be stopped, and I cannot do so on my own."

GM | Sofia is convinced there's a demon lurking within Queen's Haven, and her suspicions rest heavily on the Jousting Notes being responsible. Since their arrival, she's felt like something is clouding her ability to focus on or sense demons and undead. Worse, when she tried to investigate in preparation for tonight's concert, the troupe's manager had her removed from the village for "disturbing the peace."

Now barred from entering Queen's Haven, Sofia needs help investigating the source of the unholy disturbance. The captain of the guard, Captain Mersen, is an honest man, but he won't make a move against anyone without a good amount of evidence.

Before PCs enter the town, they're likely going to have a few questions. Encourage players when making their own knowledge checks to see what information they can gather before going forth. Additionally, Sofia is more than happy to provide information on any details regarding the town, demons, the Order of White Ash, or any other subject that will get players to aid her cause.

GM | You may want to start with an Intelligence (History) DC 12 on the history of the Jousting Notes. A successful check will reveal some facts about the troupe. Their rise to fame is well noted as a result of their incredible passion for music. They tour many places, from quaint towns to sprawling cities, and don't seem to play favorites when it comes to their performances. Their manager seems to be a recent acquisition, but it's not unusual for performers to be represented in some way. The original band members are as followed:

- **Darlene Grove (female elf)**
- **Leon King (male human)**
- **Lysindra Goldring (female human)**
- **Zane Shred (male orc)**

GM | An Intelligence (History) DC 13 on the history of The Order of White Ash (sometimes referred to as the "White Ash") reveals the significance of Sofia's position within the order. They are paladins, banded together to snuff out corruption wherever it may seek a home. More than just men and women with divine talents, the White Ash are also talented trackers. Many dedicate themselves to years of study that result in keen forensic skills, making them incredibly skilled at picking up fine details lesser hunters may miss. The *silver star* is one of many tools iconic to this

order, and ownership of such an artifact helps validate her claim of being a member.

BEFORE EXPLORING QUEEN'S HAVEN

GM | As PCs get ready to hunt for evidence of demonic corruption, Sofia will provide them with some advice and aid:

"Captain Mersen is a good man, but this community is guided more by coin than by morals. He won't be able to take any action unless you've gathered enough evidence against the demon. This should help."

Sofia holds out the vial containing the silver star, *nodding for you to take it.*

"My own senses are dulled, but this should aid you. The star shines brighter the closer it's brought to unholy idols. It is no judge of character, but an excellent tool when looking to identify the profane."

"Whatever the danger, I fear the demon may be using this concert to mask its intention. You should start by visiting the local inn, Daylight's Rest. The troupe would have taken rooms there for the evening. If there is something amiss to be found, it may be hidden among their belongings."

QUEEN'S HAVEN

GM | Used mostly as a getaway for the rich, Queen's Haven is unusually clean and well-maintained for a village of its size. Part of this is due to its larger-than-normal town guard, who serves to enforce the peace and protect their wealthy residents from the potential threat of theft.

With so many gathered in town to see the concert, it's very unlikely that PCs will attract much attention from the villagers. Still, town guards are on the look out for thieves and vandals.

> When PCs perform an action that may draw attention, be sure to use Wisdom (Perception) checks with both guard and cultist NPCs, as some areas are carefully watched by one or the other.

VILLAGE GOSSIP

GM | Queen's Haven is a hub of gossip! The concert has already begun, but PCs can use all kinds of checks to gather information from the locals. No one is being particularly secretive, so let PCs be creative on how they gather intel. A check of any kind above a DC 10 will give one or more clues:

1. "I couldn't get a room in town. I think the inn was completely bought out by the Notes! Somethin' about needing privacy."

2. "My son couldn't get a ticket, so he and his friends tried sneaking in through the cellar. Group of men standin' around back there wouldn't let 'em past."

Daylight's Rest

GM | As the only lodgings available in Queen's Haven, Daylight's Rest is usually busy no matter the time of day. Mornings and afternoons are generally filled with hungry travelers looking to fill their bellies, while those looking for a calmer drinking atmosphere settle into the bar in the evenings.

Daylight's Rest consists of two main floors and a basement used exclusively for storage. The first floor consists of a bar, spacious dining area for patrons, and kitchen. On the second floor, players can find a dozen available rooms for guests, most of which have already been taken by the Jousting Notes.

The main floor is occupied by five patrons, all of whom are demonic cultists in disguise. The barkeep is also in disguise, due to having murdered the actual innkeeper and hiding the body in the kitchen around the corner. The barkeep currently holds the master key.

1. A Wisdom (Perception) DC 15 will notice a streak of blood on the bar that wasn't cleaned up from the innkeeper's murder.

2. The moment PCs try to go upstairs to investigate the room, the cultists will arrange for an ambush. They will wait out of sight until the time is right to strike and kill PC intruders.

3. Use the cultist and priest profiles from the core rulebooks to represent the five patrons and barkeep respectively.

- **Threats**: 5 cultists (patrons) and 1 cultist priest

- **Loot:** 15 gp, plus weapons and armor

GM | Rooms are locked on the second floor but can be broken into with a Dexterity (Thieves' Tools) DC 15, or the master key. None of the rooms are labeled, but there are some clues as to which band member has taken which room.

Roll a d6 to determine which of the following rooms players enter if they choose to break in. A PC holding the *silver star* has advantage on their actions when searching a room for demonic corruption. An Intelligence (Investigation) DC 15 check in any of the rooms will find the following:

1 - BILL HORTON'S ROOM

A single desk has been overtaken by a pile of paperwork, quills, and hanging lanterns, but otherwise this room seems largely unused. The **silver star** *glows faintly in this room.*

GM | An Intelligence (Investigation) DC 14 check will reveal the following: tucked away under a pile of ledgers is an old leather tome. Scratchings across the surface seem to be written in dried blood. It is most certainly a language, but it's unclear which one it is.

GM | If a PC can read Abyssal: Scrawled across the cover is the title *Servant's Duties*. Each page goes through tremendous detail on how a lesser being can summon and empower the demonic entity known as Diafol, the Enthraller, who trades human souls in exchange for untold power.

GM | It is Bill who summoned Diafol, trading the life of a trusted band member in exchange for power. The more energy he feeds it, the more powerful he'll become, and he can often be seen close by Darlene/Diafol.

energy. Any living creature within the area must succeed at a Wisdom saving throw DC 15, or suffer 3 (1d6) psychic damage. With the demonic ward destroyed, Diafol's true identity can be detected with magical means.

DESTROYING THE EMERALD KEYSTONE

- The *keystone* must first be taken from its owner, Bill Horton.

- Destroying the emerald partially breaks the enchantment and prevents new commands from being delivered to those under the effect of an *emerald pendant*.

- The *emerald keystone* has 8 hp and a 10 AC.

DESTROYING AN EMERALD PENDANT

- Just removing a pendant isn't enough to break the enchantment. Commands made from the keystone's holder will stay locked in place for 24 hours after removal.

- The moment the *emerald keystone* is destroyed, the effects of the *emerald pendant* dissipate.

CONFRONTING DIAFOL

GM | If players don't find a means of uncovering Diafol's identity, or if they fail to force the demon to show itself, the demon will be content to stay hidden. Otherwise, if revealed, Diafol will attack.

Though disguised as an elven bard, Diafol's true appearance is far more sinister. Darlene's soul was burned out long ago, and her body is now only a vessel for the demon's power. As Darlene's body is attacked, more of the false form will burn away to reveal a twisted parody of mortal form underneath—a diseased wretch of a man. Rotten skin rips and peels away from its emaciated form, causing a fetid black substance to leak from its wounds. Despite its appearance, Diafol has incredible strength.

If revealed, it will immediately fight, wanting to preserve the control it has over its enthralled audience. Unfortunately, without its guiding voice, the enchanted audience will begin to slip from Diafol's grasp. As Diafol combats the party (see NPC stat blocks), roll an initiative position for the audience with an unmodified d20. Then roll 1d10 at the start of each round:

- **1–2:** The audience uses all its movement to frantically dash in a random direction. To determine the direction, roll a d4 and assign a cardinal direction to each die face.

- **3–6:** The audience doesn't move or take actions this turn, continuing to enjoy the "show" as though nothing was wrong.

- **7–8:** The audience uses its action to fight amongst each other in a sudden burst of violence. Most will be busy trying to attack each other, but some may wildly swing at nearby PCs. Roll 1d12 to determine how many potential audience members decide to attack PCs. Use the "Noble" profile from the core rulebooks to represent the audience. If any guards are present, use the "Queen's Haven Guard" under the NPC stat block section. Guards attack PCs at the GM's discretion.

- **9–10:** The audience can act and move normally, suddenly becoming aware of their dilemma, though they are not freed from the enchantment and cannot attack Diafol.

ENDING THE ADVENTURE

IF PCS HAVE DEFEATED DIAFOL:

With the final blow struck, Diafol's physical form begins to burn away. Sulfur fills the air as the decrepit humanoid form crumbles to black ash. Members of the audience begin to come to their senses as the demonic influence releases its grip. The surviving members of the Jousting Notes bring their performance to a sudden halt. It's not until a clear explanation is provided that the nobles in attendance begin to understand how close they came to mortal peril. They immediately demand more precautions be taken to prevent this sort of incident from happening again.

Sofia Espada, retired Knight of the White Ash, is happy to oblige. Before taking on her new role of Chief Inquisitor, she arranges compensation for the brave heroes who believed her during a time of crisis: 1,000 gold, her silver star, and a letter of commendation from the wise and well-traveled knight.

IF DIAFOL ESCAPES, OR IS UNDISCOVERED:

Without knowing where the demon has escaped to, it's difficult to say what its goals were, let alone what kind of damage it caused. Perhaps it's learned a lesson in underestimating mortals, and will keep a far distance from Queen's Haven.

Then again, there's no real way to tell if this wasn't just another part of its plan. Either way, Sofia is thankful for the aid in her investigation. She'll stay a while longer in town to help mend the wounded, though it's likely the nobles will ask she be removed again. This time for failing to properly identify the demonic threat.

Unable to provide any coin for the trouble, she offers the silver star as a token of her gratitude.

REWARDS

Cultist Spies: 800 XP (200 XP each)

Cultists: 250 XP (25 XP each)

Cultist Priest: 450 XP

Bill Horton: 450 XP

Defeating Diafol: 1,100 XP

Rescuing the Jousting Notes and Queen's Haven: 600 XP (150 XP per band member, plus the surviving nobility)

Breaking the *Emerald Keystone*: 100 XP

Destroying the Demonic Ward: 50 XP

New Magic Items

THE SILVER STAR
Wondrous item, uncommon

This pendant holds a small star inside of it, partially obscured by a cloud of mist. While holding the *silver star*, you can use an action to determine if an object or location has had a recent interaction with a demon or demonic energy. The star can detect demonic energy at least 15 feet away. However, the closer it's brought toward an item (such as a demonic tome or relic), the brighter the star will glow.

If within 15 feet an actual demon (or a gate to the Abyss), the star will glow brightly, even if not being actively used. Its brightness will vary depending on how close you are to the demonic presence.

EMERALD KEYSTONE
Wondrous item, uncommon (requires attunement)

Speaking into the *keystone* with a special command word will allow you to influence the thoughts of anyone wearing an *emerald pendant* within 120 feet of you. Anyone wearing the *emerald pendant* is charmed to obey the commands of whoever holds the *emerald keystone*. While the charmed creature is wearing an *emerald pendant* (and so long as you hold the *keystone*), you have a telepathic link with the creature. You can use this telepathic link to issue commands to the creature while you are conscious (no action required).

NPCs Stats

SOFIA ESPADA
Medium humanoid (human), lawful good

Armor Class 18 (plate armor)
Hit Points 26 (4d8 + 8)
Speed 30 ft.

STR	DEX	CON	INT	WIS	CHA
15 (+2)	14 (+2)	14 (+2)	15 (+2)	14 (+2)	17 (+3)

Skills Investigation +6, Persuasion +5, Religion +6

Senses passive Perception 12

Languages Common, Draconic, Dwarven, Elven

SPELLCASTING
Sofia is a 4th-level paladin. Her spellcasting ability is Charisma (spell save DC 13, +5 to hit with spell attacks). She has the following spells prepared:

1st Level (3 slots): *bless, cure wounds, detect evil and good*

ACTIONS
Sofia's unique condition limits her in melee; however her faith and experience as a member of the Order of White Ash means she's not completely defenseless.

Plate Gauntlet. *Melee Weapon Attack:* +4 to hit, reach 5 ft., one target. *Hit:* 4 (1d4 + 2) bludgeoning damage, plus 3 (1d6) radiant damage.

ROLEPLAYING INFORMATION
Sofia is distressed by her certainty that Queen's Haven is in immediate danger, but she'll never let it show. Time and experience have proven that cooler heads prevail. She is a woman well aware of her limitations—both physical and mental—but nothing will stop her from doing her sworn duty to defend the weak.

Bond "I've been trained to find where darkness takes root. Once I see it, I cannot look away."

Ideal "It is both an honor and a responsibility to help those less fortunate."

Flaw "It is hard to trust others when you discover how easily a mortal's heart is swayed."

DIAFOL, SCION OF ENTHRALLMENT

Medium fiend (demon), chaotic evil

Armor Class 16 (natural)
Hit Points 67 (9d8 + 27)
Speed 30 ft.

STR	DEX	CON	INT	WIS	CHA
18 (+4)	17 (+3)	17 (+3)	16 (+3)	15 (+2)	16 (+3)

Skills Deception +7, Intimidation +5, Perception +4

Damage Resistance acid, cold, fire, lightning, thunder; bludgeoning, piercing, and slashing from nonmagical attacks

Damage Immunities disease, poison

Condition Immunities charmed, exhaustion, frightened, paralyzed, poisoned

Senses darkvision 120 ft., passive Perception 14

Languages Abyssal, Common, telepathy 120 ft.

Challenge 4 (1,100 XP)

Magic Resistance. Diafol has advantage on saving throws against spells and other magical effects.

ACTIONS

Appalling Visions. Once per round, when a creature begins its turn within 60 feet of Diafol, he may force it to take a DC 13 Charisma saving throw. On a failed saving throw, the creature takes 10 (2d6 + 3) psychic damage, and cannot take reactions until the start of its next turn. Roll a d6 to determine what it does during its turn. On a 1–2, it does nothing. On a 3–4, it makes a Dash action in a random direction. On a 5–6, it attacks a random creature that is not Diafol.

On a successful saving throw, the creature takes half damage, and may resume their turn as normal.

Multiattack. Diafol makes two attacks with its wretched claws.

Wretched Claws. Melee Weapon Attack: +6 to hit, reach 5 ft., one target. *Hit*: 8 (1d8 + 4) slashing damage.

LEGENDARY ACTIONS

Diafol can make two legendary actions, choosing from the following options below. Only one legendary action can be used at a time, and only at the end of another creature's turn. Diafol regains spent legendary actions at the start of its turn.

Bone Shard Volley. Ranged Weapon Attack: +5 to hit, range 60/120, one target. *Hit*: 9 (2d6 + 3) piercing damage.

Sacrificial Devotee. Diafol calls out to one of his charmed subjects, forcing them to run to his side where he may fatally drain them of vitality. Diafol regains 6 (1d6 + 3) hit points.

Disorienting Charm. Flattering whispers fill the mind of a creature Diafol can see within 30 feet. That creature has disadvantage on all attacks against Diafol until the start of their next turn.

Shadow Displacement. Diafol slips into the shadows, melting away from sight and moving to any unoccupied space up to 30 feet away. Use of this ability does not provoke opportunity attacks.

QUEEN'S HAVEN GUARD

Medium humanoid (human), neutral good

Armor Class 16 (chain shirt, shield)
Hit Points 11 (2d8 + 2)
Speed 30 ft.

STR	DEX	CON	INT	WIS	CHA
13 (+1)	12 (+1)	12 (+1)	10 (+0)	11 (+0)	10 (+0)

Skills Perception +2

Senses passive Perception 10

Languages Common

Challenge 1/4 (50 XP)

ACTIONS

Shortsword. Melee Weapon Attack: +3 to hit, reach 5 ft., one target. *Hit*: 4 (1d6 + 1) slashing damage.

Guards of Queen's Haven are well paid to ensure the safety of its nobility. Stable coin, good meals, clean equipment, and the threat of swift replacement keep their wits sharp and loyalties assured.

ADVENTURE CRAFT: NOBODY SAID THERE'D BE MATH INVOLVED!

KAT KRUGER

So, you've written an adventure that's brimming with colorful NPCs and your storyline is filled with nuance and intrigue. You envision the three pillars of play unfolding at your table: exploration, social interaction, and combat. Before you even think to playtest your adventure on a group, how do you know if what you've written is challenging enough?

The truth is, there's a fine balance between setting an encounter to easy mode versus killing all the characters at the table. Neither is super fun, but finding the middle ground takes skill. In fact, it's probably one of the more complex challenges of encounter-building, especially for new GMs. It's also an incredibly important step to developing a balanced adventure that's satisfying to players.

Even if you're not writing an adventure, understanding the mechanics of encounter-building is helpful when making adjustments to published adventures for your players. In many tabletop RPG products, you'll likely see that an adventure is "optimized" for a certain tier of play, along the lines of "This adventure is designed for 1st- to 4th-level characters and is optimized for five characters with an average party level of 3."

What happens when your players don't meet the criteria for that optimal experience? Or a party member drops out of a game for a session? Or you have a guest player drop in? Without making adjustments, you risk having characters that are way too overpowered (OP) and breeze through the encounter or, worse, you wind up with Total Party Kill (TPK) situation.

So, what's an adventure writer or GM to do?

Well, I hate to say it, but that's where math comes in. If anyone had told me how much arithmetic was involved in adventure writing, I might have "noped" myself out of even trying. I thought the enjoyment of game design came exclusively from the creative elements. When you really think about what an adventure module is, though, it's a technical guide for a GM.

From area dimensions to DC ability checks to treasure allocation, everything you write is to provide a sort of guidebook for a GM. Encounters and, by extension, encounter math is a necessary part of the design process. Thankfully, there are guidelines available to help. The core rulebooks provide a number of handy tables.

Encounter difficulties are rated as: easy, medium, hard, or deadly. In many published adventures, you'll see boxed text for adjusting encounters based on party strength. These are helpful to GMs who won't always run the game with "optimal" numbers. When you craft an adventure, you may want to consider including these adjustments in boxed text. It's more math, but especially helpful to new GMs. What's easy to a party of five at level 3 could easily become hard or even deadly for a party of three at level 1.

Let's do some math using the "optimized" example from above: five characters with an average party level of 3.

First, we need to look at what's called XP thresholds for each character. At level 3 for an easy encounter, that's 75 XP. Do the same for medium (150 XP), hard (225 XP), and deadly (400 XP) encounter difficulties.

Next, you'll want to determine the XP threshold for the entire party. To do that, simply add up the XP character threshold by the number of characters in the party at that level. At level 3 for an easy encounter, that's: 75 + 75 + 75 + 75 + 75 = 375 XP. This still works if your party has mixed levels. Just add up the characters' XP thresholds. Do the same for medium (750 XP), hard (1125 XP), and deadly (2000 XP) encounter difficulties. These calculations will be what you use to build encounters throughout the entirety of your adventure, so keep them somewhere for easy reference.

Now, let's look at the monsters. Every creature in the core rulebooks has an XP value next to the challenge rating (CR) in its stat block. It's crucial, particularly at lower levels when the characters are still a bit squishy, to be very careful about introducing monsters that are above a party's average level. Some of these monsters may have abilities that characters simply have no way of overcoming.

With that in mind, let's throw some goblins at our characters! One goblin has an XP value of 50. We'll summon five of them to go head-to-head with our level-3 adventuring party of five. That's 50 XP x 5 = 250 XP. Compare that number to the XP threshold for the entire party and you'll find it's below easy level (375 XP). A breeze, right? But wait!

Multiple monsters means multiple attacks, which naturally adds up to a more dangerous encounter. How do you account for the increased difficulty? By using a multiplier based on the number of monsters in the encounter. An encounter modifiers table can be found in the core rulebooks.

In our example, we have five goblins. Referencing the modifier table, you'll note that for three to six monsters, the multiplier is 2. So, that means 250 XP suddenly becomes 500 XP. For our party of five level-3 characters, this falls below the medium difficulty XP threshold and, because we round down to the nearest level, it's still considered an easy encounter. However, the same can't be said for an identical number of characters at level 2, who would find this a medium difficulty encounter.

In terms of awarding XP points to players, keep in mind that this adjusted value does not reflect the XP that the monsters are worth. It's simply used to determine how difficult the encounter will be. When it comes time to track XP, you're still going to give the party 250 XP for defeating the goblin gang.

Furthermore, the modifiers assume a party size between three to five characters. If there are fewer adventurers, use the next highest modifier on the table. Conversely, for a larger party, use the next lowest modifier on the table.

Of course, if there are multiple types of monsters in an encounter, you'll want to make further adjustments. Add the monster XP together, use the appropriate multiplier, and you'll be able to determine how difficult the encounter will

be for your players. That being said, if you don't think they'll have a meaningful impact on the outcome of an encounter, you don't need to include monsters whose CR falls well below the average CR of the other baddies in the fray.

Your adventure will no doubt feature more than one encounter. In that case, you'll want to take into account the XP that the party has for an entire adventuring day. Again, there's a handy table for that in the core rulebooks that you can easily reference. For our level-3 adventuring party of five, we're looking at 1200 XP per character in a day. That's roughly how much you can throw at an adventurer in a given day before they have to take a long rest.

Other factors come into play when encounters are more complex, such as waves of enemies making incursions without giving the characters the opportunity to rest. Allocating XP for an adventuring day will help guide you in making decisions on how much to throw at your players before they're tapped out of spell slots and other resources.

Finally, keep in mind that when designing an adventure, there are four tiers that you'll write for: tier-1 (levels 1–4),

Illustration by Sarah Bollinger

tier-2 (levels 5–10), tier-3 (levels 11–16), and tier 4 (levels 17–20). Adjusting encounters works best when keeping these tiers in mind. For example, a tier-1 adventure isn't meant to be played by tier-3 characters.

What happens when you don't have the time to make adjustments in gameplay or otherwise need to wing it? Again, the core rulebooks are your friends here. You can find a table that shows damage severity and level. Severity is categorized as: setback, dangerous, and deadly. Using our sample adventuring party of five at level 3, a setback would cause 1d10 damage to one character. The entire party could therefore take a total of 5d10 damage without the encounter becoming a lethal one.

With this knowledge, you can find monsters at an appropriate CR and cross-reference the damage "budget" that you have to shop around. What you'll be looking for is a damage output that a creature is capable of dishing out which is equal to or less than what the party can take.

It's still a bit of math, but it's faster than going through all of the aforementioned calculations. Similarly, in a published adventure that you're running as a GM, you can make adjustments by looking at what the attacks of the encounter monsters are and then adjusting based on what your party is capable of fending off before it becomes dangerous or deadly.

Now that I've explained all the math involved, you have the foundational knowledge from which to build encounters. While all of it is important to understand, there are online calculators that will do the calculations for you! You'll still need to do the legwork of tracking down monster stats to add to the encounter and running the numbers to make adjustments for a given party, but now you've got the basic toolset to challenge your players in just the right way. Happy adventure writing! ⬢

RUNNING THE GAME: NIGHT MOVES

MK REED

The party needs to rest, but in a world of magic and peril, only a fool would just sleep through the night. You can, of course, use your standard night attack with monsters and bandits, or you can see how your players react to noncombat challenges that test the other skills they've rolled up. Or just mess with them a little and see if they actually hold themselves to the ideals they claim to embody.

RANDOM CAMPSITE FEATURES

ROLL A D12 TO GIVE YOUR CAMPSITE TERRAIN SOME FEATURES.

1. There's a small stream to one side, and anything crossing through it would make splashing noises.

2. There's a fire ring and a flattened area with a bed of leaves or pine needles where someone has camped before.

3. There's a huge old tree that's collapsed and is perfect for building a lean-to off the road.

4. The site is bordered by thorny blackberry bushes on one side.

5. The site is in the ruins of a small cottage, with no roof but some walls and a fireplace.

6. The site is over a tiled floor of a ruined building; flower motifs are visible in the tiles and felled columns can be used as seats.

7. There's a large boulder with multiple sets of initials carved into it to the side of the camp.

8. Steep cliffs rise 20 feet over the campsite, and they can't be climbed without sending down a spray of pebbles and rocks.

9. The grass in this field is 3 feet high and provides cover low to the ground.

10. A 10' x 10' platform that is 15 feet high can be climbed to keep off the ground at night, but there's no place for a campfire in this hunter's blind.

11. The campsite has a small well, fire ring, and a night's supply of firewood. It seems to be maintained by someone. There's a small box affixed to a post by the well with a slot for coins. The box does not contain any coins.

12. A wagon with broken wheels tilts at an angle and provides some shelter to sleep under.

SCRY A CAMPFIRE

CHALLENGE: PLAYER PARANOIA

One of your players' relatives or acquaintances is concerned about them and convinces a priest or wizard to check in on them while they eat for the night (or casts scrying themselves if they're a powerful enough magic user to do so). Have that player make a Wisdom save, and on a fail describe what each character within 10 feet of them looks like at that moment, unless they're invisible or otherwise undetectable. How are they dressed? What's their mood? Are they safe or in danger? Do they seem comfortable and happy or are they distressed about something? Take notes, and then move on. If they meet up in the future, have that NPC bring it up—your provincial dwarf's mother might find it concerning that her daughter is hanging out with dragons and cat people. Otherwise, it's just DM secrets that will make your players pay slightly more attention to what's going on.

RACCOON ATTACK!

CHALLENGE: GENEROSITY VS. RATIONS

During the night watch, your most nature-loving PC is visited by a group of at least three raccoons looking for food. The raccoons will take any rations offered by the PC, but will not be satisfied with the portion given, and will

Illustration by Sarah Bollinger

continue to ask for more. When they're no longer given any more food, they'll sniff out the party's supplies. They'll eat and grab everything they can until a party member makes an attack. The raccoons will cut and run as soon as they're attacked, hauling off as much as they can carry in their lil' paws.

TRAVELER IN DISGUISE

CHALLENGE: ALIGNMENT

As the party stops for the night, an old traveler asks if they can stop by the campsite and share the group's food. It's your religious PC's god, testing their follower's adherence to their faith's practices. If they're welcomed and treated well, they'll give a small gift to the player, though standards for behavior may vary depending on the god.

- **Everyone is respectful**: The party is blessed from dawn to dark.

- **Only the worshipper is respectful**: They find a healing potion left next to their pack in the morning.

- **The party members are jerks**: They are surprised by a skunk first thing in the morning and are sprayed. Social skill checks are at disadvantage for the day.

- **The party threatens or attacks the traveler**: This weak-looking stranger has 1000 hp & hits 'em with 9th-level spells.

WITCHES' BREW

CHALLENGE: INVESTIGATION, LIE DETECTION

The party notices a small path into the woods off the road and follows it to a very small shed, about 5 foot by 5 foot. The roof sticks out a few feet as an awning, so it has plenty of dry firewood underneath, and there's a small fire circle. Inside is a still and a few barrels full of liquid, a pair of stools, some long spoons, and a pair of cups. It's an inviting camping spot.

Around midnight, a pair of middle-aged women show up in dark cloaks. Greta and Homelza claim to be witches, but this is a bluff so that the party doesn't attack. They're moms who like to drink and gripe together away from their families, and this band of intimidatingly dressed weirdos is at their secret clubhouse. They're cautious but only carry walking sticks and have no desire to actually fight. The "witches" will ask the party to leave their belongings alone and then they'll leave for the night if they feel uneasy about staying. If the party is friendly, they'll drop the ruse and stick around for a drink, dropping a little helpful knowledge about the nature of someone in the area in their gossip. If your party is the "fight first, ask questions later" type, the women will dodge attacks or hide, and move to cover in the trees, with advantage for their knowledge of the terrain. If it's a massacre, their husbands and families will be looking for them at sunrise, and they know exactly where their wives hang out.

STRANGE CRIES

CHALLENGE: WILD GOOSE CHASE

The PC on watch hears something crying in the night that sounds like it might be a baby. It is in fact a small, pixie-sized black bird that startles easily and moves a short distance away each time a person comes near it. It is very hard to spot, especially at night: a DC of 20 for a character without darkvision, or 15 with. It will try to stay at least 60 feet away whenever possible. If a chase leads to combat, it has one hit point and an AC of 19, +9 from Dex. If caught, the bird shuts up. If that hit point vanishes, it has some stylish tailfeathers the color of the night sky.

BIRD'S NEST

CHALLENGE: INVESTIGATION, ACROBATICS/ATHLETICS

There's something shiny very high up in a tree, but your strong or limber PCs should be able to climb up to it. If they're able to climb up 40 feet, they find:

Roll a d6:

1. A silver key
2. A 20 gp gem
3. A tin toy soldier and a metal fishing hook
4. A bird's nest with golden threads woven in
5. 7 gold coins
6. A string of small pearls, worth 25 gp

MAGIC MUSHROOMS

CHALLENGE: NATURE OR SURVIVAL

Your nature-lover took the Nature or Survival skill to use it, so throw some fun finds their way. There's a single mushroom by the side of the campsite. Pick a DC from the table below, ask for a Survival check, and see if they correctly identify the species. You can either set the DC based on how strong an effect you'd like to throw at your players, or use their roll to determine how amazing their find is. If the mushroom is ingested, it produces the following spell effects on the eater, as though the spell had been successfully cast.

DC 10

The mushroom heals for 1d4 points. It's large enough to share a bite among all party members, but only works once per person per day.

DC 15

Roll a d6:

1. *Sleep*
2. *Calm emotions*
3. *Zone of truth*
4. *Suggestion*
5. *Fear*
6. *Detect magic*

DC 20

Roll a d4:

1. *Misty step*
2. *Mirror image*
3. *Sleep*
4. *Hideous laughter*

DC 25

Roll a d6:

1–2. *Legend lore*
3–4. *Telepathic bond*
5–6. *Mind blank*

DC 30

Roll a d6:

1–2. *Faithful hound*
3–4. *Gaseous form*
5–6. *Summon fey*

Hard Mode: Have your player roll Arcana checks to correctly identify the effects. If they pass the Survival check but not Arcana, they know the mushroom is safe to eat and has some useful effect, but they can't properly identify what it does.

Roll a d4:

1. *Weird*
2. *Time stop*
3. *Maze*
4. *Holy aura*

MAKE YOUR GAME HARDER

If you've been skipping night watch encounters in your game, consider adding them in, especially as your players get to higher levels. As your players get accustomed to breezing through levels with all their spells slots, scaling the encounter to stay challenging gets a little more interesting when your barbarian is low on rages or your wizard's spent a few of their spell slots. You can only take one long rest per 24 hours, so something that uses an ability or two might not feel like a big deal at the time to the party. But if you're able to surprise them with their next encounter before they take another rest, it can make the challenge a lot more dicey. ◈

RANDOM NONSENSE:
PARTY OF ONE

GEOFFREY GOLDEN

MY QUEST TO REDISCOVER ADVENTURE GAMEBOOKS

For the last few years, we've been experiencing a role-playing boom. Board game sales are up. New gaming cafes are opening across the country. Podcasts and streaming shows are turning RPG gamers into household names. But for all the love and attention given to tabletop gaming lately, there's an offshoot of the genre—a redheaded, paperback-bound stepchild—that's been unjustly forgotten during this D&D resurgence.

* * *

When I was growing up, none of my friends played D&D. We were all about our video game consoles. The Fred Savage movie/shameless Nintendo commercial, *The Wizard,* was targeted to me specifically. I was definitely a Nintendo kid, but I was also (weirdly) a story kid. I pored over game manuals looking to learn anything I could about the heroes, villains, and worlds of my favorite games. I didn't just want to play a game, I wanted to play a *story*.

At a Scholastic Book Fair, I discovered something really cool: a *Nintendo Adventure Book*. It was similar to a *Choose Your Own Adventure (CYOA),* which I also enjoyed, but "leveled up" with puzzles to solve, items to collect, and Koopa Kids to foil. The book felt a lot like a game, and thus began a lifelong fascination with the adventure gamebook genre.

Adventure gamebooks are a combination of CYOAs and tabletop roleplaying games. The reader is asked to make choices, sending them one way or another on a branching narrative path. In addition, the books weave in elements from RPGs: readers create characters, learn magic spells, collect helpful items, and slay vicious monsters with dice!

For a time, gamebooks were incredibly popular. One of the first and best remembered series was *Fighting Fantasy*, created by Games Workshop co-founders Ian Livingstone and Steve Jackson (the British Steve Jackson, not the American Steve Jackson, creator of *Munchkin*—so many Steve Jacksons!). *Fighting Fantasy* launched in 1982, spawning 59 titles and selling 20 million copies throughout the '80s.

During the '90s, when D&D became more of a niche hobby eclipsed by video games and VHS tapes, the best-known adventure gamebook series was discontinued. *Fighting Fantasy* ceased publication in 1995 after 59 titles, followed in 1998 by its nine million-copy-selling rival, the *Lone Wolf* series.

Over the years, I've slowly amassed a small library of gamebooks. Unlike most of my old video games cartridges, lost to moving sales and game trade-in shops, I've managed to hold onto these strange and wonderful books.

With the rise in popularity of roleplaying games, I wondered if my love for adventure gamebooks was just the rose-colored glasses of nostalgia, or if this art form is really worth revisiting. I decided to re-play some of my favorite adventure gamebooks from my shelf and discovered some new favorites in my research. Here's what I found...

ADVENTURE GAMEBOOKS ARE A GREAT WAY TO GET STARTED WITH RPGs.

Imagine you've never played a roleplaying game before in your life (I know that might be difficult as the reader of a magazine called *Rolled & Told*.) Many tabletop roleplaying games are complex, with lots of rules to learn and decades worth of lore to dig into. When I try to convince RPG newbies to play a tabletop game with me, I'm often met with expressions of skepticism—or *pure terror*.

So, as a new player, how do you know if you want to invest your time and energy into playing tabletop roleplaying games? I think adventure gamebooks would serve as an excellent gateway.

The rules pages for gamebooks in my library are typically around two to five pages long, written in plain language. In the gamebooks I've played, even when it's part of a series, there's no expectation that you already know how to play. To be "standalone," the books treat each reader as a brand new player.

Sometimes the rules are written cleverly, in a conversational style. In the cheeky opening of *The Castle of Darkness* by J. H. Brennan (#1 in the *Grail Quest* series), Merlin the wizard gives you the instructions as if you were his pupil.

> "Don't fidget!" Merlin instructs, before educating you on how to fight. "The way you fight in my Time is a bit peculiar. You have to roll dice. Two dice together, or one die twice. Doesn't matter which. If you score more than six on your two rolls added together, it means you've hit your enemy. Landed him a whopper on the snout or wherever."

Simple and easy-to-understand mechanics help new players get a feel for what's fun about roleplaying games. In *The Citadel of Chaos* by Steve Jackson (#2 in the *Fighting Fantasy* series), you build a character and choose from a list of spells your character knows. At specific points in the book, the player can cast a spell to avoid danger or power up during battle, but each spell can only be used once per game. This gives the reader the *feel* of using magic in an RPG game with none of the complexities.

One anxiety I've noticed from new players is the concern that they're "holding back" a group of expert players by being confused or asking too many questions. The reader of a gamebook is on a solo adventure, and can focus their energy on solving puzzles, winning battles, making story decisions, and having fun! Hopefully, after playing a gamebook or two, the new player would feel more comfortable with the roleplaying format.

Illustration by Sarah Bollinger

HOUSE RULES: REIMAGINING CLASSES

STEVE KENSON

The twelve core character classes cover a wide range of archetypes and roles, giving players a lot of options when it comes to the type of character they want to play in the game. Even so, there are hidden opportunities to further customize or modify the existing classes to get even more "mileage" out of them when it comes to creating unique characters. They are found in the fictional conceits of how the classes are described versus the mechanical implementations of what the classes do. In video game terms, character classes are prime opportunities for "re-skinning" in order to expand what they can offer to players. Consider the following possibilities and take in a wider vision of character creation for your games.

BARBARIAN

Savage warriors empowered by rage, barbarians are lightly armored, tough fighters. Although their key ability is called "Rage," does it have to be? Consider these potential re-skins of the barbarian:

- Rather than primal rage, the character has learned to enter into a deep trance, turning the movement of battle into a primal dance full of grace, rhythm, and power. In this trance state, the "battle dancer" is stronger and faster, and does not feel pain. The Path of the Berserker can represent a character whose dance is a frenzy of energy, while the Path of the Totem Warrior may "dance the aspects" of different beasts, much like some martial arts styles.

- The character is a vessel for spiritual power, which comes over them in battle. They might channel the spirit of an ancestor, spirit guide, or tribal totem, or the divine power of a deity. Their "rage" is in fact the throes of spiritual possession, in which the character might not even be truly conscious, their ordinary mind displaced.

BARD

Musicians, magicians, and jacks of all trades, classical bards are strongly tied to music, but the class often makes mention of "oration" when talking about their abilities, suggesting some potential re-skins:

- They are a true leader who can inspire their company to greatness, soothe and tend their injuries, and have the knowledge and experience to negotiate peace when the battle is done. Their inspirational words are their weapons as much as their arms and armor.

- "Words can cut deeper than swords," say the masters of the duel, although it is usually the sword that finishes a foe. Still, a swashbuckling duelist learns more than a few tricks here and there: a few odd spells, a knack for inspiring speeches, and a Renaissance approach to a wide range of knowledge. The wit of a duelist of the College of Lore can truly cut a foe to the quick!

- The bard's power lies in knowledge of the runes, sacred sounds and symbols, and perhaps even a whole "secret language" of magic or sacred poetry. Similarly, a "cantor" might be a divine singer of sacred songs and reciter of scripture to guide and inspire others.

CLERIC

Agents of divine power, clerics are often seen as priests in an existing religious hierarchy, but that does not have to be the case. Consider the following:

- A cleric might follow an ideal or concept rather than a deity. As such, where the cleric's Divine Domain is more important than any particular deity, religious dogma, or mythos. Similarly, a cleric might serve an entire pantheon, drawing spells and blessings from diverse deities. They could even be the devoted agent of an institution, such as a cleric of the Throne or Crown of a particular ancient nation.

- Rather than an ordained priest of a temple or church, a cleric might be a "holy hermit" or a similarly inspired prophet, someone chosen by the gods as their agent, whether they want to be or not. A prophet's purpose is to serve the god's will in the world, which may include shaking up the existing hierarchy a bit.

DRUID

Divine priests of nature, druids (like clerics) have the potential to embody other natural forces or concepts using their existing abilities.

- A devoted "animist" can perceive and interact with the spirits inherent in all of nature. They can call upon them as allies to work their magic, which ranges from the spirits of plants and animals coming to the character's aid, to the spirits of beasts lending their essence or form.

- The druid might even be an embodied nature spirit! Mythology is full of spirits taking on human or humanoid forms, and a nature spirit might incarnate in such a fashion. Druid's spells can be used as examples of the spirit's innate powers, and class abilities can represent the spirit's link with the natural world.

FIGHTER

The fighter is one of the more "generic" classes as is, but still offers some opportunities for reimagining.

- The emphasis on the fighter as presented is on skill and training, but a fighter could just as easily be "naturally gifted" and "talented." This could be just an accident of birth, or the result of a supernatural blessing or heritage of some kind.

- Speaking of supernatural blessings, some of a fighter's class abilities could be re-skinned as innately magical in nature. Perhaps the fighter has preternatural speed for their Extra Attack, or can magically heal themselves using their Second Wind, and so forth.

MONK

The monk is typically an Asian-style martial artist and ascetic. Monk class abilities tend to focus on unarmed combat and mind-over-body effects, pointing towards potential different points of view:

Illustration by Tara Kurtzhals

IN VIDEO GAME TERMS, CHARACTER CLASSES ARE PRIME OPPORTUNITIES FOR "RE-SKINNING" IN ORDER TO EXPAND WHAT THEY CAN OFFER TO PLAYERS.

- Rather than Asian ki, the monk might exercise a kind of "psychic" discipline, the power of the mind enhancing the body through focus and meditation.

- It almost goes without saying that the Way of the Four Elements tradition bears a strong resemblance to the "bending" techniques of certain animated martial artists. It would be easy to imagine orders (or "nations") following the Four Ways, or even a setting where Way of the Four Elements monks are the only wielders of magic.

PALADIN

Although seen as "holy warriors" the key elements of the paladin are their fighting abilities and their devotion to a cause or ideal greater than themselves. As with clerics, paladins might be divinely-empowered in ways other than conventionally dedicating themselves to a particular deity or church.

- The paladin is well-suited for a "fiend hunter" type of character who wanders the land and shows up in town to deal with a monster plaguing it before continuing on their way. Some might even hunt a particular quarry, like demons or witches.

- The character's paladin class represents an otherworldly heritage or nature. They could be an angel in (or possessing) a mortal form, or the spirit of an ancient knight or warrior returned to life with extraordinary powers to fulfill some purpose.

RANGER

The ranger is a hunter, tracker, and dedicated foe of certain creatures, but can be seen in a few different ways, such as:

- Rather than hunting monsters in the wild, a ranger might rely on stealth, archery, and mastery of terrain to

waylay unwary travelers through those selfsame wilds. This might be to line a highwayman's own pockets, or to rob from the rich and unscrupulous and give to the poor and needy.

- Although a ranger's combat prowess is considerable, their magic represents a strong connection with the natural world. Some of this can be considered an inherent ability or a working knowledge of the magical qualities of herbs, animals, and terrain rather than "spells" per se. The class's primeval awareness ability reinforces this.

ROGUE

Along with the fighter, the rogue is one of the most flexible classes in concept. The easiest re-skinning usually involves removing some of the rogue's criminal associations.

- Cunning, quick thinking, with an expertise in skills like Deception, Insight, Persuasion, and Stealth, and a knack for literally stabbing people in the back—a rogue makes an excellent master of courtly or urban intrigue.

- While rogues are usually associated with civilization, their skills are also applicable to the wilderness. A rogue focused on stealth, quick movement, and infiltration could be a scout or explorer, or perhaps even a "tomb raider," an expert at delving into trap-laden ruins.

SORCERER

The core of the sorcerer class is "innate arcane power." There are a number of different ways to interpret that beyond just bloodline or heritage.

- The sorcerer can represent a character marked, touched, or transformed by magical forces in early life, perhaps even before their birth. Examples may include a blessing or curse placed on a child, a role in a prophecy, a faerie "changeling" substituted for a mortal child, or a brush with supernatural forces, such as demonic or ghostly possession that was cured but still left its mark.

- Sorcerers are typically isolated examples of "arcane heritage," but a sorcerer could just as easily be an example of a kind of arcane sub-race—people who all possess innate magical potential, with some of them developing it into true levels of power. This "arcane folk" might have the standard racial traits of an existing "parent" race, but the magical power that sorcerers wield is common, and even the average member of the race knows a couple of cantrips.

WARLOCK

The warlock bargains with a patron for arcane power, but that is not the only arrangement suitable for the class as presented.

- Perhaps the most obvious re-skin of the warlock class is that many elements of the warlock embody the fantasy or fairy-tale, which is particularly well-suited for warlocks with Fiendish or Fey patrons.

- Another interpretation of the warlock's "pact" might be the spirit-bargains and relationships forged by shamans and spirit-workers in other cultures. After falling into a "shaman's sickness" or similar crisis, the character meets with different powers in the spirit world and learns to forge agreements with them, returning to the mundane world with magical power.

WIZARD

Wizards work their magic through comprehensive study and preparation, making them some of the most flexible of spell-casters, which offers some possibilities for re-skinning their arcane trappings.

- In particular, a common element to reimagine for wizards is the venerable spellbook. The key is that it's a permanent record of spells a wizard can study. Beyond that, a "spellbook" could just as easily be a set of carved sticks, bones, rune stones, a mala or necklace of semi-precious beads, a cloak or mantle of elaborate embroidery, bead-work, or weaving, or any number of other things.

- Wizardry is the arcane art most like a science, with its emphasis on research, study, and experimentation. The wizard class makes an excellent base for a re-skin for an "arcangineer" or tinkerer character who produces various sorts of gadgets and devices capable of producing remarkable effects. These are generally just special effects of the wizard's spells, with re-skins of spell focuses and arcane components. ⬡

RANDOM NONSENSE: HOMEBREW HOMESCHOOL

BROOKE JAFFE

A Crash Course in Content Creation

A waterbender smothers the fire of a dragon as it breathes over their party. A druid befriends soot sprites in the ashes of a hearth. A bard discovers that electricity, when channeled through their guitar, makes for a pretty rockin' instrument.

Waterbenders and soot sprites and electric guitars may not be content endemic to your tabletop system, but you can still bring them into your game! How, you ask? Through Homebrew!

What Is Homebrew?

Homebrew is what we call unofficial content made for a tabletop system by fans or players. "Homebrew" is the broad term—it can refer to anything from a new item to a new monster, race, or feat.

So, other than creating cool stuff for your campaign based on your favorite media, why use Homebrew content?

First, it lets you customize your game to your table. Every party is different: different people, different play styles, aesthetics, and experience levels. Being able to craft things for those people, things that speak to what they want to get out of a play experience, helps personalize gameplay for your players and gives them more of a stake in the world. If your player makes a character who's a former pirate with an ancient curse, then wouldn't it be cool to make a curse mechanic that affects their gameplay? It helps cement that character's personal features in the world: both narratively and mechanically.

Second, the designers who create content for the official sourcebooks can't, and won't, think up everything you can. They don't know your table, and they can't predict everything your party will do. You can fill in the gaps of official content with your own ideas and create a level of adaptability that can take your campaign in new and exciting directions!

Last, but not least, it can spice up your campaign's world. Everyone has played standard classes, fought standard monsters, used standard spells—but what about throwing in something new? Homebrewing novel and exciting monsters, classes, and weapons is far from an exact science, but for GMs, having the ability to generate new content can mean that difference between a game that feels like standard medieval fantasy and something truly unique.

How Do I Start Building My Own Homebrew?

Let's break it down into phases: Ideation, Prototyping, Playtesting, and Revision. If any part of that sounds complicated and jargon-y, don't worry—we're going to take it step by step.

ADVENTURES IN IDEATION

Everything begins with an idea, and ideas begin with inspiration! What are you using for inspiration? Is it a setting, a myth, a character from your favorite book? Find something that gets you (or your players) excited.

Now, consider what are the essential parts of that

concept you want to focus on? What makes that thing so exciting to you, or to your player? Write these down. They're going to serve as the architecture of your Homebrew. Are they aesthetic? Are they mechanical? Think about why you feel strongly about those points in particular. Write down a couple of words about those reasons. If it's an aesthetic, consider the kind of language you use to describe those features and consider implementing that in your design. For example, if you want to make a pirate class, think about seafaring terms: how pirates talk, dress, act. Keep all of those in mind for when you're building out the features of your class. It'll lend spice and style to your work!

PROTOTYPING FOR PLAY

Now that you have an idea of what you want to create, let's start building prototypes.

What kind of content are you making? If you're building a new class, make a list of all of the features of a standard build. Classes have at-will abilities that recharge on a short or long rest. Classes give proficiencies in different skills, armor types, and saving throws. Does your class have magic? If so, is it a half-caster or a full-caster? What spell list can they choose from? How many abilities do they get as they level up, and how do their initial abilities scale with experience? Look at a canon class to make a list of what aspects you'll need to specify to make sure your class can stand alongside any canon class from the book.

Do this with any other kind of Homebrew. What features come with a particular race? What about magical items —

their power, their school of magic, their cost? Once you know what you have to decide, we can start putting ideas into place.

To continue with the pirate example, I decided that any good pirate worth their salt should know how to

sail, and probably knows how to navigate, too. In order to put that into my new pirate class, I give all pirates proficiency with boats, and advantage on Survival or Intelligence checks related to navigating through the open ocean. Since they use both simple blades and also ranged fare like early firearms or light crossbows, my pirates have proficiency in simple melee weapons and simple ranged weapons.

Pay close attention to how what you're making aligns with existing material. Does your new spellcaster class have a d12 as their Hit Dice? That's the same as a barbarian; you might want to take a look at how that compares to sorcerers or wizards, and adjust accordingly. Is your new evil ent monster supposed to be fought by a small party at level 3, even though its stats look comparable to a CR 13 storm giant? When in doubt, make use of free online tools. There are calculators for CR and databases of content to reference and compare. A lot of these sorts of imbalances will show themselves in playtesting, but if you can save yourself the trouble by keeping a sharp eye out and learning how to self-edit, your creative process will be much smoother.

If the thought of coming up with something totally new and off-the-wall still feels a little intimidating, I recommend taking something you like that already exists in the game and modifying it. Change the abilities with new names, vocabulary, or a different kind of damage to give them a new flavor. It's a simple and easy way to breathe new life into existing content, and is a great first step towards becoming more confident in your Homebrewing skills!

> **"**
>
> **IF THE THOUGHT OF COMING UP WITH SOMETHING TOTALLY NEW AND OFF-THE-WALL STILL FEELS A LITTLE INTIMIDATING, I RECOMMEND TAKING SOMETHING YOU LIKE THAT ALREADY EXISTS IN THE GAME AND MODIFYING IT.**

THE VALUE OF PLAYTESTING

Once you have your first draft of a build done, get a few friends together and try it out in a one-shot game, or in an encounter that's comparable to one in the game you're ultimately trying to create for. It may seem like a bit of a pain to go do lots of testing before getting

Illustration by Tara Kurtzhals

> ## " "
>
> ULTIMATELY, WHEN YOU IMPLEMENT HOMEBREW
> CONTENT THE KEY IS TO KEEP COMMUNICATION WITH
> YOUR PLAYERS OPEN TO GET FEEDBACK. IF THEY AREN'T
> HAPPY, LISTEN TO THEM AND STAY FLEXIBLE!

to use your shiny new Homebrew content, but trust me: playtesting is invaluable, and will save you a lot of trouble down the line.

Why, you ask? Well, playtesting has a lot of benefits. First, it helps you discover problems you can't anticipate. Any GM can recall a time when they spent lots of time planning an encounter or a plot, only to have their party do something that they didn't expect and throw everything off their perfectly-plotted course! Homebrew is no different. Players are always going to find ways to use (and abuse) your content that you never thought of. Playtesting lets them run amok in a controlled environment and not your actual campaign.

Second, you get another pair of eyes on your work! Sometimes things that seem perfectly clear to you make no sense to someone else. When in doubt, look things over with a trusted player or a fellow GM.

Finally, playtesting often helps generate new ideas. Do

you end up using one ability or feature particularly often? Maybe make it the central mechanic! How can you play with that to make it more versatile, or more fun?

THE ART OF REVISION

With a solid playtest under your belt, go back to your initial concept. Did your Homebrew evoke the feelings or experiences you set out to capture? Talk to your playtesters. Did they get those feelings, or have those experiences? Did it feel overpowered, or underpowered? Did they have fun?

Listen to their feedback and decide what, if anything, needs work. Take your Homebrew back to the drawing board, tweak it, and test it again! More often than not, you'll have to do a lot of playtesting and revising and playtesting again to get something that feels right. It may seem exhausting, and sometimes you might even get a little frustrated—but know that each iteration takes you closer and closer to your goal.

A NOTE ON OVERPOWERED ("OP") CONTENT AND BALANCING

Balancing is far and away one of the most difficult parts of any kind of game design. It's subjective, and fickle, and in the end, there's no right answer except the one that means your player's experience is the experience you set out to evoke. With Homebrew, it's easy to let things get out of hand. You want your creations to be the coolest! But you also don't want to dishearten your players by making some seriously OP stuff.

For example, I was in a campaign where our paladin was a 500-year-old haunted suit of armor dedicated to a god of competition and battle. He was awesome, and the character was great—but he had a LOT of OP Homebrew content that made him so powerful that any given fight had to be calibrated to him specifically. Many of the other players felt alienated. Why bother taking part in a fight if this one guy could practically win it on his own, anyway?

Now, there are a few ways to solve this problem. One is to nerf the OP player's mechanics—which can work, but doesn't feel good for the person getting nerfed and has the potential to continue feelings of inequity between the person singled out and the rest of the party. Narrative arcs can soften that blow if it's worked in elegantly, but your mileage may vary depending on how story-focused your party is.

In the end, we went with another solution: level the playing field. No one is "over"-powered if everyone is, so create Homebrew content for everyone that lets each of your players feel as cool and special as the next! This can sometimes backfire and mean a more difficult job for the GM, trying to juggle lots of powerful characters. But as a GM, I tend to prefer players all feeling as badass as possible—even if it means I have to build my encounters around it.

Ultimately, when you implement homebrew content, the key is to keep communication with your players open to get feedback. If they aren't happy, listen to them and stay flexible! The game is about having fun, after all, so the most important thing is always if you and your players are all enjoying your campaign. If that means having to scrap an idea because it threw things out of balance, or having to go through a few more cycles of testing and revision, then it's worth it.

IN CONCLUSION

Part of the beauty of tabletop gaming is that, because it's analog, you don't have to be a programmer to get your hands dirty and play around with the gears that make up the system. Unlike video games, where all of the calculations and randomness and stat-crunching is happening inside the bowels of a computer, in tabletop the GM and players serve as the medium through which the game happens; and you (yes, you!) are more flexible and more powerful than any game engine out there! You can change things on the fly, create new and exciting original ideas, modify this game at-will—so why not try it out?

Homebrew your heart's desire. It may look intimidating, but I promise you, you can do it, and it's worth it. ✪

SITES & SETTINGS: SETTING THE ENVIRONMENT

RACHEL DUKES

Tips to Brighten Your Burrow and Host Your Party's Next Adventure

The three pillars of adventure are exploration, social interaction, and combat. The next time you host your party's campaign, use the following cunning tips to optimize your living space to ensure peak social interaction (and that exploration and combat stay in-game). The pointers below will get your burrow party-ready for campaigns of any length or complexity.

Brightening Your Burrow

Are you a level one wizard? I sure hope so, because your first task is to cast *clean*. Clean those stains, dirt, grime, mud, and other tiny things in the shared spaces you'll be hosting your party members in. It doesn't need to look like a townhouse or the finest inn, but no one wants to spend their day in what looks or smells like a squalid, leaky stable.

Speaking of stables—make sure to dust with a wet rag and sweep up dirt and pet hair in case anyone on your team has allergies. Whether it's an aerem rabbit, commerce cat, or blind dog, you don't want the local fauna adversely affecting your adventure.

You'll need a central space to play that's large enough for your adventure grid, snacks, and drinks. For smaller parties, this could be a card or coffee table. Larger parties may require a dining or folding table.

Use common intuition—don't offer four chairs if there are eight members of your party. Be mindful that your party may have members of differing size and mobility. Everyone should have a comfortable space to adventure from. Plan accordingly.

Drink

Can't fathom what to serve your party to quench their thirst? This short list will have your drink menu on loch!

POND DEW
1st-level divination

Casting time: 5 minutes
Components: 2 cups water, 2 cups sugar, 2 cups grape juice, 1 cup orange juice, 2 quarts ginger ale
Range: 16 servings

Actions: Combine sugar and water; stir until sugar is dissolved. Add juices. Stir. Add chilled ginger ale and stir immediately prior to serving.

Creates an invisible, magical eye that hovers in the air for the duration.

You mentally receive revealing information from the eye. You understand the literal meaning of any language that you hear or lies spoken by those around you. You see the truth behind magical illusions.

TINKERER'S TINCTURE
1st-level evocation

Casting time: 10 minutes
Components: 7 ounces hot tea, 1 tablespoon honey, 1 teaspoon lemon juice, grated cinnamon, ground cloves, grated nutmeg, lemon wedge for garnish
Range: 1 serving

Actions: Pour honey, lemon, and spices into mug. Top

with hot, brewed tea. Stir. Garnish with lemon wedge.

A healing concoction. Flame-like radiance descends on you. You regain hit points equal to 1d8 + your spellcasting ability modifier.

BLOOD HUNTER'S BLEND
2nd-level necromancy

Casting time: 5 minutes
Components: 2 ounces fresh lime juice, 2 ounces fresh orange juice, 2 ounces pineapple juice, 1 ounce passion fruit nectar, ice, straw
Range: 1 serving

Actions: Combine ingredients in a blender with ice. Blend thoroughly. Pour into glass. Garnish with a fruit slice, sprig of mint, and a cherry. Serve with a straw.

The drinker is protected from decay and can't become undead.

FAE FIREBALL
3rd-level evocation

Casting time: 5 minutes
Components: 1/3 cup apple cider, 1/3 cup cranberry juice, 1 ounce grenadine, ¼ teaspoon edible gold glitter, ice
Range: 1 serving

Actions: Combine all ingredients in cocktail shaker, then fill shaker with ice. Shake until contents are mixed and shaker is cold (approximately 30 seconds). Pour into glass and serve.

Fills the drinkers with faerie light. Drinker can inflict fire damage up to 20 feet away with their pointing finger for the duration.

DRAGON'S MILK
3rd-level transmutation

Casting time: 2 minutes
Components: 1 ounce fresh lemon juice, 3 ounces water, 2 ounces orgeat syrup (contains almonds), ice
Range: 1 serving

Actions: Combine ingredients into shaker with ice. Shake until contents are mixed (approximately 15 seconds). Double strain into glass with ice.

The drinker, along with everything they're wearing and carrying, turns into a cloud of dragon smoke for the duration. The drinker can pass through small holes, narrow openings, and even mere cracks. The drinker can fly at a speed of 10 feet.

PETALWOOD PALOMA
4th-level enchantment

Casting time: 5 minutes
Components: ½ ounce ginger syrup, ½ cup pomegranate juice, 1 ounce grapefruit juice, ½ ounce lime juice, ginger beer, 8 mint leaves, pomegranate seeds, crushed ice
Range: 1 serving

Actions: Combine ginger syrup, pomegranate juice, grapefruit juice, and lime juice in shaker. Shake until contents are mixed (approximately 15 seconds). Pour over ice and top with ginger beer and pomegranate seeds. Garnish with mint.

The drinker can bless up to three party members for the duration. When a blessed party member makes an attack roll or a saving throw before the spell ends, they can roll a d6 and add the number rolled to the attack roll or saving throw.

RIVER'S REWARD
Abjuration cantrip

Casting time: 1 minute
Components: 8 ounces of water, ice
Range: 1 serving

Actions: Pour into glass over ice. Enjoy!

Bolsters the drinker with toughness and resolve. The drinker's hit point maximum and current hit points increase by 3 for the duration.

FOOD

Can't stand another night of takeout from the local tavern? Try these snacks that are easy to make, clean to eat, and won't break the banquet!

CRUDITE PLATTER

Casting time: 20 minutes
Components: Seasonal fresh vegetables and a dipping sauce of your choice

Actions: A simple platter of sliced or whole raw vegetables, served with a dipping sauce (traditionally a vinaigrette, ranch dressing, or hummus, but follow your heart's desire). Vegetables typically include celery sticks, carrot sticks, cucumber sticks, bell pepper strips, broccoli, radishes, cauliflower, fennel, or asparagus spears.

Rinse the vegetables and slice them into strips or halves where appropriate. Serve on a platter, with vegetables arranged by color surrounding a bowl of dipping sauce.

A 5-foot invisible sphere of anti-magic surrounds the eater. Until the spell ends, the sphere moves with the eater, centered on them.

CHARCUTERIE PLATTER

Casting time: 15 minutes
Components: Smoked, dry-cured, or cooked meats with selections of cheese (2 ounces per person), grapes, sliced apples, or cornichons (tiny French pickles), crackers, baguette

Actions: A platter of meats and cheeses. Choose 3 of each, varied in texture and taste (typically parmesan, brie, gruyère, or goat cheese for cheese; and prosciutto, salami, soppressata, or chorizo for meat).

Arrange on a platter with grapes, sliced apples, or cornichons. Serve with crackers or a sliced baguette.

Bestows vitality. For the duration, the eater has advantage on Wisdom saving throws and gains maximum hit points from any healing.

TOMATO AND MOZZARELLA CAPRESE SKEWERS

Casting time: 30 minutes
Components: 1 pint cherry tomatoes, ¾ ounce fresh basil, 4 ounces mozzarella (cherry-sized), 1 tablespoon pesto, 1–3 teaspoons olive oil, flaky salt and freshly ground black pepper, toothpicks
Range: Approximately 16 servings

Actions: Wash and dry tomatoes. Fold basil leaf around tomato, then spear with toothpick. Add a mozzarella ball to the toothpick. Repeat. Whisk pesto with enough olive oil to create a thin sauce, drizzle over the mozzarella. Sprinkle with salt and pepper.

Bestows freedom of movement. The eater's movement is unaffected by difficult terrain. Magic cannot reduce their speed or restrain them.

BANANA BREAD

Casting time: 1 hour 30 minutes
Components: 2 cups all-purpose flour, 1 teaspoon baking soda, ¼ teaspoon salt, ½ cup butter, ¾ cup brown sugar, 2 eggs (beaten), 2 ⅓ cups mashed overripe bananas
Range: 12 servings

Actions: Preheat oven to 350 degrees Fahrenheit. Lightly grease a 9x5-inch pan. In a large bowl, combine flour, baking soda, and salt.

In a separate bowl, cream together butter and brown sugar. Then stir in eggs and mashed bananas until well blended.

Stir banana mixture into flour mixture (until moist). Pour batter into prepared loaf pan. Bake in preheated oven for 60 to 65 minutes, until toothpick inserted into center of the loaf comes out clean. Remove from oven. Let bread cool in pan for 10 minutes, then turn out onto a wire rack.

Imbues the eater with positive energy to undo one debilitating effect. Can reduce the eater's exhaustion level by one, raise their ability scores by one, or raise their hit point maximum by one.

SOFT MOLASSES COOKIES

Casting time: 23 minutes
Components: 1 cup packed brown sugar, 1 cup butter (softened), ¼ cup dark molasses, 1 large egg, 1 teaspoon vanilla extract, 2 ½ cups all purpose flour, 2 teaspoons baking soda, 1 teaspoon ground cinnamon, 1 teaspoon ground ginger, ½ teaspoon salt, ¼ cup granulated sugar (for rolling), parchment paper or non-stick cooking spray
Range: 24 servings

Actions: Preheat oven to 325 degrees Fahrenheit. Line a large baking sheet with parchment paper. If you don't have parchment paper, use non-stick cooking spray.

Combine butter, brown sugar, egg, vanilla, and molasses in a bowl. Beat with a hand mixer until well combined, approximately 2–3 minutes. Add flour, baking soda, salt, and spices into the bowl and mix until the dough forms together, approximately 1 minute.

Shape the dough into spheres that are about 1 ½ inches across. Roll the dough balls in granulated sugar and then place on the baking sheet 2 inches apart.

Bake for 13–15 minutes. Remove cookies from the oven, then the tray, and place them on a wire rack to cool.

Fills the eater with divine light. The eater has advantage on all saving throws, and other creatures have disadvantage on attack rolls against them for three turns.

Don't forget the napkins! And be sure to talk with your party about food allergies—there's no instant healing spell for stomach upset!

Equipment

Make sure you party is adequately prepared for battle. Gather as many sets of pens, paper, and dice as you have members in your party (in case folks forget theirs).

If no one has done so, you can use some artisan's tools to create custom initiative tents for your party members. They're useful for gameplay and they serve as a small token of appreciation that your team can always see.

During Your Adventure

Campaigns are about cooperation, crafting a good story, and having fun. Stay invested in the story you're creating. Pay attention to your party members and what they're doing, don't just wait for your turn to play. Consider your choices for gameplay in advance as it relates to the scene unfolding in front of you. Make decisions that help your party members and help move the story forward.

Read the room: check in that everyone is having fun. Make a point to lift each other up and help each other succeed at your goals. Work together to have an awesome session and celebrate your wins!

The Epilogue

With the day's quest completed, it's time for all accomplished adventurers to get some well-deserved rest. But, before everyone returns to their own realms, villages, and kingdoms, do a group check and be sure to cast *clean* one more time (no one should have to clean dirty dishes alone!), and thank the GM for another exciting session! ⬡

Illustrated by KikiDoodle

ADVENTURE CRAFT: ADVENTURE CRAFTING

SHING YIN KHOR

There are particular emotions that I feel when the snacks get cleared off the gaming table to accommodate the roll-up grid mat. The comforting smell of dry-erase marker and the slight screech of pen against plastic fill the room as we all anticipate a dungeon being drawn out in front of us!

There's a joy in placing my painted miniature on the table, which I painstakingly found by sorting through game store bins for exactly the right details, and then modified with that weird green putty! These gestures herald the start of a fight, both exciting and intimidating, depending on how many monsters our GM seems to be gleefully placing on the table. As a visual thinker and a long-time enthusiast of making things, I get really excited seeing a scene come to life, and even more so when we all get to tell a story with it.

When I was introduced to Dungeons and Dragons about a decade ago, I was immediately drawn to the potentials of three-dimensional maps and integrating my craft into my newfound hobby. Obviously, part of the joy of roleplaying games is that they do not require anything beyond pen and paper. But as a maker, I love the idea of having an affordable, but creative, toolkit that can still surprise my friends at the table. The very first roleplaying games I played as a kid were marvels of the interior imagination, and we made a whole lot of magic without anything other than some dice and paper. Now that I am older and have both disposable income and a large dining room table, I am delighted to indulge in my propensity for theatrics and cool objects.

It doesn't take a lot to bring little sparks of physical crafting magic to the table. All it takes is some basic crafting skills, a willingness to get a little messy and to giggle at yourself, and a high tolerance for hilarious failures.

MODEL-MAKING BASICS

The scale of most mass-produced roleplaying miniatures is approximately 1:64 scale, also known as 3/16-inch scale. This is a good thing to keep in the back of your mind as you start down the brave new path of crafting your own RPG-related objects, such as terrain and landscapes, new characters, and effects.

If you would like to build your own walls and furniture and keep them in scale, an architect's scale ruler will become very helpful. An architect's scale ruler, used by most model makers, does the less-intuitive calculations of scale for you, since you can read it just like a regular ruler when building your own miniatures and terrain. That said, keeping to a strict scale is absolutely not necessary and you can rely on your intuition to scavenge objects that are approximately the right size.

If you want to look for terrain pieces in less traditional places, S scale (1:64) is not a very common scale for both dollhouse and miniature train hobbyists. But it is a scale that matches up to a roleplaying game miniature! You can find S scale things in stores intended for dollhouse and train hobbyists that may be useful in your roleplaying games, such as miniature people (great for civilians and townsfolk!) and structures. They will often run more

Illustrated by KikiDoodle

contemporary in style, but there are often elements such as fences, barrels, hay bales, and other landscaping elements that would look perfectly in place in even the most historically accurate medieval campaigns. Taxidermy stores and catalogs are also a good source for terrain crafting ideas and have been used by miniature-crafting enthusiasts for decades. One of my favorite things available from taxidermy stores is sculptable dirt putty, which is wonderful for quickly covering a large map area with graveled pathways and well-worn dirt roads.

SCULPTING AND PAINTING

Miniature painting and customization materials are expensive and come in very small quantities. If you are creating larger sculpted pieces, like terrain or buildings, you have alternatives.

If you have used the "Green Stuff" readily available at game stores to modify your gaming miniatures, then you've already taken the first steps into sculpting elements for your maps, too! Green Stuff is an epoxy putty, and you can get larger tubs of a similar material under the brand names Apoxie Sculpt and Magic Sculpt. They are both two-part mixable epoxy clays, although they handle slightly differently. Please wear gloves! Apoxie Sculpt is a bit more similar to the rubbery feel of Green Stuff, while Magic Sculpt behaves more similarly to ceramic clay, but the concepts are very similar. These can be used to sculpt

large terrain pieces, and neither requires any baking or firing to chemically cure to a very hard and sturdy piece.

When building larger objects, such as terrain, the cost of miniature paints and primers can add up quickly. Miniature paints are often more pigmented and have more adhesion than other oil- or acrylic-based paints, but these qualities are not necessary for painting larger works! Buy the paints you can afford—the quality does generally increase with price, although most student-grade paints will be sufficient.

In lieu of using an airbrush to cover large areas, I often use Liquitex spray paints, which contain artist-grade pigments, and are matte and easy to layer. Ask for custom spray nozzles at the art store to control your spray flow, although it won't be easy to get down to the detail that an airbrush can manage. For primer, I usually pass on the expensive primers found in game stores and buy automotive primers found in hardware stores. They go on a little thicker than hobby primers, which can help mask minor sculpting errors, but can also eliminate very detailed work.

Most importantly, remember that making things is supposed to be fun, and even the wonkiest looking build will be delightful and special to your friends at the table!

BEYOND THE STORE-BOUGHT GRID MAP

The standard square grid map is simply a large sheet with marks at one-inch intervals. In scale with miniatures, these one-inch squares represent five-foot squares. Coincidentally, this is also exactly what cutting mats and quilting mats are, which can become quite cheap with the correct combination of fabric store coupons and discounts.

An alternate way to make a modifiable and interactive grid map is by getting a sheet of clear acrylic from a hardware store or clear vinyl from a fabric store. These are sometimes sold as clear table covers as well! You can draw or mark the grid yourself with a permanent marker, but most importantly this let's you add lots of interesting papers and effects underneath the map, allowing you to build a detailed and visually engaging world for your players that can be modified with every play session.

The scrapbooking section of any large craft store is the secret motherlode of map textures. The popularity of scrapbooking in recent years has led to a wealth of interesting papers—it'll be easy to find grass, brick, stone, marble textures, and many more. Layer these under your clear map to create detailed and lushly textured environments.

A walk through these craft stores will reveal a wealth of ideas and props to bring to your table. Grass mats and rocks are in abundance, as well as gravel, shells, wooden and brass findings, and more. What could you do with sheets of crinkly sparkly paper? Cast spells and build magical pathways or rivers? Perhaps your character holds a special amulet, or a weathered spell book. Building these props by hand can create a more intimate connection to your characters as well as fun props to playact with at the table. In addition, with the increased interest in the steampunk and medieval aesthetic over the last several years, jewelry and scrapbook aisles of craft stores are filled with wonderful themed trinkets and charms. These can be given to players as rewards for completing quests, as inspiration points, or just as story props—there are lots of bronze keys, corked potion jars, patinaed treasures, and many items that would not be out of place in a medieval fantasy treasure horde.

SOME SUGGESTIONS FOR RIDICULOUS THINGS TO CRAFT FOR THE TABLE:

- *Glue a monster figure to a windup toy or Hexbug for a monster that moves randomly.*

- *Steal your players' figures and cast them into clear gelatin in ice cube trays for an immersive gelatinous cube experience.*

- *Instead of just telling your players what items they find in a dungeon, why not make some gilded boxes for them to open?*

- *You can modify the board game Operation to be a puzzle where players steal items from an ogre or other very sleepy monster.*

- *Distribute healing potions in charming corked bottles at the end of a horrible fight, which can be filled with fancy layered mocktails.*

NOT JUST FOR GMs!

While many of the suggestions in this article may seem geared towards GMs, it is just as enjoyable to surprise your table as a player. Imagine casting your spells by using shiny crinkly paper (from the craft store's gift wrap section) or being able to physically hand a fancy healing potion to another party member (a small bottle from the craft store's home decor section).

One of the greatest joys of playing spellcasters is making their spell books. Why not take a stab at hand-binding some paper to make a lovely book? If your ranger has a familiar, why not also have them exist in goofy puppet form? Bringing a bit more of the universe to the table isn't just about physical objects—in my first D&D game, I played a cook (also a ranger), and I still regret that I didn't know how to cook well then, because I definitely wanted to create increasingly complex themed stews for each gaming session. In that same game, my partner was a rogue and apothecary, and often had various bottles and jars at the table to illustrate the potions that he would craft.

Just remember—it is always impolite to dump glitter on anyone's table. ⬡

RUNNING THE GAME: MMORPG IRL

GRACE THOMAS

Creating Massively Multiplayer RPGs in Real Life

We play RPGs because we, as players, want our stories to matter. We want our stories to be able to affect the world around them in a dramatic fashion, as our day-to-day lives don't seem to make a dent on the real world. Maybe I'm being a bit too grandiose, but at the very least, this description sincerely matches my experience. When I got into RPGs around the age of ten, I was a lonely, bullied geek who was afraid of everyone. The sprawling, summer-long campaigns I participated in at my local gaming store, filled with dozens of players enthusiastically working together to succeed, helped me begin to break free from that shell.

Here's how it worked, in broad strokes: players were broken up into groups of six to eight for weekly sessions. Two to three times during the campaign—usually at the beginning, middle, and end—everyone would gather, absolutely packing the room, and play together. Those communal sessions were the most fun I've ever had playing an RPG. No matter how many characters were in the mix, I still felt like my story mattered. At the time, I don't think I realized what a monumental feat that was. Even at that age, though, I certainly sensed there was a kind of magic to it all.

Groups were structured depending on the game. The first summer I participated in, we played the second edition of Mutants & Masterminds, the classic superheroes and villains RPG. So groups were split up between heroes seeking justice, villains bent on world domination, and rogues that were just looking out for number one. I played a speedster in a group of villains that was not just a simulacrum of the Flash villain, Zoom, but pretty much just the character himself. He was even named Dr. Zoom, but somehow, I didn't realize that I had created a blatant rip-off. Be easy on me, I was in elementary school and my two favorite things were The Flash and thinking I was way smarter than I actually was.

I played in four of these summer-long campaigns, and some went better than others. Each one was enjoyable, but a couple got bogged down in storylines too complex to have enough room for everyone to feel like they were playing an important role. For instance, one year we played the pulp RPG Savage Worlds, and the task our group was given for our end-of-the-campaign gathering was to basically find some blueprints for a Nazi super weapon that was being dismantled by another group. It felt a little anticlimactic, like we were doing something that could have been accomplished in some session a couple weeks back.

I'll circle back to how to pull off a truly great event day for such a massive campaign, but first I want to outline the best structure for all of the regular sessions in between.

The best storylines for games like these are those that are able to give each group a distinct identity that sets it apart from the rest. For instance, if you were playing a *Star Wars* RPG, you wouldn't just have a few groups of Jedi, a few Sith, and a few Rogue. The space between these groups' identities is where the juiciest moments will come from when they meet—and it needs to be a larger and windier space than generated simply by the difference between good and evil.

Give your players strong parameters at the beginning and their creativity will flourish as they create their characters. By assigning groups before character creation, you give them a general direction that creates greater diversity among characters overall. Tell everyone you're playing Pathfinder without any specific guidance, and you'll end up with a whole slew of uninspiring archetypes coupled with hyper-specific ideas that may not fit into the flow of any group you have planned.

You may think a good alternate route would be to design the story and groups after characters are created, but logistically that's just not feasible. This is a huge venture that you need to start preparing for months in advance. Some won't be excited that the exact character they had in their brain won't work out, but in the end, they'll forget that because of the fun this structure creates. You're encouraging more possibilities, not less. You're jumpstarting your players' imaginations with a prompt, instead of leaving them with a blank page to wander around and doodle the same old squiggles that idle, unchallenged minds create.

You also need to give each group a specific purpose to go along with their identity, while also fitting into the larger framework of the campaign. One group is on the run from the law and needs to find the group of scoundrels that actually committed the crimes they've been accused of—another group is that group of scoundrels, and they're trying to hunt down and kill these fall guys before their cover is blown. Another group is the law, trying to piece together what is actually going on, while yet another group investigates a seemingly unrelated string of disappearances in a town across the way that becomes wrapped up in the rest of this mess. After you've established their purpose, let them loose. You give the players the parameters of the reality they're playing in, but they give you the story. It is your job to be the world reacting to that story, not the one telling it.

One of the most engaging tools that the GMs used during these campaigns were forums created for each one, where players could post in-character about what had gone on in their sessions, and interact with players in other groups. This really made the world seem alive, and it was great to gain perspective on the awesome scale of each campaign. Maybe someone posts a journal entry that canonically slipped out of their bag for other players to see. Or maybe a group of law enforcement makes a post that's the equivalent of a wanted poster for a criminal they're seeking that another group just might have seen during one of their own sessions.

Illustrated by Ahmara Smith

> **A NECESSARY COMPONENT OF PULLING OFF THESE EVENTS IS CONSTANT COMMUNICATION BETWEEN EACH GM. SET UP A TIME FOR WEEKLY MEETINGS, FACE TO FACE OR DIGITALLY, WHERE YOU CAN ALL MAKE SENSE OF HOW WHAT HAPPENED IN YOUR INDIVIDUAL GROUPS HAS AFFECTED THE WORLD YOUR STORY LIVES IN ON THE WHOLE.**

Encouraging this type of in-between session communication allows for way more story to be covered than the ten to twelve sessions alone could contain. Plus, these forums can spur players to make choices that they wouldn't have without this well of context.

Another ploy you can try to keep the campaign connected is having certain players guest in other groups' sessions. This can be the product of necessity when a player has to skip one of their own group's sessions because of other obligations. It can also be a fun opportunity for a player who has the time to take advantage of it. Maybe a character was kidnapped by a band of roving barbarians at the end of their group's last session and ends up in the town where the other group is looking for that exact same band of barbarians to right a different wrong. Maybe a character was stranded on a planet because they took too long to use the bathroom and the ship accidentally left without them, and the characters from the other group picked up on their BM-induced distress signal. The possibilities are endless.

Your regular sessions are important, but you have to put even more work into event days, the crown jewels of campaigns like this. Event days do not just match up to, but exceed the fun your players have during their weekly sessions. Some of the things you should do to make this happen doesn't have anything to do with how the game is played. First and foremost, you've got to make it a potluck. You're going to be gaming for eight to twelve hours straight if not more, morning, noon, and night. Communing over food made by each other forms an instant bond between folks who might not have met before, even though they're ostensibly playing in the same campaign.

Having an idea of which different big moments will happen in the story before beginning the campaign is fine. The NPCs you control will have goals, ambitions, and plans that your players are figuring out as the game goes along. But make sure you're adapting to the story your players are telling. The best event days come from acknowledging the stories your players have created and letting them know you're paying attention across the board. The huge twists and turns that happen during these gatherings should be spawned from a combination of the general arc of the campaign you had planned and the choices your players have made up to this point.

A necessary component of pulling off these events is constant communication between each GM. Set up a time for weekly meetings, face to face or digitally, where you can all make sense of how what happened in your individual groups has affected the world your story lives in on the whole.

To keep track of everything that has happened with the kind of detail required to keep players engaged, it's important to keep a written record of each session. One possibility to ease the workload is to have two GMs assigned to each group. One can do the regular dungeon mastering while the other serves as a scribe, recording things down as they happen as to not miss a story beat. If that doesn't sound like the most enticing job in the world to you, don't fret. Feel free to switch roles every session or every other session. As long as you and your partner have a clear vision that you've built together for the scenarios you've crafted, it should work out just fine.

If your mega campaign is popular, you might find that you don't have enough GMs to run groups of a reasonable size (like four to six people). I've been in groups of eight for campaigns like this, and that is generally too much. Here are a few solutions to this problem you should consider:

- Schedule group sessions every other week so that DMs can comfortably run two groups, with one on the other's off week. That doesn't necessarily cut down on the prep work all that much, but it's an idea worth floating with your group.

- Set a hard limit. You'll have to turn some interested folks away, but next year you can prepare for a bigger crowd, and hopefully this will teach prospective players to sign up earlier next year.

- If you absolutely cannot avoid overstuffing your groups, then try to have in-game puzzles that your players can try to work out while waiting for their turns and that don't halt the game for everyone else until they're solved. Consider even bringing a physical representation of the puzzle for them to solve. For instance, maybe a character has discovered a magic locket that they just cannot get open and they have to solve a Hanayama puzzle to do so. Or maybe there's a code that must be deciphered to go forward. If you go with this route, make sure your players know this will be a facet of the game as they create their characters so they can adjust their skill points and the like accordingly.

When it comes down to it, the golden rule of these massive campaigns is the same one every GM should follow no matter what the size of their group: treat every player like you'd want to be treated if you were playing the game. Make every single player's story count. I hope you run your own IRL MMORPG soon! ⬢

RUNNING THE GAME: FIRST-TIME PLAYERS

E.L. THOMAS

10 RULES TO FOLLOW WHEN RUNNING ADVENTURES FOR FIRST-TIME PLAYERS

As game masters, it is our honor to be the first to introduce new players to our hobby of roleplaying. Playing an RPG for the first time can be daunting. There are piles of rules mixed with math skills, tactics, and a lot of social interaction. All of that does not come easy to everyone. When running a game for first-time players, you need to ease players into it yet still try to feature the great parts of the game. Here are a few of the rules I follow when running games for first-time players:

RULE #1 RULES LITE

Use just the bare basics for rules. Don't mess with opportunity attacks, cover and concealment rules, or concentration rolls. If you want more than the basics like hit, damage and saves, stick with advantage, disadvantage, and inspiration. These mechanics are what makes 5E different from other RPGs, and even other editions. It's enough to give a good feel for the game and not overwhelm new players.

RULE #2 MAKE IT SHORT & SMALL

Don't go in for a marathon session the first time, or even the first few times you play. Two hours is more than plenty to introduce new players to the game.

Also, trying to teach more than four new players at once is challenging. If you have a veteran player or two that can help you teach the game, then you can run a mostly new table with more than four new players. But I don't recommend more than four if it can be avoided. If you have six or eight folks that want to learn the game, run two different sessions.

RULE #3 MAKE IT FUN

Focus on the most exciting aspects of the game: combat, a crazy NPC or two, or a few skill-uses that feature what the players are good at. The main thing you should try to do is just make it fun for new players. If the game is fun, they will come back for more.

RULE #4 PRE-GENS ARE THE WAY

Pre-generated characters are the easiest tool to get new players into the game. Making characters can be great fun, but it can be a bit time consuming when making your first one. It requires access to rulebooks, or even multiple rulebooks if more than one player is trying to make a character at the same time. It also requires either some reading or a decent knowledge of the rules for character creation. More importantly, if you provide the pre-gens, then you can perfectly tool the adventure to the characters' strengths and make them feel super ready for anything. It also lets you build a balanced party.

RULE #5 STICK WITH CLASSIC CLASSES

If you're playing with four new players, Cleric, Fighter, Rogue, and Wizard are the way to go. If there are more than four, add in Ranger, Bard, and Paladin, as needed.

The easier the learning curve, the more likely a new player will not get confused or overwhelmed. While barbarian, druids, monks, sorcerers, and warlocks are great, they are more specialized than some of the more basic classes. I recommend you learn how to make an attack with a longsword or a fire bolt spell before you try out other classes. If you play with more than the above listed basic classes, players will see that there are much more complicated rules. Barbarians require a player to learn how long a rage lasts and what that means. Does a druid changing into an animal mean that you need a new stat block, or how do KI points work when you are playing a monk? If you need a guide, classes in the Systems Reference Document (SRD) are the best place to start. They give you plenty to play with, and best of all, a new player can just grab the PDF, or print out the pages they need, for reference.

RULE #6 DICE FOR EVERYONE

If possible, make sure each player has a set of dice to use. Sharing dice is alright but tends to slow down the game. Also, who doesn't like to have their own dice? It also helps in teaching which of these crazy dice is used for which weapon and character ability. The assorted polyhedral array is, in part, one of the biggest things non-gamers have said they find confusing and inhibiting. When running, take time to point out which dice is which, even holding up your own as an example. Think about plain language and work game terms into instructions. "Roll 1d20 + to hit the number listed by your greataxe to hit the bandit" is clearer than "Roll 1d20 to hit the bandit."

When teaching dice to new players, it's way easier if every dice in a set is a different color, rather than some cool match set. Helping a new player with, "Roll a d8, it's the green one," is much more effective than, "the d8 is the diamondy-looking one...no that's a d10..."

RULE #7 KEEP IT CORE

For books that you and the players have access to, and for when you build your PCs, use the core rulebooks only. You went with the fundamentals with your pre-gen PCs, do the same with books. There are piles of great supplements and secondary publisher's resources for 5E, but you are trying to teach new players the bare basics, so no need to delve any deeper than the three core rulebooks for a quite some time. You can go up to 20th level PCs, just using what is provided in the SRD, without even having to buy core books!

RULE #8 GET ON THE TRAIN: ALL ABOARD!

While I'm not usually a fan of the players having no choice in their adventures, it is a good idea to not give brand-new players any choice when the adventure starts. Be it boxed text like:

The smell of mold and rot stings your nostrils. The pungent odors forcefully raise you. As you awaken, you find yourself laying on the cold, damp stone floor of a small alcove. A nearly spent torch sputters, smoking beside you, providing only flickering dimness. In the fading light, three twisting corridors lead off into dreary gloom.

Such an intro sets the newbies into the story, without the whole trope of starting in a tavern, wasting two hours role-playing out buying ales and meeting mysterious strangers.

Or the start of the adventure can be as simple as you just announcing, "ROLL INITIATIVE!" and goblins come running out from every direction. Either method gets the job done, the dice or minds rolling, and players right into playing the game.

While I normally always caution against railroading when

teaching a whole table of newbies, you want to have a short play session to avoid boring or overwhelming the players. So, you need to force at least the start of the adventure. If you give the lazy GM question of, "So what do you guys do?", new players are most likely going to get frustrated, feel self-conscious, or just be clueless. This kind of railroading focuses more on setting the table and serving dinner. We all want to eat, you as the GM just picked the time and menu.

RULE #9 SET THEM UP FOR THE WIN

You only get one chance to introduce someone to our hobby, so make sure they like it. No PC casualties. Consider using enemies that look scary but go down easy, say half hit points for most or maybe 1 hp minions. Also, lower the average damage for most of the bad guys to a max of 3. Keep one or two bad guys at full power. Also give out inspiration as much as possible.

For the first couple of sessions, reward them inspiration for great ideas, funny comments, getting dice or rules right without asking, and any attempt to roleplay. I mean, if they win, they will want to do it again. This also lets you have fun bringing the hammer down on them once you have hooked them with a few wins. That first hard battle after so many wins is always memorable.

RULE #10 EVERYBODY GETS A TROPHY

Whatever rewards you are giving, make sure everyone gets some. If this means adding in a few extra potions or scrolls or some 50 gp gems, make sure every character gets a cool (if not minor) piece of treasure or loot.

In this instance, I like to front-load the treasure in the first adventure, meaning: make sure there is one minor magic item and a potion or scroll per player. Sure, that is heavy on treasure for such an adventure, but treasure sometimes seals the deal as to whether or not a player comes back for another game session. Also, it's not like it really costs you as the GM anything to amp up the loot for the first couple of games.

Easy ways to do this without giving out piles of magic are rewarding them with silvered weapons, the above-mentioned potion or scroll, pricy gear or armor, alchemical items (alchemist fire, acid flasks, poisons), splint mail, or

a breastplate. You can even go with weird or odd items (look at trinkets in the core books for inspiration). Sure, a solid glass ball with no opening that has a swimming clockwork fish inside isn't much, but it is cool and could be an adventure hook! Maps and other promises of future treasure or adventure are good also.

Our hobby of roleplaying games is one of the coolest, most social hobbies around. If done right, it can also be one of the most inclusive and age-spanning hobbies as well. It's a hobby that teaches creative thinking and social cues, and best of all, it's a place where lifelong friendships are forged, and storytellers are born.

As game masters, it is our duty to make such a grand gift accessible to any who wish to learn its ways. Embrace that duty, because you just might learn a few things yourself as you are teaching the game to others. ⬡

RUNNING THE GAME:
ADVENTURES WITH KIDS

FINLAY LOGAN

Creativity. Reading. Social skills. Math. Problem-solving. Resilience. Teamwork. Those are just a few of the skills that researchers say kids can improve by playing tabletop roleplaying games. Who knew that a storytelling game about fantasy heroes and monsters would turn out to be so good for kids?

I'm a sixth-grade teacher by day, and it was actually one of my students that got me back into RPGs after a long break. His enthusiasm convinced me to organize a lunchtime game, and it wasn't long before I was running up to four separate games a week at school. The players ranged from sixth to eighth graders and varied widely in experience level, from totally new to "memorized the rulebook" pros. But one thing they had in common was their exhilarating excitement for the characters and story they got to create.

It wasn't that long ago that parents worried that playing RPGs would turn their kids into evil demon-worshippers. But now we know that, in addition to being a lot of fun, gaming actually helps kids develop in many positive ways. With tabletop gaming growing more popular every year, many people are looking for ways to get the young people in their lives involved in gaming.

Before wrangling a group of kids and setting off for adventure, however, it's important to consider some of the ways that gaming with kids is different than gaming with adults. Kids make awesome roleplayers—they're creative, spontaneous, and high-energy—but running a game for them requires some adjustment on the part of an adult GM. GMs who want to introduce the kids in their life to roleplaying games can make the experience more positive by anticipating these needs and planning for them. While this might sound like extra work, in the end it will make the game even more fun for everyone.

Read on to learn strategies for making your game more responsive to kids' needs. Don't have kids in your life? Many of these tips can also be helpful when running games with adults!

STRUCTURE AND ROUTINE

To adults, kids may seem chaotic, but deep down they actually need (and thrive on) predictable routines. Knowing what to expect in a given situation helps kids feel more in control and confident, which means they're going to be a better player and have more fun. You can help your players out by trying to be consistent as much as you can. Institute some simple group rituals, like always having pretzels before your game, or the game starts when the GM puts on a silly hat. Kids are also obsessed with fairness, so try to apply the rules consistently and explain any exceptions clearly. However, that doesn't mean you need to run your game in any one particular way! In my experience, kids are fairly good at adapting to new or "house" rules, especially if you explain the rule and why it's needed. Whatever your particular rules and routines are, explain them and stick to them, and your game will be off to a good start!

ATTENTION

Kids tend to have more energy than adults and less capacity for sitting and listening for long periods of time. Fidgety, distracted kids aren't focusing on the story and aren't having fun! To make sure they actually get to enjoy the game, keep your sessions high-energy, relevant, and short.

High-energy means using your voice and body language to show how excited and enthusiastic you are about the awesome story you're telling. To keep your session relevant, keep the player characters central to the story. Keep exposition short and sweet. Finally, don't ask kids to sit at the table for too long. Instead, play through a small chunk of the story, then take a break. If you can end on a cliffhanger, even better! How long should you play for? Ask yourself if these particular kids can sit through TV episodes, or classes in school. Some kids might be able to stay engaged in an exciting session for an hour, but others might need a break every twenty minutes.

SOCIALIZING AND TEAMWORK

Kids and adults love roleplaying games because it's a chance to tell an awesome story with your friends. Just like adults, kids need time before, during, and after a gaming session to hang out and talk with the other players. However, sometimes kids need support to create and join a fun social conversation. Some kids are shy, while others talk too much, not giving others a turn. If your players don't know each other well, you can start your sessions with a silly ice-breaker question (related to the game or not) to get conversation going. While the game is going on, you might need to make sure everyone gets a chance to shine. A talking stick or some other object can

help kids remember to take turns and not to interrupt. As the GM, you can help kids learn to work together and support each other by explicitly encouraging and rewarding cooperation in the game. Award bonuses like XP or inspiration dice, or voice an NPC who commends them for their teamwork. Or, when the players are facing a challenge as a group, simply ask them, "How can you help?"

IDENTITY

Kids are engaged in the important work of exploring their identity. Whether it's elementary-aged kids learning about their unique talents, or adolescents questioning authority, RPGs can be a powerful tool to help kids through this process. As the GM, you can support them by creating space to do this in a safe, nonjudgmental way. Celebrate the characters they create by making art, writing or discussing their backstories, and creating encounters that let their characters do awesome things. Combine the typical fantasy explorations and monster battles with social encounters and dilemmas that give them a chance to grapple with real world problems. Need inspiration? Watch their favorite TV shows and see what kind of issues the characters face. Most importantly, model and teach respect for different identities: games are a great opportunity to teach pronouns, tackle stereotypes, and celebrate all characters.

Illustrated by Geneva Benton

> **IT WASN'T THAT LONG AGO THAT PARENTS WORRIED THAT PLAYING RPGS WOULD TURN THEIR KIDS INTO EVIL DEMON-WORSHIPPERS. BUT NOW WE KNOW THAT, IN ADDITION TO BEING A LOT OF FUN, GAMING ACTUALLY HELPS KIDS DEVELOP IN MANY POSITIVE WAYS.**

READING

Many roleplaying games put a lot of emphasis on reading. Just making a character involves reading and understanding several pages of tiny, informationally dense text with lots of uncommon words. The character sheet itself is crammed with tiny text and abbreviations. I teach kids with dyslexia and other language disabilities, so RPG rulebooks are inaccessible to many of my students. But even for typically-developing kids, not all kids of a similar age read at the same level. Some kids may devour books while others find them too daunting and would feel intimidated by the need to read an entire sourcebook before they could even play a game.

Online character creators are a great tool because they reduce the burden of reading and understanding the rules. Whip up a character in minutes, then help kids highlight the key info on their sheet. Alternately, photocopy the relevant pages from the book so your fledgling wizard isn't overwhelmed by 200 pages of irrelevant text. You can also make a "cheat sheet" for each character with just the essentials like special abilities, spells, and attack/damage rolls. Another tool to help kids who can handle the amount and complexity of language are PDFs and screen readers.

MATH

Arithmetic is another well-known component of RPGs. Many people point out that tabletop games can help kids practice math, but just like reading, the frequent need to work with numbers can be a burden for those who are still working to memorize basic facts. One strategy is to simplify rolls for ability checks, attacks, and damage by removing the modifier. If that seems too simplistic, a

printed number line can help kids add and subtract more easily. Using physical tokens or checkboxes to represent hit points and gold can make these quantities feel more real while also making it easier to compute how much health or money a character has left.

UNDERSTANDING AND REMEMBERING

A lot happens during a typical RPG session, and it can be hard to follow all the action. On top of that, you need to remember all those details until the next session! For kids, that can add up to a lot of work for their brains. One way to simplify things is to make sure that the players' interactions with the story are memorable. Give NPCs easy-to-remember names, descriptions, and motives. Make locations distinct from one another using lots of sensory details.

Another big help for memory is to record information. During a game, even simple maps scribbled on a sheet of printer paper can make the action easier to follow. Make a list of important NPCs and objectives and hang it up in your gaming space like a real-life quest log so kids can refer to it easily. To help kids understand and remember the main parts of the story, they can write or draw events from the session. Before the next session, work together to do a recap so that everyone starts on an equal footing.

COMBAT

Talk to ten GMs and you'll get eleven opinions about whether violence in games is appropriate for kids, and if so, when and how much. It's a tricky subject because, unlike in video games, in an RPG the players have a huge amount of control over the story, and have the ability to explore the concept of actions and consequences much more freely. That freedom means more responsibility, so it's important that the story the players tell makes them feel like awesome, powerful heroes, and not scared or upset. It's definitely worth taking the time to think about what type and amount of combat will be best for you, your kids, and your game.

Here are some suggestions to make combat safe for kids. First, definitely don't reward or glorify wanton violence against innocent targets. Roleplaying a party of murderous vandals isn't a good look for adults, and it's totally inappropriate for kids. If you want to give kids opportunities to use their super cool magic weapons and combat abilities, give them good reasons to fight: conquering evil, saving innocents, liberating the earth, that sort of thing. When it comes to dealing damage, avoid gritty, realistic gore and opt for Saturday morning action cartoon theatrics instead.

Also, reconsider using humans and humanoid creatures as enemies; I replace guards, bandits, pirates, cultists, and so on with undead, evil plants, constructs, aberrations, and corrupted beasts when possible. If you give your evil awakened shrubs glowing red eyes and withered stabby branches, they will be even more menacing than a run-of-the-mill bandit. (Note: do not use animals as enemies in kids' games unless you want the party to adopt them. All of them.)

Finally, if the amount of combat inherent in games like D&D isn't a good fit for your players, remember that there are lots of gaming systems available now, and many put less emphasis on combat, or don't include it at all!

Of course, no two kids are the same, so use these suggestions as a starting point. As your adventures unfold, you'll inevitably discover the tips, tricks, and modifications that make sense for your game and your players. Don't be afraid to scrap a strategy that isn't working, or to try something totally new. Remember that, at the end of the day, the most important rule of playing RPGs with kids is to HAVE FUN! Keep that in mind and, with any luck, your kids will have a new favorite hobby that will last them a lifetime. ⍟

RANDOM NONSENSE: SPIRITUALLY SPEAKING

TELINE GUERRA

It's Friday night, and while most people in town are headed out to dinner or to the theater, at one house on the street, something special is happening. Five people have come together to have an otherworldly experience. What is going to happen tonight is very important to the host. One person is in charge. They sit at the head of the table, but what is about to happen depends on everyone there buying in and participating. There is excitement. Snacks. The drapes are pulled. Maybe candles are lit for the atmosphere.

The person in charge starts to talk in a deep voice with a funny accent. You'd think the next move would be to roll some dice. You'd be wrong.

In the 1850's, a century before tabletop role players started writing out rules, people were gathering around their tables to escape their regular humdrum lives in a slightly different way: by contacting the dead. You've seen it in movies—the séance with lightning flashes and tables being lifted into the air. The reality was a bit more mundane, and an awful lot like your gaming group.

Spiritualism began when two young girls, Maggie and Katie Fox, claimed they could talk to spirits of the dead. The spirits would answer in knocks: once for yes, twice for no. Later, they'd admit it was all a hoax, but by then, spiritualism had taken off. Some mediums did stage shows, some worked one on one, but the tabletop séance was the most popular venue.

A medium, the game master of the spirit world, would lead the proceedings. The medium set the tone of the evening, talking in a spooky voice and lighting candles. Once the séances got underway, the medium would reach out to a spirit guide. The spirit guide would be someone like Julius Caesar, King Tut, or Cleopatra, and would speak through the medium. The attendees would know when the spirit guide had arrived when the medium started speaking in a strange voice, maybe using a different accent. The spirit guide was the non-player character (NPC) of the séance.

Lewis Carroll wrote *Alice in Wonderland,* which not only showed his unhealthy fixation on young girls, but was also a ground-breaking fantasy novel. These luminary heroes also had an interest in spiritualism. For Lewis Carroll, who was also a career mathematician, spiritualism was a form of science. And he wasn't alone in that thinking. A number of prominent mathematicians and scientists considered spiritualism an extension of their studies. Or, to put it another way, spiritualism was very attractive to nerds. Sir Arthur Conan Doyle quit writing his hugely successful Sherlock Holmes stories to more fully dedicate his time to spiritualism. He said he hoped he would be remembered more for his work in spiritualism than he was for his writing. Well, that didn't work out how he hoped.[1,2]

Those who went to séances also had similar motivations to your average dungeon delver. It was a chance to get together with friends and do something unusual. While some people were looking to talk to a specific lost relative, most were there for the novelty. They were happy to talk to whoever showed up. The most important part of the evening was the ambiance. A séance was spooky, startling, and different.

The medium would have everyone sit around the table and hold hands. The lights would be lowered or put out, and the medium would call out to the spirits to come. Then, people would start hearing knocking sounds coming from under the table. The table would spin, sliding across the room and pinning people against the wall. The spirit guide would appear, speaking through the medium's mouth, and telling the attendees which spirits had arrived and what messages they had brought back from the beyond. They would describe the afterlife. And they would leave behind ectoplasm, a mystical substance left behind by the presence of spirits, which would mysteriously disappear before the lights came back on.

At the end, everyone felt like they had been transported somewhere else, though all they had actually done was sit around a table for a few hours. Which, once again, sounds like a description of a great night of fighting dragons and collecting treasure in our minds.

The reason these events are so similar is that they both address a fundamental human need. We need other people. We need to tell stories. We need to explore ideas like magic and death. We need to play with these ideas, try them out in a new light, to help us understand the rest of our lives better. Playing with these ideas in the safety of someone's living room allows us to experiment in ways we can't do in the real world.

In the 1850's, the rise of industrialism meant more people were cogs in the machine, stripping their work of meaning. Science was explaining away all the interesting phenomena of the world,

relegating imagination to the sidelines. The popularity of roleplaying games is no accident. In fact, these games are good for us. More than ever, people can be replaced by computers, and everything spooky can be easily explained away. But human beings need to feel a sense of purpose and wonder. Add to that how disconnected our modern life can be, and a weekly game of heroes becomes essential.

Seeing these similarities between séances and roleplaying gives modern game masters a chance to learn from some real masters of ambiance. Here are a few lessons you can learn from nineteenth century spiritualists:

HOLDING HANDS IN THE DARK

Step one to a good séance was to get those dang lights off! At the time, that meant turning down the gas lamps, pull the drapes, and hold the event at night, lit by candles. Candles naturally flicker and sputter and create moving shadows that, to the overactive imagination, could be anything.

One very simple trick you can use in your game is to include darkness. Did your players enter an unlit dungeon? Have the players who can't see shut their eyes. The psychological power of darkness was a medium's most powerful tool. Use it.

Illustrated by Geneva Benton

ECTOPLASM

You may know of ectoplasm from *Ghostbusters*, but the idea originally came from—you guessed it—nineteenth century spiritualists. During an appropriate moment in the seance, ectoplasm would appear, touching the people at the table. It was proof—tangible proof—that the spirits had actually visited them.

Doyle called it "a plastic substance, not yet fully understood, which comes from the body of the medium." He also said, "I have held the ectoplasm between my fingers, and it seems to be alive, vitalized." [3]

But what was this mysterious substance?

Cloth. Long pieces of cloth. Mediums would hide this cloth in their mouths or...other crevices of their bodies, and at the right moment, they'd pull it out and pass it around the table, saying, "Oh, wow! Ectoplasm!" Add in the dim lighting and the mood, and *bam!* People around the table touched this cloth and it felt alive and otherworldly.

Props don't have to be big, impressive things. They can be common things that are just lying around your house. The fact is that handing your players a "dragon claw" is cool, even if it is really only half a plastic fork. What matters more is the mood of the game. If the mood is right, a little tangible addition can go a long way to making things feel real.

KNOCKING

From the beginning, knocking was central to the idea of talking to the spirits. The trick to making the knocks feel like they were coming from the beyond was simple. Mediums knocked on the bottom of the table. Or they knocked with their foot while they held hands with someone else. It seems too simple, but knocking was one of the most reliable tricks a medium had to startle and convince people that a presence had arrived. A knock, a bang, a bonk on the underside of the table will startle your players, and get their hearts racing. Online libraries can provide your game with roars and other sound effects. Several great companies offer long sound effect tracks of battles, dripping caves, spooky music, and other things that you can play during your game. Sound effects add to the overall feeling of otherworldliness.

SEEING IS BELIEVING

Another interesting aspect of spiritualism was spirit photography. Photography was new, and not many people understood what could be done with it, so a simple double exposure could blow their minds.

A medium took portraits, and when the photo was developed, another image would emerge, too. Sir Arthur Conan Doyle sat for a portrait, and when it was developed, a young man hovered over him. He was convinced it was the image of his late son.

Interestingly enough, around this time, Elsie Wright and her cousin Frances Griffiths took a series of five photos that showed them sitting in their garden, surrounded by faeries, tiny women with wings. Years later, they would admit that they had cut out pictures from a book to create the double exposures, but the photos blew people's minds and led to a widespread belief in fairies. The controversy and excitement around those five photos gave fantasy stories another big boost, leading to the fantasy books we read today and the worlds we play our games in.

Rule books are illustrated for a reason. Showing your players pictures of the monsters they face, and the NPCs they talk to adds another layer. Your players may know the pictures aren't real, but they can spark the imagination all the same.

EVERYONE BUYS IN

Doyle convinced his good friend Harry Houdini to sit for a séance with Jean Doyle, Sir Arthur's wife, as medium. Jean wrote out a long letter that was supposedly dictated by Houdini's mom.

Only problem? The letter was in English, a language Houdini's mother barely spoke.

Houdini was furious. He ended his friendship with the Doyles and became a lifelong opponent of all things spiritualist.[4]

Doyle thought he could win Houdini over, but the game only works when everyone buys in. Sure, you might want your brother to play in your game as you might be having trouble getting enough players for your table. But if someone at your table isn't into the game, they can ruin things for everyone.

When people want to be carried away, they will be. When they don't want to believe, they won't. It might be harder to put together a gaming group with people who love the game, but it is worth it. A whole table ready to buy in creates the perfect atmosphere for magic.

So, the next time you get together for a little tabletop action with your friends, take a moment to reach out to the spirits of mediums past. After all, they helped pave the way. If there's anywhere spirits hang out, it's wherever people gather to make a little magic. ⬡

1 Diniejko, Andrzej. "Arthur Conan Doyle's Interest in Spiritualism."*The Victorian Web*, Nov. 14, 2013, http://www.victorianweb.org/authors/doyle/spiritualism.html.

2 Strauss, Mark. "An Actual Recording Of Arthur Conan Doyle's "Spirit" From A 1934 Séance." *io9*, Gizmodo Media Group, May 6, 2014,https://io9.gizmodo.com/an-actual-recording-of-arthur-conan-doyles-spirit-fro-1572329022.

3 Cafazzo, Debbie. "A Study in Spiritualism: What happened when the creator of Sherlock Holmes visited Tacoma." *The News Tribune*, Tacoma News Tribune, Dec. 30, 2015, https://www.thenewstribune.com/news/local/article51980580.html.

4 Perry, Marsha."Conan Doyle and Spiritualism." *Conan Doyle Info*, 2019, https://www.conandoyleinfo.com/life-conan-doyle/conan-doyle-and-spiritualism/.conandoyleinfo.com/life-conan-doyle/conan-doyle-and-spiritualism/. (7 February 2019).

RANDOM NONSENSE:
UNDERWATER ADVENTURER'S GUIDE

ALINA PETE

The sea is a mysterious place that holds more dangers than the fiercest volcanic mountain range or frozen tundra. The first and greatest of these is the risk of drowning! How can you take your adventuring party deep under the waves and stand any chance of survival? This helpful guide will give you a variety of options!

The rules for underwater combat are quite different than those for standard combat. Any creature without a swimming speed will have disadvantage on all melee rolls, unless they are equipped with a dagger, javelin, shortsword, spear, or trident. This means characters will need to find different weaponry for their underwater trip, since the creatures they'll be facing will have advantage against them. Ranged combat is also more difficult underwater, since a ranged weapon will automatically miss a target beyond the weapon's normal range. Also, all creatures and objects fully immersed in water have resistance to fire damage! This will make things difficult for anyone who relies on fire magic to damage their opponents.

Obviously, the spell *water breathing* is the easiest way for your group to survive underwater. If you don't have anyone in the group who can cast it, it is also available in potion form. However, the potion only lasts for one hour, so a group who needs to stay underwater for long stretches of time will need to stock up on potions or use the items listed below.

Moving underwater will also provide a challenge, since most characters don't have an innate swimming speed. This means that they'll need to spend one extra foot of movement for every foot they move, effectively halving all movement speed (though casting the spell *freedom of movement* will alleviate these penalties). There are items that can magically give characters a swimming speed, as well as oceanic mounts for your characters to ride. These options will help your group get to whatever watery destination their quest takes them.

Here are some useful undersea items from the core rulebooks:

- *Ring of Swimming*
- *Trident of Fish Command*
- *Gloves of Swimming and Climbing*
- *Cloak of the Manta Ray*

NEW ITEMS FOR UNDERWATER ADVENTURING

BOOTS OF THE FROG
(Wondrous item, common)

These boots seem ungainly at first, with long webbed toes sculpted to resemble the feet of a frog, but when you step into water, the boots will suddenly come to life! You gain a swim speed of 30 feet while the boots are wet, and the ability to hold your breath for two hours. However, the boots cannot be removed until they have completely dried off, which means that anyone looking to make a quick escape over land will have to contend with the long toes slowing their movement speed to 5 feet until the boots can be removed.

BELT OF MERFOLK SHAPE
(Wondrous item, uncommon)

While wearing this belt, your lower body changes into a long, scaled fish tail which allows you to swim easily through the water. In this form, you gain a swim speed of 40 feet and the ability to breathe both air and water, though your stats and skills remain unchanged. While wearing this belt, all Merfolk will automatically sense that you are not true Merfolk, and this deception may make them suspicious and prone to attack.

FIGURINE OF WONDROUS POWER, MOON RAY
(Wondrous item, rare)

(For rules on activating a *Figurine of Wondrous Power*, see core rulebooks. For creature stats of the Moon Ray, see below.)

This item is a small statue of a creature that looks like a manta ray with pearlescent marbling across its wings. When activated, it transforms into a Moon Ray, which persists for up to five hours. The Moon Ray is a Huge creature that can fit up to six Medium-sized creatures upon its back, and moves through the water with a swim speed of 60 feet. The Moon Ray is an independent mount and will swim to whatever undersea location the character who summoned it commands. Moon Rays are gentle pacifists and will not initiate combat. If the Moon Ray is attacked, it will disengage and flee, making every attempt to evade its attacker, until it senses the danger has passed, or until the character who summoned it has made a successful DC 15 Handle Animal check. Once the figurine has been used, it can't be used again until 27 days (a full moon cycle) have passed.

PEARL OF THE ABYSS
(Wondrous item, very rare)

A perfectly black pearl with a white starburst emblazoned on it, a *Pearl of the Abyss* only grows in the deepest ocean trenches, inside specially-cultivated Shadow Oysters. When activated underwater, the pearl generates a 10-foot radius sphere around itself, marked by a shimmer of bubbles, which lasts for 24 hours or until the pearl is deactivated. Any creature inside this sphere becomes incorporeal to the water, drifting downwards (along with the pearl) at a steady 10 feet of movement until they reach the seafloor. Though they are incorporeal to water, creatures inside the sphere can still be attacked and can interact with objects (such as terrain, structures, and items) normally. All those inside the sphere can then walk along the bottom of the ocean as though it were normal land, and do not need to breathe or worry about the crushing pressure of the deep ocean so long as the pearl is active.

BATHYSPHERE
(Wondrous item, legendary)

An invention of gnomish manufacture, the *Bathysphere* is a spherical vessel large enough to seat seven Medium-sized creatures. A crystal juts from the ceiling of the interior of the craft, containing a small air elemental that provides unlimited fresh air for the passengers. Another cluster of five crystals project from the rear of the craft and contain small water elementals that propel the craft through the water at a speed of 50 feet. Each crystal has an AC of 20, 80 hit points, and is resistant to slashing damage but vulnerable to thunder damage. If these crystals are cracked (hit points reduced to zero), the elementals contained within them will escape and may

Illustrated by Geneva Benton

turn on the *Bathysphere*, venting their frustration at being trapped for so long.

(Optional Rules) Underwater Challenges

There is a reason that sailors fear the sea—it is a tempestuous place where alien creatures lurk unseen, ready to strike. But there are more dangers under the water than just the creatures that live there. The sea itself may be the greatest challenge your adventurers face. Here are some optional rules to provide additional challenges when your party is heading beneath the waves.

Vision in the Depths: Visibility underwater can be worse than in the darkest cave. Even near the surface, ripples of light distract the eye and swirling particles in the water make everything foggy and indistinct. While diving in clear, shallow waters, a character's range of vision drops from two miles to 500 feet. Diving in murky water can reduce the range of vision to 100 feet or even less. Sudden movements that stir up bubbles or silt can reduce visibility to zero, forcing characters to fight completely blind.

As characters dive deeper, the light of the sun quickly fades into twilight and then to pure blackness. Half a mile under the ocean, everything is completely dark. Darkvision still functions, but at half its usual range. Creatures at these depths are attracted to dim lights and repelled by bright light, so summoning a magical light to help guide your way is a calculated risk.

Navigation: Characters who are skilled in using the constellations to navigate will be completely lost underwater, and there are few landmarks to help guide the way in the open ocean. All Survival checks to guide the group through underwater realms are at a +5 DC unless the character has a specific familiarity with the area.

The Cold: The deep ocean is extremely cold, and unlike the tundra, you can't wrap yourself in furs to keep warm. Characters must succeed on a DC 10 Constitution saving throw every half hour they spend exposed to deep waters, or gain one level of exhaustion. Characters with resistance or immunity to cold damage automatically succeed on the saving throw, as do creatures that are naturally adapted to living in cold water. However, characters without a natural immunity can coat themselves in bear or whale grease to give themselves a +5 bonus to their saving throws against cold water. At the

GMs discretion, certain magic items or spells may include resistance to the underwater environment.

Strong Ocean Currents: The deep ocean has a network of strong currents that flow like underwater jet-streams. Although these can be perilous, they can also aid strong swimmers. Trying to swim against the flow slows the character down by 10-20 feet of movement, depending on the strength of the current. However, if the character swims with the flow of the water, it can add 20-30 feet to their movement speed so long as they stay within the stream. Entering and leaving an ocean current requires the character to make a successful Athletics check, or they are tumbled about by the water and unable to act for one round. Particularly strong currents may require a Strength/Athletics check to control movement at all.

Underwater Mounts

The sea is vast, and you will need a way to cross the fathomless depths relatively quickly. Befriending and riding a tame sea creature is an option for your group's travels in the deep ocean.

COELACANTH *Large beast, unaligned*

An ancient, armored fish with strong jaws and lobed fins for walking along the seafloor. The coelacanth prefers deep, cold waters and rarely comes to the shallows. However, its docile, steadfast nature makes it a true workhorse of the sea, and domesticated giant coelacanths are often used by deep-water Merfolk as beasts of burden. Coelacanths can be ridden by three Medium-sized creatures at a time.

Armor Class 16 (Natural Armor)
Hit Points 65 (10d10 + 10)
Speed 10 ft. Swim 30 ft.

STR	DEX	CON	INT	WIS	CHA
18 (+4)	13 (+1)	13 (+1)	1 (-5)	1 (-5)	4 (-3)

Skills: Perception -3

Senses darkvision 40 ft., passive Perception (7)

Challenge 2 (450 XP)

Water Breathing. The coelacanth can breathe only underwater.

ACTIONS:

Bite. *Melee Weapon Attack*: +6 to hit, reach 5 ft., one target. *Hit*: 20 (3d10 + 4) piercing damage.

MOON RAY *Huge celestial, neutral good*

The Moon Ray is a huge, pale manta ray with opalescent mottling across its back. They are independent mounts and will swim to whatever undersea location the rider commands, so long as the character can picture the location in their mind. Moon Rays are gentle pacifists and will not initiate combat. If the Moon Ray is attacked, it will disengage and flee, making every attempt to evade its attacker, until it senses the danger has passed, or until the character who summoned it has made a successful DC 15 Handle Animal check.

Armor Class 14 (Natural Armor)
Hit Points 60 (8d12 + 8)
Speed Swim 60 ft.

STR	DEX	CON	INT	WIS	CHA
17 (+3)	15 (+2)	13 (+1)	1 (-5)	10 (+0)	10 (+0)

Skills: Perception -+2

Senses darkvision 60 ft., passive Perception 10

Challenge 2 (450 XP)

SPECIAL ABILITIES:

Water Breathing. The Moon Ray can breathe only underwater.

Swift Dash. When taking a Dash action to escape combat, the Moon Ray travels an extra 30 feet per round.

ATTACK:

Tail Strike. Melee Weapon Attack: +3 to hit, reach 5 ft., one creature. *Hit:* 9 (2d6 + 3) piercing damage.

Stunning Sting. Melee Weapon Attack: reach 5 ft., one creature. *Hit:* 6 (1d6 + 3) piercing damage, and the target must succeed on a DC 15 Constitution saving throw or become Stunned for 3 rounds.

The ocean is a place full of unexpected challenges and dangerous sea creatures, but it's also the resting place for ships full of treasures and lost underwater civilizations, so there's plenty of incentive for your group to brave the deep. Hopefully, these items and tips will give your group some ideas for their next adventure under the sea! ⏣

SITES & SETTINGS: THE FIVE SENSES AND THE SWEATING SWAMP

SHEL KAHN

Imagine walking into a moldering dungeon: the still air warm, but slightly clammy against your skin; the tang of decay in your mouth as you breathe it in; a distant dripping echoing hollowly through the cavern and ringing in your ears. Your eyes, slowly adjusting to the murky room, suddenly alight on the dim but unmistakable shape of a ghoul, leaning casually against a wall, half-smiling at you with a sinister glint in her eye. You begin to realize that metallic smell in your nose wasn't just fungus and dust—it was the fresh blood staining the hands and face of your new problem.

If you can almost smell that blood in your own nose, and you want to make your players feel as immersed in your story as you are in mine, this article is here to help!

Here's the trick I'm using: I'm appealing to all five of your senses, giving you every category of information I can. I'm sharing useful information—it's dark, it's damp, and there's a ghoul covered in fresh blood who can see you better than you can see her. It's the kind of information you give a player and can immediately ask afterwards: what do you do?

Describing all five senses is something you might not be thinking about at the table, but giving your players five potential channels for imagining how their character is experiencing your story is guaranteed to make them feel more immersed. Some players are going to find it a lot easier to feel engaged in a world they can imagine through their nose or their hands as well as their eyes, and all your players are going to remember that description that made them gasp or yell, "Eww!"

Of course, you don't want to read your players an essay each time they enter a new space—they'll just start zoning out. Instead of using all five senses in each description you give, try instead to keep descriptions short, while changing up what sense you appeal to. This works especially great if you have five players. Each player character walks into the room, and as the GM, you let them know what they're up against: the first character sees the chair, desk, and bookshelves; the second one hears a clock ticking; the third one smells dried glue and old leather; the fourth one tastes the dust in the air; and the fifth one feels the soft, old carpet against their boots.

In the spirit of useful demonstration, I'm going to help you take your players to the unsettling and much-rumored Sweating Swamp—not through stats, but through a full five senses' worth of adjectives that will help you set the mood and immerse your players in a visceral way.

THE SWEATING SWAMP

The Sweating Swamp is named for the extreme temperatures within its murky moors and fens. Bubbling out of a mountain plateau, the high altitude of the swamp means the air is never warm, and icicles cling to the trees most of the year. But beneath the swamp's soil boils a dormant volcano, whose subterranean heat stews the waters up into yellow clinging fogs. Despite its strong smell and uncanny feel, the Sweating Swamp is the safest path through the mountains, and your adventurers find themselves reluctantly traversing it. To incorporate this into an ongoing campaign, have the swamp show up on the map blocking the path through a mountain range, at a high altitude and right in the way of your players.

Within the swamp are a few well known landmarks:

THE PEAT BOGS

The famous peat bogs of the Sweating Swamp look like small clearings filled with spongy peat, covered with a film of thin ice. The bogs will look like the easiest paths through the swamp to new travelers. In some spots, the crust of ice will easily support a traveler's weight; in others it won't.

Beneath the ice, the peat is sticky and soft, and travelers who fall into it will find themselves slowly sinking.

DESCRIPTORS

- **SIGHT:** Ruddy brown earth, topped with a frosting of ice between one and ten inches thick.

- **SOUND:** Eerily silent until the whip-crack loud warning snap of the ice as it starts to break.

- **SMELL:** The ice smells clean and cold. Once the ice breaks, however, the steamy warmth of the peat pushes its rotting scent of old tea leaves and compost mixed with rotten eggs up into the air.

- **TASTE:** Inhaling this strange steam coats your mouth with a greasy bitterness.

- **TOUCH:** The edges of broken ice cut like torn metal, but the peat itself is warm and soft to the touch as it pulls you under.

THE LOWLAND FOREST

A forest covers most of the Sweating Swamp; the trees are perched on boulder-sized clots of earth, while wet or frozen pools thread between them.

The trees are mostly a stunted mix of cedars and spruces, with grasping branches and clumps of hanging lichen.

Sometimes the ground is solid underfoot. Other times a misstep could lead to being knee-deep in knotted roots and warm water.

DESCRIPTORS

- **SIGHT:** The drooping branches of the cedars form uneven archways, while the spruce limbs hang across the path like barricades.

- **SOUND:** The wind blows incessantly through here, giving the forests a constant chorus of whistling, groaning, and squeaking trees.

- **SMELL:** The strong aroma of cedar and spruce is everywhere, sneaking into noses with intense turpentine scents. The fetid stench of the peat bubbles up from the steaming pools.

- **TASTE:** The thick smell of the evergreens coats the inside of all the airways, giving an extra chill to the tongue with its menthol-ic effect.

- **TOUCH:** The cedar boughs bend as you push by, with splintering bark that gets under the skin. The stiff spruce branches are covered in sharp needles and sticky sap. The sap gets caught in clothing and itches.

THE WATERFALL OF KNIVES

A notorious section of the path through the Sweating Swamp leads travelers along a bridge at the bottom of a cliff face, underneath a natural wonder called The Waterfall of Knives. This overhang is the ever growing and collapsing frozen outflow of a waterfall. Whenever a large icicle falls, water gushes out again, until that water freezes back into icicles, slowly pushing the overhang further and further out.

If they arrive at this spot in the dark of night, adventurers will find a waterfall frozen solid, a looming mound of icicles. If they try to cross through here in the daytime, the heat of the sun makes the icicles more fragile, and spraying water will sneak out between the cracks, streaming out in an arc over the path and creating a lot of slippery ice on the frozen river bridge.

DESCRIPTORS

- **SIGHT:** Freed from the dark mire of the forests, the frozen parts of the waterfall glitter brilliantly in sunlight or moonlight.

- **SOUND:** A perpetual clinking and snapping fills the air of this river crossing, as the ice responds to the pressures of the water beneath it. A new icicle falling is often announced by a cascading series of cracks; the water flowing freely will make the whole frozen structure sing with an uncanny harmony.

- **SMELL:** If the water is frozen, this crossing is a realm mercifully clear of any of the noxious smells stifling you elsewhere. If the water is running, however, you can still smell that steeped-leaf scent, bitter but less fetid.

- **TASTE:** The ice, if you choose to eat or melt it for drinking water, is beautifully clean and fresh. The running water has a bitter, aromatic flavor, heavy with spruce and cedar aromas.

- **TOUCH:** The running water is unbelievably cold. The icicles are sharpened by the wind into vicious knives, as sharp as any dagger.

THE CEDAR CRYPT

Towards the end of the swampy forests, your adventurers will notice the trees getting older and larger, and the ground becoming firmer and safer. Then they'll come across an enormous, twisted red cedar whose trunk has been torn open at the bottom, where it is rotting into a steaming pile of sawdust and fungus.

If this is investigated, a trap door is found within, which leads down into the Cedar Crypt.

Descending into the crypt, you find two human-built underground rooms. The first room is large and stone-lined, where remains of grave goods are scattered around—empty stone coffins, stone jars broken open, and silver grave-coins spread around carelessly.

The second room leads off the first through what looks like a hand-dug hole in the wall and is little more than a den dug into the damp, peaty earth. It's empty except for humanoid hand- and footprints.

If your adventurers have snuck in quietly, the swamp ghoul will still be resting in the hand-dug den. If they have been carelessly loud in their exploring, she'll have hidden herself behind a smashed coffin, ready for a surprise attack.

DESCRIPTORS

- **SIGHT:** These crypt rooms are pitch black unless you bring your own light. Even with magical or firelight, there's a strange haze in the air that haloes the light and fogs your vision.

- **SOUND:** Throughout the stone-lined room, you hear the dripping sound of water echoing against the walls, and if you stand very still and listen, you hear skin on stone as something nearby is slowly, sneakily moving.

- **SMELL:** The scent of rot and death is strong down here. Mixed with the strong funk of the peat and sap from the cedar's roots, the stench sweats from the stones.

- **TASTE:** There's a metallic tang mixed with the haze in the air, and when you breathe in it settles in your mouth like the taste of blood.

- **TOUCH:** The walls and floor of the stone-lined room are slippery with warm dampness, and the stones feel a little insecure in their placements. The hand-dug den is soft all around, and heavier adventurers will sink slightly in the peat if they enter.

THE SWAMP GHOUL

The ghoul hunts the swamp at night, and will attack travelers who stay the night if they don't keep a fire lit.

If your adventurers engage the ghoul in combat out in the swamp, she will run away when bloodied to hide in her peat den.

In a fight within the crypt, the ghoul will fight to the death.

DESCRIPTORS

- **SIGHT:** The ghoul is a glossy, pearlescent grey, her skin taut over a desiccated form, draped in damp, red, peat-stained fabrics. If she's outside, that fabric is rimmed with frost.

- **SOUND:** The ghoul can move incredibly quietly, but if she's feeling sneaky, she might lick her lips with a horrible damp sound. When she has been seen, she screeches from peat-filled lungs, gurgling chunks of earth out of her mouth.

- **SMELL:** There is no mistaking the smell of the ghoul, once you know what she smells like: the tang of fresh blood drying on her face from her last meal mixed with the sulfurous rot of the bogs.

- **TASTE:** No one recommends tasting a ghoul, but if for some reason you do, she tastes bitter, nauseatingly sulfurous, and so salty.

- **TOUCH:** Her draped fabric scraps are damp to the touch. The ghoul herself is uncannily firm and strong, her undead musculature rippling with unearthly power along her skeletal frame.

Hopefully this haunting swamp is inspiring more than nightmares for you! Remember, as you add scents, tastes, and textures to your worlds, keep the descriptions brief and useful. The added dimension of all five senses is sure to make your players excited, enticed, and occasionally a little grossed out, but beware, once you describe one important smell, you may find yourself asked to describe the smell of every new room your players explore! ⬡

MEMORABLE MONSTERS: ROLEPLAYING DRAGONS GREAT AND SMALL

ANDREW G. SCHNEIDER

Dragons! Nothing strikes dread into the heart of adventurers everywhere than rumors of a dragon. Yet far too often they devolve into little more than large, flying lizards when confronted by a group with tin cans and pointy sticks.

Dragons are big creatures with big personalities. This article of roleplaying advice for GMs takes an in-depth look at pseudodragons, faerie dragons, metallic dragons, and chromatic dragons; their flaws and foibles; and how best to get them to jump off the page and into your players' imaginations well ahead of the moment someone says, "Roll initiative."

PSEUDODRAGONS: THE BEST FAMILIARS

"It's kind of like a dragon, but smaller?"

Though they're the size of a housecat, pseudodragons feel that they deserve every bit of dignity, wealth, and wonder as their larger cousins. Their size and solitary lifestyle means they are little threat to a party of adventurers, so it's important instead to lean on their personality. What better way to showcase these diminutive drakes than to bond with a party member? Who doesn't want a dragon friend?

When roleplaying a pseudodragon familiar as an NPC, be sure it expresses its opinion frequently. Remember, they communicate via images, ideas, and emotions. Be frustrated when the party misses an obvious clue, fierce

in the face of adversity, and smug when everything goes according to your plan. And do it all from a reasonably safe distance. Unless it serves a greater purpose in the story, the fragile companionship of a pseudodragon will add welcome emotional weight to any campaign. Take that companionship away for no reason, and your players may suffer hurt, heartbreak, and be less willing to form emotional bonds in the future.

SAMPLE PSEUDODRAGON TRAITS

1. My master is my most valuable possession, while all other party members are part of my larger horde.

2. Magic is in my blood. I mimic my master's spellcasting gestures, especially in combat.

3. I engage in epic battles against mice and other small vermin while the party deals with larger threats.

4. The world is begging to be explored. Let's go, Master, and check it out.

FAERIE DRAGONS: PRANKSTERS AND CHEERLEADERS

"What's that laughter? Hey, who tied my shoelaces together?"

Just a little larger than a breadbox, a faerie dragon doesn't have the temperament to bond itself as a familiar, but one can still inject a needed dose of levity and good cheer to even the dourest situation. Faerie dragons often come into conflict with bonded

Illustrated by Michael Harris

the rarest of moments, whereupon the tiny dragon goes from prankster and heckler to friend. The faerie dragon will do its utmost to guide and protect these friends, its most valued possession, and steer them clear of danger. And when the party does triumph over adversity, the dragon will be there to celebrate and sing their praises.

SAMPLE FAERIE DRAGON PRANKS

1. Swapping the materials of spell component pouches with packets of fresh herbs used for cooking.

2. Undoing the buckles on the fighter's armor.

3. Painting funny faces on shields.

4. Interrupting a ritual casting with a sudden noise or light.

METALLIC DRAGONS: MISGUIDED INTENTIONS

"I know it looks like a good idea, but trust me," his eyes glowed molten gold, *"you don't want to do that."*

pseudodragons; the pseudodragon works to help the party while the faerie dragon just wants to have fun.

A faerie dragon's sometimes contentious relationship with an adventuring party goes through three phases:

Once a faerie dragon notices an adventuring party in its territory, it will evaluate their sense of humor by playing a number of relatively innocuous and non-damaging pranks. So long as the party proves good-natured, it may—out of curiosity or loneliness—follow a party on its adventures.

In the second stage of a faerie dragon's relationship with adventurers, the dragon plays the archetypal fool, heckler, or Greek chorus. It offers timely insight into, and commentary upon, the party's decisions and adventures. If said commentary—which may or may not have basis in fact—causes the party to doubt, argue, or change its mind, so much the better for the faerie dragon's fun.

A party that tolerates the second, more vocal phase of a faerie dragon's attachment may find themselves in

Metallic dragons occupy a problematic place in any campaign. Well-intentioned, good-aligned shapeshifters of enormous power, they can easily play the part of guide, mentor, and savior to a party; directing them to their next quest, shaping their advancement, and rescuing them from certain doom. This is a fine role to play, but without proper care, the dragon will gobble up all the spotlight in what is ultimately the players' story. To downplay a powerful dragon ally, be sure to follow the standard mentor fantasy tropes. That is, the mentor discovers or brings the party together, nurtures them through hardship, and then sacrifices themselves so the party might live. Gandalf's stand against the Balrog in J.R.R. Tolkien's *The Fellowship of the Ring* may be one of the more famous instances of this mentor arc, but examples can be found across fiction literature.

Alternately, a metallic dragon can be set up as a formidable adversary. Not normally inclined to set themselves against a party of heroes, the crux of a metallic dragon's enmity is time and perspective. Adventurers are bulls in the china shop of the world—they dive into their challenges, gain power rapidly, and can wreak huge changes

> A DRAGON'S STRENGTH AND MAJESTY ARE LIKELY ENOUGH
> TO DISSUADE THE CHARACTERS FROM HUNTING IT TOO
> EARLY, BUT IF THEY DO—WELL, THE NEXT PARTY TO COME
> ALONG MIGHT BE A LITTLE MORE CAUTIOUS.

to the world in a matter of months! Dragons, on the other hand, take the long view—their plans evolve over decades, and their understanding of cause and effect in the larger world is theoretically more complete. Those caravan-raiding goblins might actually be serving as an essential check on the yeti in the nearby mountain pass. That lich, in addition to devouring souls, might also be working on a cure for a deadly disease. In the question of immediate versus ultimate good, adventurers tend to pursue the former, while metallic dragons almost always prefer the latter.

When using a metallic dragon as an enemy, bear in mind that the dragon likely has its claws in any number of plans, and won't immediately spare much effort for the adventurers. Perhaps it delivers a cryptic warning, or has minions or organizations it controls confront the characters. What's important is that the dragon is a power, a presence in the characters' lives that acts against them intermittently, and who holds ideas that are absolutely, and fundamentally at odds with the party's vision of the world (unless you want the dragon to transition to the previously detailed mentor arc). Only when the adventurers have thoroughly exasperated the dragon, disrupted his plans, defeated its minions, and made a mess of the world for future generations, should you have the dragon reveal himself in his majesty and strike at the characters directly. Hopefully, by then, they'll be strong enough to survive.

SAMPLE METALLIC DRAGON GOALS

1. Curing a disease that resists normal magic.

2. Subtly preparing a society to withstand a foreseen catastrophe.

3. Ridding a land of invasive species, while promoting an ecological balance with native creatures.

4. Promoting humanoid innovation so that giants become irrelevant (because giants deserve it).

CHROMATIC DRAGONS: CLASSIC EVIL

"The smoking cave in the side of the mountain, the scattering of bones around the entrance, they all knew what lay within: Their quarry, the dragon!"

The above scene is classic, and for good reason: a good dragon battle is the climax of so many great stories, why not make it yours? But while some sessions call for an impromptu encounter and a new set of dragonscale armor, the more frequently the adventurers encounter the same chromatic dragon, then the more exciting it will be to finally defeat them.

At the most basic level, follow the draconic rule of three: have the adventurers encounter a draconic foe at least three times before it perishes or eats the adventurers for lunch. For a first encounter, showcase the dragon from a distance, then allow the adventurers to sift through the devastation it wrought. The second encounter ideally foils one of the dragon's plans or hunts, preferably outside. Perhaps the dragon decides that its investment in the situation isn't worth its life. Or perhaps the adventurers are routed by its superior maneuverability and breath weapon, and realize that in order to be victorious, they need to control the battlefield. Only then comes the hunting, tracking, and the dramatic fight to the death in the dragon's cave.

For chromatic dragons as long-term villains, bear in mind that while their hunting territory might only span a couple hundred miles, their greed and ego are unlimited. Counted among the most powerful creatures in the world, they often attract minions and servants who work in turn to expand their holdings. The presence of a powerful dragon—by the actions of the monsters that serve it or the political machinations it fosters—can be telegraphed long before the adventurers spot a single scale. As a campaign structure, it helps to think of a pyramid. The dragon is at the top, naturally, and every adventure has the characters moving up the layers (and lairs) of minions and schemes—either deliberately or haphazardly—until they are ready to face the dragon itself. Then follow the draconic rule of three for an exciting and well-deserved climax.

SAMPLE CHROMATIC DRAGON OVERSIGHTS

1. Adventurers are far too plump to fit down that convenient chimney in my lair.

2. I like to get up close and personal when I fight. My scales will protect me.

3. Minions are extensions of my will; they'd never betray me.

4. I'm not arrogant like other dragons. I actually am the most powerful creature in the world.

Mind you, dragons do not need to be mysterious villains or behind-the-scene manipulators. It's not a problem (it might even heighten the tension) if the adventurers know from the very beginning of the story that they'll be facing a dragon. A dragon's strength and majesty are likely enough to dissuade the characters from hunting it too early, but if they do—well, the next party to come along might be a little more cautious.

From friends to foils, mentors to implacable foes, dragons can occupy a wide range of roles in your campaign. Whatever their role, drop a touch of roleplay into your draconic encounters and they're sure to become the memorable fire-breathing life (and death) of the party. ⬡

RUNNING THE GAME: BRIDGING GENERATIONS: FAMILY GAME NIGHT

RENEE RHODES

"I want to be a poodle."

I blinked at my grandmother during character creation. Her poodle, Bella, was curled comfortably in her lap, caring far more about the cuddles than the character sheets on the table.

Sure, I'd told them that they could be anything. We were bending the rules in an attempt to make character building quick, and to make the game as relatable as possible. I told them to imagine any character from television or real life that they'd like to be.

Otherwise, it had turned out somewhat like I'd expected. My cousin, who was two years into nursing school, created an elf cleric. My younger cousin wanted to play a human rogue, a prankster in life and at the table. And my mom, playing an elven princess sorcerer with a wand for her arcane focus, inspired by her deep love of the wizarding world? Pretty predictable. I hadn't seen the poodle part coming, though. But, okay, the entire point of this session was for my family to try—and enjoy—the game that I'd learned to love. It was to help them understand why I'd become so invested in gaming. To do that, I wanted to give them flexibility. If that meant my grandmother played her poodle, so be it. And she did.

Bella, the bard poodle, inspired others through her motivating barks, attacked enemies with her bite, and was more concerned with being awarded toys and treats than gold at the end of the quest. It was stranger than most of my experiences running the game, but she loved it. Actually, everyone loved it.

My family doesn't always see eye to eye, but we like to play games. (Sometimes we even get a little too competitive.) We also like to sit around the table after meals, sharing stories and laughing. Tabletop roleplaying seemed like a no-brainer next step. They were skeptical at first. It was the holidays after all, and our schedule was going to be very full of eating, watching Christmas classics, and…playing other games.

It's already tricky for a storyteller when everyone around the table expects something different from the game. Whether it's a preference for strategy and challenging combat scenarios, or for delving into character backstories in emotional roleplay, players enjoy the game more when the session considers their gaming expectations.

A group spanning generations takes the storytelling difficulty to the next level. The youngest player at our table was 13. The oldest was 74. Their ages affected their perspectives coming into the session; their expectations were influenced by the experiences or images they'd had of gaming throughout their lives.

On the oldest end of that span, my grandmother's expectations were tinted by what she'd heard about gaming—mostly horror stories. She'd never wanted to learn what it was like for herself because the news had portrayed it so negatively. Her hesitance was all over her face.

Maybe one of the reasons she was willing to try it was because it kept my cousin away from the computer for an hour. The youngest of the group, my cousin, was an avid Fortnite player. He played online all through the afternoons. At dinner, he had his phone close at hand to check memes.

A decade older, my other cousin wasn't familiar with the game beyond the representation she'd seen in pop culture—a group of boys playing in the basement.

Those family members in the middle of the spectrum were the most open-minded. My mom and aunt were key in persuading the others to play. They'd heard horror stories, too, but they were more willing to look past and discover for themselves.

Because each player came to the game with such different perspectives, I had to compromise. I worked to craft a game suited to the specific range of players by taking their expectations and perspectives into consideration for the adventure.

In each game, I learned which aspects of the adventure work best for which member of the family. I learned how to adapt my style so that they each have fun. More importantly, I've learned to be flexible and communicative in the adventure so that we all have fun together.

Some of the key things I've learned can help when playing with family with a multigenerational span:

FIND OUT HOW LONG THEY ARE WILLING TO PLAY

While I'm perfectly content to sometimes play for hours with my groups, that might not fly with a multigenerational family. The youngest might get restless, ready to move on to the next event. Mid-aged players may game for hours—it's not that far off from sitting at work or school. Older players may physically struggle to sit for long stretches.

Ask up front how long they'd like to play and consider building in breaks accordingly. An hour game may not need a break, but breaks during longer games allow the players to move and stretch, go to the bathroom, or grab a snack. They can come back to the game refreshed.

From character creation to final reward, my family games have never lasted longer than an hour and a half. For us, that was the least stressful option for the players, but also each session left them wanting to come back to play more.

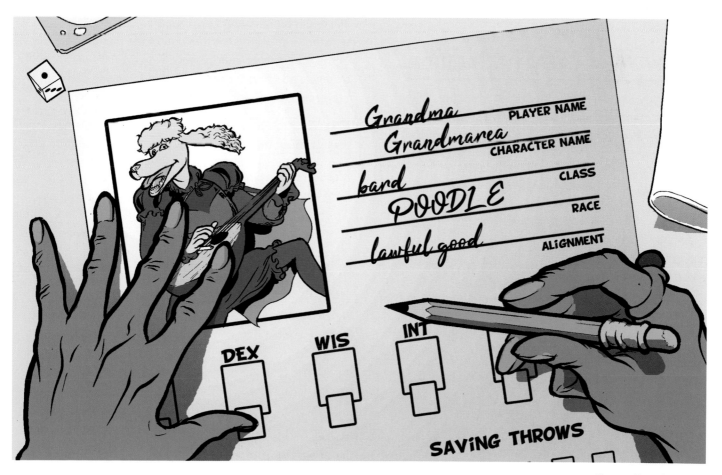

Illustrated by Michael Harris

CATER THE GAME TO THEIR INTERESTS

Make a list of things you know your family members love. Each person has different interests that you can allude to in-game to sustain their interest. Primarily, though, if there are shared interests, you can focus the adventure around those. Does your family rally around sports? You can build a sporting event or fantasy sport into the game. Does your family like to laugh? Try keeping the tone of the story and plot elements light and goofy.

My family has a love for escape rooms, mysteries, and action movies, so I tried to create quests with an element of mystery, a dash of action, and at least one puzzle reminiscent of an escape room.

ALLOW THEM CREATIVE FREEDOM

I frequently use the "rule of cool" at my table. When players suggest a creative alternative solution to an encounter, I'm likely to allow it if it's "cool," unique, or out-of-the-box, even if the solution clashes with the rules. Because multigenerational players come to the table with varied perspectives, they will act in ways that feel honest to them. My advice? Let them.

Especially if your multigenerational players are new players, they aren't likely to know the rules. Even if they aren't new, their unique idea may be worth breaking the rules for something really cool (or silly or intriguing!) to happen in the story.

My family laughed together each time a new wild idea was brought to life in game. When my grandmother actually howled a battle cry as Bella charged into combat, we all almost fell out of our chairs laughing.

JUDGE WHERE TO FUDGE THE RULES

To springboard off the last point, it's okay to fudge the rules if it helps your players understand. Multiple pages of character information and a heavy rulebook can be intimidating to anyone. A multigenerational game may have players of any age who feel that intimidation weigh more heavily based on their perspectives, experiences, and perceived skill sets. That's okay, and it's important that no player feels punished for that.

To be honest, elements like rations, currency conversion, and encumberment may be okay to forego in your game. The same could apply for multiple elements of combat, like opportunity attacks or reactions. This might mean constantly changing the function of the game based off of the reactions of your players. However, it's also okay to slowly add back rules you've skipped if you sense the players are comfortable with what they know.

My grandmother didn't care one bit for the rules. It wasn't about that for her (which is fine, we could do the math on her die rolls). For her, it was all about being in this fantasy world, just having fun, frolicking like a poodle at playtime. I was happy to adapt the rules on the fly to make that happen for her.

COMMUNICATE YOUR OWN EXPECTATIONS

Be open with your family from the beginning about how you want to run the game, and what you want from your players—like a mini session zero. A longer session zero before a campaign starts is a good time to introduce characters, discuss expectations, and review safety mechanics for your game. Even in situations where there might not be time for a full session zero, it's still good to go over your goals with the players.

Encourage things like questions, teamwork, and roleplay. Tell them that sometimes creativity can be the greatest solution to their problems. Encourage them to use the tools you provide to help them feel comfortable. Ask them a question or two about their character to start a roleplaying mindset. Communication will help everyone enjoy the game better.

While it's important to communicate up front, it's also valuable to keep those lines open during the game. It's okay to pause and review the rules if someone is struggling to understand. If the players all disagree, it's okay to talk through options out of character. This may be considered meta in other situations, but it can also be incredibly valuable for a multigenerational game.

In one game, my nine-year-old cousin wanted to kill all the bad guys simply because he found them annoying. We ended up having a discussion around the table. Ultimately, no one else in the party wanted to fight them, so we decided to try their way first and keep his option as "Plan B."

These suggestions aren't exclusive to families either. You're just as likely to encounter multigenerational spans in your local game store or in your online campaign. If you find yourself running a game with a wide age range amongst the players, consider using some of these tips to meet them at their perspectives and expectations. You can absolutely bridge those generations and adapt a game so that they will all enjoy it.

It's important to bridge the generations where we can. Gaming is given more legitimacy when those who have negative perceptions, like my grandmother, can overcome them. And younger gamers, like my cousin, will be the future of tabletop gaming if we introduce them in a way that they feel comfortable. Anyone can love the game and share the love with others. Not to mention, there's joy in bringing more and more people to the table!

The games with my family were a joy, and I learned from each of them. I learned the types of adventures my family loved, what kinds of stories they loved to tell, and what kinds of stories I want to tell across generations in the future.

In the meantime, gaming will continue to allow us to weave epic tales in a game store or around our family dinner table. And it'll leave us with memories to cherish—like Bella the bard poodle's battle howl. ◉

well. Terrible graffiti covers the stairs and carved archways of the structure. The water itself only fills to about half of the third level; the stepwell drops four stories into the ground, leaving one level dry, the next half-full, and the last two submerged. Anything captured or stolen by the occupant lies hidden in a niche, deep in the first level, concealed with trash and severed branches, but not too difficult to find (DC 12 Intelligence [Investigation] or DC 15 Wisdom [Perception]). Rededicating the site automatically reveals the cache but requires eliminating the threat posed by Arunarel (Ah-RUNE-ah-REL).

THE INTERLOPER

Having killed the previous custodian, Arunarel camps on the first floor, where he attacks anyone foolish enough to attempt using the site, or to try venerating the gods it once honored.

ARUNAREL, ONI EREMITE

Large giant (oni), lawful evil

Armor Class 17 (chainmail)

Hit Points 144 (17d10 + 51)

Speed 30 ft., fly 30 ft.

STR	DEX	CON	INT	WIS	CHA
20 (+5)	12 (+1)	16 (+3)	14 (+2)	12 (+1)	15 (+2)

Skills Arcana +6, Deception +10, Perception +5, Stealth +5, Survival +5

Senses darkvision 60 ft., passive Perception 15

Languages Common, Giant

Challenge 9 (5,000 XP)

INNATE SPELLCASTING

Arunarel's innate spellcasting ability is Charisma (spell save DC 14). The oni can innately cast the following spells, requiring no material components:

At will: darkness, invisibility

1/day each: charm person, cone of cold (10d8, as if using a 7th-level slot), gaseous form, sleep

Magic Weapons. Arunarel's weapon attacks are magical.

Regeneration. Arunarel regains 10 hit points at the start of its turn if it has at least 1 hit point.

ACTIONS

Multiattack. Arunarel makes two attacks, either with its claws or its glaive.

Claw (Oni Form Only). Melee Weapon Attack: +9 to hit, reach 5 ft., one target. Hit: 9 (1d8 + 5) slashing damage.

Glaive. Melee Weapon Attack: +9 to hit, reach 10 ft., one target. Hit: 24 (3d12 + 5) slashing damage, or 18 (2d12 + 5) slashing damage in Small or Medium form.

Change Shape. Arunarel magically polymorphs into a Small or Medium humanoid, into a Large giant, or back into his true form. Other than his size, his statistics are the same in each form. The only equipment items transformed are his glaive, which shrinks so that it can be wielded in humanoid form, and his clothing. If Arunarel dies, he reverts to his true form, and his glaive reverts to its normal size.

Arunarel's polymorphed form is similar to Vikras, the other site's custodian. He claims to have just chased away bandits who defiled the site, and plans to cleanse it the next morning, ambushing any who stay.

In oni form, he stands nearly 10 feet tall, with hairless cerulean skin, milky-white eyes, and obsidian claws, teeth, and nub-horns. His ragged cloak is made of yakfolk hide.

THE BOON

Should the characters clear the site of its evil-aligned occupier, remove the remains from the standing stones, and reconsecrate the stepwell (a DC 15 Wisdom [Religion] check and a bless spell, or equivalent), the powers once venerated here notice, providing the characters either advantage on three rolls of their choice, or the ability to succeed once on a saving throw after learning their roll fails.

Those who leave the shrine in its dark state and perform a minor veneration of the powers it now glorifies (two DC 15 Wisdom [Religion] checks before a failure, or a bless from an evil-aligned caster), gain the one-time ability to impose disadvantage on a foe for one minute. There is no save for this effect, and it does not take an action.

ADVENTURE SEEDS

There are many ways such a grim, unfortunate location might be incorporated into your game.

SCRATCH MY BACK

The evil-aligned creatures occupying the stepwell arrived after another creature took their original lair; perhaps a cave, watchtower, or other structure. If the group negotiates with the occupiers, they learn removing those invaders

Illustrated by Michael Harris

from the old lair would cause these creatures to go home without a battle. Depending on the characters' concern for damaging the site, or defiling the waters with more bodies, this might be an excellent alternative and a way to learn about a greater evil in the area. It may also cause other conflicts, as individuals learn all it takes to get the characters to perform a task is to take over the stepwell.

ACT OF FAITH

The creatures sent to this stepwell came after receiving a divine message from the characters' own good-aligned deities. Their presence here is meant as a test of faith, and they carry a message warning the party about their inaction at a previous encounter, engagement with a particular NPC, or visitation of a specific locale. They have been sent to punish or fight the party and leave their broken forms as a testament to the consequences of their behavior. If the group can defeat them and reclaim the site, they will pass the test.

Will your PCs seek out tranquility or delve into the inky blackness in search of redemption? Present them these options and find out! ⬡

SITES & SETTINGS: THE ADVENTURE COMES TO YOU

JEREMY MELLOUL

THE STRANGE AND FANTASTIC ARE INCREDIBLE TOOLS TO DELIGHT YOUR PLAYERS AND EXPLORE THE UNEXPECTED.

As a Game Master, it's always useful to have a few encounters in your pocket to use either as an exciting change of pace or to stall your players while you finish preparing the next chapter of your campaign.

To this end, let me introduce you to the Magical Traveling Feyre. It's a fantastical festival that you can easily drop into your home games, perfect for any adventuring party, regardless of their character classes or backgrounds.

TUATHA'S TRAVELING FEYRE

Come, weary traveler. Journey a little further and delight! Tuatha's Traveling Feyre has come to town, offering you a portal into a world beyond your imagination. Step into our wondrous grove and behold the incredible sights we have gathered for you from across the realms—all for your enjoyment!

Tuatha's Feyre occurs in the Realms of Fey, a separate plane of existence more susceptible to the influence of the forces of nature and magic. Portals between the two planes are rare, but Tuatha's magical abilities allow her to link her Feyre's campgrounds in the Realms of Fey to any other place in the world—allowing for visitors to travel between the two realms.

In order to establish the portals, she plants a grove of trees and uses her nature magic to propel its growth. Over the course of a single day, the seeds go from saplings to towering ancient trees.

As the grove grows in the Realms of Fey, so too does it grow in the mortal plane that your heroes occupy, usually appearing on the outskirts of a city, or even in environments where such a grove is out of place, like snowy tundras, or barren deserts.

When both groves are fully formed, the sympathetic link they share causes a portal to form at both dawn and dusk, through which travelers can pass.

Often, if word has sufficiently spread, there are campsites built around the grove in the mortal realm, where travelers gather from all over to participate in this event and trade stories of the things they've experienced "on the other side."

The Feyre typically lasts anywhere from a week to a month, and when it disappears, it only returns the following season.

THE FEYREGROUNDS

The portals between the two groves only remain open for half an hour at dawn and dusk. Every time the portals open, it is a celebrated event marked by a swell of magic. First, music begins to play around the grove, coming from no discernible source. Then the trees themselves move. Their branches curl to form a circular gate and the space between the wooden limbs fills with magic, an opaque pool of bright, swirling colors, forming the portal. As the music reaches its crescendo, dozens of pixies fly out from the portal, littering the grove with their laughter. They take the stunned audience by the hand and lead them into the Feyregrounds.

- **Staying Past the Portal's Close:** It is said that those who stay too long in the Realms of Fey can lose themselves to the plane's magic. They sometimes return, weeks or months after they first set foot in the plane, even though they only believe that a few days have passed. There are even stories of people returning from these extended trips into the Realms of Fey only to lose all memory of what they experienced on the other side.

Upon crossing through the portal, visitors are greeted by a grove identical to the one in the world they came from. The rest of their surroundings, however, are totally changed. There are festive, multi-colored tents and dozens of performers playing music, spinning flaming instruments, and juggling swords.

The Feyreground tents vary in size. Some are small, just large enough to hold a single stand for food or drink, while others can accommodate a small audience. They form a circle around the grove, where there are tables for visitors to rest beneath the trees. The largest tent lies to the north, and hosts the Feyre's largest shows and attractions.

The realms itself also adds to the Feyre's mystique, the entire sky stuck in the plane's eternal twilight.

PEOPLE & PERFORMERS

TUATHA, THE FEYREMASTER

Tuatha is an energetic sprite—a small, winged, fey being. She carries herself with a lot of grace, but also with the same mischievous air that most sprites are known for. Tuatha relishes bringing people into the fantastical Feyre that she's painstakingly created, taking great pleasure in delighting visitors. She is often dressed in colorful costume, woven with vines that seem to move and twist on their own. She understands that she, too, is a part of the show she has created, and enjoys that greatly. In addition, she is very protective of the family of performers she has gathered.

KEZIO, THE FORTUNE TELLER

Covered in tattoos from head to toe, at first glance Kezio seems imposing. But his shy and reserved demeanor undercuts his appearance. In fact, he often beams warmly when someone wanders into his tent to have their fortunes read (see the *augury* spell for guidance). He finds the world a scary and dangerous place, and is grateful for his ability to shed a little light on what may come.

OTHER ENTERTAINERS

There are many other performers at the Feyre who entertain the visitors by demonstrating their talents as strong-folk, knife jugglers, fire dancers, and more unusual vocations. Here are a few to get you started:

- **ANGEL:** Angel is a short, but athletically built, human. He dances with fire poi, swinging tethered weights in a rhythmic pattern while they are lit on fire, drawing people in with his exceptional routines. He is most often seen shirtless, his pink and purple hair marking him in the crowds.

- **BOLIVAR:** The young, half-elf Bolivar loves getting one over on visiting adults. He performs many mundane acts of magic, using cards, coins, and his dexterous sleight-of-hand ability to amaze and impress.

- **THE GREAT ZASS:** The strongest woman at the Feyre, the Great Zass prides herself on her prodigious power. She is an oread, a mountain nymph, and wears the hide of a dire bear on her back. She tends to pick on visiting adventurers, using them to demonstrate her strength by challenging them to push her off balance. Zass is not above wagering some coin to goad a prideful challenger.

- **MERRICK:** Merrick most enjoys performing and drawing attention to themselves. A druid of great talent, they can wild shape into just about any animal, having traveled far to study all manner of beasts. Merrick's performances often gather a crowd that shouts out requests in an effort to stump them.

- **SOLVEIGH:** This graceful and beautiful elf leads a small troupe of other dancers and musicians around the Feyregrounds, spinning and dancing, pulling visitors out of their comfort zones and into her arms—forcing them to dance with her for a spell before she continues on her way. Her very appearance and personality are as fluid as her movements, changing distinctly between the seasons, as she pleases, or as the music she dances to moves her.

SHOWS & PERFORMANCES

THE FEARLESS FOUR

A thrill act in the Main Tent, this performance features an assortment of death-defying acts including flying trapeze, tightrope walking, knife throwing, sword swallowing, and a fair amount of illusory entertainment to add ambiance to the show.

- **PERFORMERS:** Jero / Redhawk / Haly / Strix

BLINK & YOU'LL MISS IT

A show of immense skill and coordination, in which Neja, a dryad (a fey creature with the appearance of a woman with bark-like skin), leads her blind dog, Flash, through an incredibly challenging obstacle course filled with magical traps!

- **PERFORMERS:** Neja & Flash the Blind Dog

THE LIGHT FANTASTIC

The only show at the Feyre that does not actually take place on the grounds, "The Light Fantastic," is a festival of merriment led by Trip, the merry satyr, that takes the audience out into the wilderness of the Realms of Fey. Along the way, there are many drinks to be had, and the song Trip plays from his harp is known for its ability to bewitch those who listen to it, putting them into a sort of trance as they are forced to dance to his tune until his performance ends.

- **PERFORMER:** Tripamuck "Trip" the Satyr

OTHER FEATURES

CARNIVAL GAMES

If you wish to include carnival games for visitors to play, you can adapt them from the "Ghost Carnival" adventure from *Rolled & Told's* October 2018 issue.

VENDORS & SHOPPING

There are also many vendors who set up shop at the carnival. Many simply provide food and drink to be enjoyed—collected from all the realms. Some, however, make their business trading exotic goods collected over the Feyre's wide-ranging travels. They have an exotic collection and may just carry some rare, magical items relevant to your players' quests, or others that you simply wish to include in your games.

When your players win a game or spend some time perusing the vendor stands, allow them to roll a d6 and compare the result against the table below to determine which of these fey items they find!

RESULT	ITEM NAME	DESCRIPTION
1	Starlight Weapon	Forged with the essence of starlight, these weapons shine with a dim light for 30 feet while drawn. On a hit, they deal additional radiant damage equal to one weapon damage die.
2	Hero Figurine	This small, wooden sculpture of a hero holds great magical strength. When the command word is spoken, it comes to life, growing to humanoid size and manifesting as an animated armor (see core rulebooks) construct. It follows the commands of the one who activated it for 10 minutes, or until they speak the word again, at which point the construct reverts to its figurine state. The figurine can only be activated once per day, and if the construct is destroyed, it can no longer be called forth.
3	Lullaby Instrument	As an action, while playing this magical instrument, the wielder can subject everyone capable of hearing the music to the effects of a 3rd-level *sleep* spell. The performer cannot do this again until they complete a long rest.
4	Muse's Mask	This shifting mask fully obscures the wearer's face, instead showing one of two faces—one laughing and comedic, the other crying and tragic. While wearing the mask, the wearer has advantage on Insight checks made against any humanoid that is not immune to being charmed.
5	Rings of Dreaming	Usually found in a set, the Rings of Dreaming allow their wearers to enter the same dream state, allowing them to communicate there, or share a dream or nightmare they've had.
6	Teleportation Tapestry	This beautiful, surreal tapestry of a far-off place is actually a sewn teleportation circle. When the proper command word is spoken, the depicted landscape shimmers, allowing any creature that steps into the tapestry to appear in the depicted place. These tapestries are very rare and often found in pieces. Only a dedicated group of adventurers stands a chance of reassembling such an item and gaining access to whatever far-off destination the treasure portrays.

Journey Into the Unknown

Tuatha's Traveling Feyre can provide a much-needed break from tense adventuring, but its light-hearted nature doesn't prevent it from serving a more narrative role. You can use the Feyre to introduce story hooks or integrate clues relevant to quests your players are already on.

Perhaps someone the party is looking for is hiding out as one of Tuatha's performers. Or perhaps the party needs to venture into the Realms of Fey and decides to use Tuatha's Feyre as a crossing.

Of course, there's nothing wrong with using Tuatha's Feyre as a lighthearted break. A bit of fun with little connection to the rest of the adventure can usually make for a really entertaining session. 🎲

SITES & SETTINGS: THE TRANS-KINGDOM SKYWAY COMPANY, LTD.

GARETH-MICHAEL SKARKA

The party left the Temple of the Priest-Lord of the Church of Light and wandered through the streets of the city, looking for an inn where they might spend the night before heading out upon their quest.

"The journey will be arduous," said the paladin. "The Priest-Lord says that to recover the Chalice of Ulm, we must journey to the Spinecrest Mountains—and they lie many leagues to the east."

The ranger nodded, and rested her palm on the hilt of her sword. "Through the Forest of Graymire. Orc-infested...and worse."

The thief spoke up, gesturing with his thumb at a faded parchment advertisement, wheat-pasted to the wall of the stable they were passing. "Guys, I think I've found our solution..."

THE TRANS-KINGDOM SKYWAY COMPANY, LTD.

Historically, many overland journeys weren't undertaken alone, but rather by traveling with a caravan, a commercial venture that regularly traversed the route between destinations, ferrying cargo and passengers. The caravan offered safety in numbers (and usually the added safety of hired security), as well as a guide who was intimately familiar with the route.

There's no reason why the same shouldn't be true in your fantasy world.

The Trans-Kingdom Skyway Company is a business run by a former adventurer who operates a travel and cargo

service using a magical treasure that she acquired during her past exploits—a flying ship!

THE ZEPHYR
Unique caravel-sized magical airship

Size: 100 ft. long, 25 ft. wide
Speed: 10 mph/100 ft. per round
Crew: 12   **Passengers:** 20   **Cargo:** 100 tons
AC: 15   **HP:** 500
Damage Threshold: 20

Trans-Kingdom Skyway Company runs the *Zephyr* along regular routes (as suited to your particular campaign), and carries passengers and cargo between destinations. Passengers are carried for a flat fee of three silver pieces per mile traveled, which includes the use of a cabin (which is shared with another passenger), as well as two meals per day. Cargo is negotiated on a case-by-case basis—often for a negotiated 15% of the sale price of the cargo.

THE SHIP

The *Zephyr* resembles a sailing vessel—three decks high, 100 feet long, and 25 feet across at its widest point. Like many sailing vessels, it has masts—but uniquely, this vessel has four. Two masts rise vertically from the top deck, as one would expect. Two additional masts, however, extend horizontally outward, giving the appearance of a set of wings. The sails on all four masts provide the *Zephyr* with its primary method of propulsion, in the traditional fashion. Without sails, or in instances of lulls in the wind,

Illustrated by Ahmara Smith

The middle deck is divided as follows: the forward section features 10 small cabins, each with room for two passengers. The rear section features the similarly-sized officer's cabins, as well as the ship's kitchen. The large center area of the middle deck is used for several purposes simultaneously—this is where ship's goods are stored, where the crew and passengers dine, etc.

The lower deck of the *Zephyr* is the cargo hold, which can be accessed by hatches in the decks above, as well as through a hatch in the side of the vessel that leads directly into the hold (which would certainly not be found in a seagoing craft).

The *Zephyr* is not an armed vessel. It carries no weapons of any kind, beyond those carried by the crew and passengers.

THE CREW

The *Zephyr* has a crew of about a dozen: The Captain, two officers, and eight to 10 hired hands.

THE CAPTAIN · VIXIS RHEE

Vixis Rhee spent years adventuring as a ranger before she and her party discovered the Zephyr, gathering dust in the treasure room of an evil cloud giant. After defeating the creature, the party took the flying ship, and chose to retire from the adventurers' life.

Vixis felt that they'd earned a quieter, safer life. She had spent some time years ago as a hired guide for caravans, leading them through the wilderness to their destinations. This gave her the idea for forming the Trans-Kingdom Skyway Company—a caravan venture that avoided the most common dangers of overland travel by making the journey by air.

Of course, since then, she's discovered that life is never quite that easy. Air travel has its own unique dangers...but deep down, she's glad of that. Life would be boring if it was too safe.

Personality: Vixis is, in many ways, the archetype of the stoic, taciturn ranger, despite leaving that vocation years ago. Her manner is direct (some might say abrupt), especially when acting in her official capacity as captain. She is loyal to the long-time friends who serve as her fellow officers, and fiercely protective of the *Zephyr* itself, and its crew.

Appearance: Vixis is a dark-skinned, human woman of medium height. She usually wears a large tri-corner hat, as well as leather armor (a holdover from her ranger days),

the magic that keeps the *Zephyr* aloft can also propel it forward, but only at around 2 mph/20 feet per round.

The top deck is open to the air, with the exception of the sterncastle, a structure covering most of the rear quarter of the vessel. Within the sterncastle is the captain's cabin. The area atop the sterncastle is the quarterdeck, which features the ship's wheel that controls the *Zephyr's* altitude and direction.

RUNNING THE GAME: COMICS FOR DUNGEON ENTHUSIASTS

LISA OLSON

HOW TO GET THE MOST OUT OF LOCAL NERD STORES

If you're holding this copy of *Rolled & Told* in your hands, my guess is you're already pretty familiar with the idea of collaborative storytelling. It's the great RPG-legitimizing buzzword for the 21st century, explaining, in non-nerd centric academia, what makes a roleplaying game experience so unique: the idea that a group of people create their own narrative together, or the participation of the consumer in their storytelling experience. The later definition allows a collaborative story to go beyond an RPG a bit—it brings in narratives like video games, or an escape room, and other types of stories where the experience of participating in the story is just as important as the story itself.

I recently had the great joy of working in a large comic and gaming store for four years. I walked in as a comics specialist with no real experience in tabletop or RPG anything, and as an enthusiastic nerd, it was obviously all of a few seconds before I was hoarding dice and falling in love with a whole other realm of wonder. And the thing that made my job the most fun was the realization that the community of people around the store was one of the best tools for me, as a businesswoman, to utilize. I've read dozens of articles over the last handful of years about how millennials prefer to spend their money on experiences rather than stuff. And on the surface, maybe that is scary for someone who sells stuff

to hear, but all the stuff that I was selling was the basis of collaborative stories.

A local game shop's gaming space is really the first and easiest place to tackle this idea. Both publishers of the top two fantasy-themed RPG systems have organized play systems around their official, ongoing campaign stories. You can create, register, and track your own character, and then drop in to any shop in the world that participates in the programs and play with the people there. Both groups were a big presence in my shop's game room. I personally learned a lot about both games from seeing people every week and listening to their adventures while I shelved books and chatted with shoppers.

One of the things I love the most about these two organized play systems is how they lower the barrier to entry for new players. As a recent know-nothing myself, I can say with extreme confidence that not having much background makes approaching any RPG very intimidating. Even as an employee at a store that sold and ran the games, I looked at the decades of backstory and universe of character options as deeply impenetrable.

It took me a lot of reading online to get comfortable enough about the world to agree to sit down and play, because it's a lot to take in. And my own reluctance really helped me to understand my role as an employee at one of these stores, to be that of a Nerd Sherpa: a guardian of all the necessary Adventure Supplies. It was my job to make getting into this stuff as easy as possible. I honestly believe that should be the guiding philosophy for all local game stores and local comic shops. It's good customer service that leads to good sales, and empowering the community around your store to participate with each other can be very powerful.

One of the best things I ever did at my store was to create a gaming group called the Shieldmaidens. I spoke to women almost every day at the shop, but they were vastly underrepresented as a casual population in the gaming room. I asked women if they were interested in changing that, and what would make them more likely to participate. A lot of our clientele were not extroverts dying to run into a crowd of strangers to ask for help learning to play a complicated, largely social game. And because they weren't seeing other women and beginner games happening, they assumed it wasn't something that happened at all.

So I created a private Facebook group for the women I'd spoken with. They invited their friends and we made a poster for the store. The idea was for anyone passing through to regularly see this group of femme-identifying people in the game room, and to know that it was something they were welcome to join.

Now the Shieldmaidens Facebook group has a couple hundred members. There are at least two regular RPG campaigns that run most weeks, with people who craft and hang out while they watch the campaigns. There are campaign-off days, where people bring and share board games, and local conventions have begun requesting that the Shieldmaidens do panels and host games at their events.

One of the more common posts on the Facebook page is when

someone who has never played will ask if it's okay for them to come watch or sit in or have someone explain the game. The answer is always, "Yes! Anything you want!" And I did very little—all I did was set up the group, reserve table space, and introduce people to each other. I made sure that they understood that I, as an extension of the store, was at their disposal to get them any resources they needed, and would create events to share on the store's social media platforms. With my support, the Shieldmaidens became an independent force of nature and enthusiastic walking billboards for my store. That's the definition of a win-win.

That's a pretty high-level example that requires a lot of things, though—enough open gaming-room space to run the event, enough of an existing social network to pull that group from, a full-time employee with the connections to that group; it's all very situational. But there are other ways to encourage participation and interaction without having to rely on some of those resources. You just have to think outside the box a bit.

Illustrated by Michael Harris

> YOUR LOCAL GAME SHOP IS JUST LIKE ANYTHING ELSE IN YOUR GAMING ARSENAL—IT'S A TOOL THAT'S LIMITED ONLY BY YOUR IMAGINATION AND YOUR WILLINGNESS TO PUT SOME EFFORT INTO IT.

If your store has a game room and runs regular game demos, take similar (if not the same) story nuggets to run a fifteen-minute tabletop roleplaying encounter. The encounter can be to run some kind of obstacle course or fight a monster, but do it in four or five different game systems so that players can try the same thing in the different systems side by side. Maybe even have the same character prepared for each game, so they can see how the character sheets differ and how the same skills are utilized by the different systems.

Maybe your store is small and doesn't have a gaming room. You can always stream an after-hours game played in your store. Ask local comic creators, local radio or TV personalities, or a local news reporter to sit in on your game and record it. You could do a series of one-shots that way. Ask a local comic creator to illustrate scenes or characters from those games. Have an art contest for your community to illustrate a scene or character from those games. Create playable character sheets of your store employees. Encourage people to play them in their own games, report back on your employee's adventures, and share brief little write-ups about those games in your newsletter.

Another way I really pushed the idea of expanding the experience for gamers in our store was doing a lot of cross merchandising with comics. While a comic book is not as obviously participatory or collaborative as a roleplaying game, I think of them as similar because of the collaboration in the creative process. A comic book is a true meeting and sublimation of two different creative pursuits—the written and the visual—into a singular narrative product. There's also the letterer, the colorist, and the editor, molding their visions into a cohesive whole. The process of making a comic can feel very much like a great adventuring party on an epic quest. And reading the resulting pages is very much like watching *Critical Role* every week.

Comics and RPGs are similar in that the journey really is more important than the destination. No one necessarily knows how or when either will end, and it's everything that happens in between that matters. That's why I'm always a little disappointed when I encounter a gaming store with no comics, or a comic shop with no games—they're so deeply related and feed off each other so well, it's a shame to love one and not the other.

One of my favorite and most successful displays in the store was called "Comics for Dungeon Enthusiasts." It was situated right in the middle of the store, between the normally very separate comics and game sections. It was a rotating mix of RPG Beginner Boxes and collected volumes of comics that pair with comics like fine wine with gourmet cheese. It was a great way to draw someone in with something they already like, and to introduce them to the equally wide world of another collaborative storytelling form. There are decades of officially licensed comic books based on the two dominant RPG systems in every game shop, and long running comics based around people playing RPGs like *Order of the Stick* and *Knights of the Dinner Table*. Then there are series very tapped into the RPG sensibility like *Rat Queens*, a cross between a rollicking RPG adventure and the movie *Bridesmaids*. *Die* is a new comic about a group of kids transported to the world they're gaming in, where things take a dark and deadly turn. It also will have an actual original gaming system they're planning to be released in the future! Classic high-fantasy, sword-and-sorcery stories are alive and well in gorgeous series like the magically inclined, *Prince Valiant*-esque *Sleepless*. In *Highest House*, a young boy is brought to an ancient, powerful citadel and starts to hear it speaking to him. Recently translated and printed in English, *Elves* is a best-selling comic from France that will drop the jaw of anyone who even glances at it, and *Scales and Scoundrels* is an all-ages-friendly adventure that I wish there were a thousand more volumes of. Then there's sword and sorcery with a modern and hilarious twist in *Nimona*, which was also nominated for a National Book Award in 2017. The list goes on and on, and you've probably got a local shop that would be happy to keep adding to it for you.

If any of the game or shop activities I mentioned sound like fun but you don't own or operate a comics or gaming shop, get in touch with your local shop and tell them about it. Don't have a local comic or game shop? Go visit a local librarian and talk to them about it. Your local game shop is just like anything else in your gaming arsenal—it's a tool that's limited only by your imagination and your willingness to put some effort into it. It's staffed and patronized by a willing multitude of new allies and adventures just waiting to be discovered. So go forth and game! ⬡

Critical Role, Order of the Stick, Knights of the Dinner Table, Rat Queens, Bridesmaids, Die, Prince Valiant, Sleepless, Highest House, Elves, Scales and Scoundrels, and Nimona are the trademarks of their respective owners, which are not associated with Lion Forge.

RANDOM NONSENSE: SHARPENING YOUR SWORDS WHEN YOUR PEN IS DULL

MATTHEW ERMAN

I'm lazy. I'll be the first to admit it. If left to my own devices, I tend to do a variety of things that aren't helpful to the betterment of my craft. Hell, maybe I'm lazy because I'm constantly in a two-day window of existential crisis. Who knows? But without a deadline or project to keep me focused, I just kind of...uhhh...do nothing. I do nothing, real hard.

Some backstory: I'm new to comics. With a handful of anthologies and only one series under my belt (as of this writing), it has been a huge learning curve to understand the ebb and flow of this kind of industry. Work can be sporadic. It can come without any warning, or you may be out of work for months without landing anything substantial. The comic industry is pretty unique in that way. It requires your active participation to get work as well as to create the work. This past year has been a whirlwind of trying to set up projects for my future, and the ones that I've lined up are so far off that it is hard to predict when I'll be actively writing scripts; but I still have to write. I have to. It's in the job description.

So you're reading this thinking, "What the hell does it have to do with anything?" "Who is this jabroni prattling on about nothing?" Well, I'll tell you right now, writing "fantasy campaigns" has changed my life. It has helped me hone my craft as a writer, experiment with bizarre storytelling devices that I've never considered, understand my players' interests (this is huge), and be more confident in my ability to create something that is truly captivating. I'm going to go over three writing skill sets I use every moment I am crafting an adventure for the players.

I.) CREATIVITY

Creativity is a vital component in running campaigns. Creative solutions are needed every moment of gameplay, and as a GM, you need have a variety of things prepared, as well as the ability to improvise.

How do you create magical items that are interesting and unique?

Context! Having context or NOT having context is such an awesome tool to employ when making homebrew items. I use a mix of random generators and tables to create the base structure of my items, and then I think about context, which informs what kind of magical properties my items will have.

Our players are in a green hag's theater, so I'll ask myself, "What makes sense to be here and what doesn't?" The answer to the first question can lead to items like magic costumes that bind players when worn, enchanted wall ornaments, closets full of strange trinkets from an old play, or scripts with magic phrases baked into the dialogue. These make sense, will deepen the context of your location, give the players flavor for where they are, and expand the world by showcasing a consistent history within the location. It's a theater, so there should be theater-related items.

The most fun part, though, is adding items that are out of context from the location. It's a balancing act, and you don't want to do too much of it. Having your players find a magic comb that permanently makes someone resistant to water, yet they always have sopping wet hair, creates an intriguing mystery. Creating context around that item makes the discovery even more impactful! A skeleton in a dark closet clutches tightly to this comb, and their clothes show they're from a seafaring people. A note revealing that they were looking for a lost treasure creates the seeds to a future mystery. The goal is always to world-build with your items. Deepen the immersion, expand the history and the lore of what your players are doing, and create moments where a player can think back sessions later and ask an NPC, "Hey, do you know anything about this comb?"

Opening a treasure chest? Roll a d10 and see what item you get from this list!

MAGIC ITEMS

1. **Je'Par Dee's Puzzle Box:** It is cursed; whoever is holding this during a long rest can only speak in the form of a question. Speaking anything other than a question inflicts 1d4 damage to the bearer of the curse. The curse can only be broken by sacrificing an item equal in gold pieces worth to the player's level x 10.

2. **Bag of Goblin Hair:** It smells bad and is full of unsavory oils. They seem to be constantly generating goblinoid oil. Your hands are covered in an un-washable oil for one hour. While greasy, you have "butterfingers," which gives you disadvantage on attack rolls that require using a weapon.

3. **Shifting Flower Amulet:** The bearer may change minor aspects of the physical appearance of this item. Smells like a freshly blooming flower, very fragrant in a 15-foot radius around the wearer.

4. **The Slumbering Giant:** A small blue stone affixed onto a silver earring band. When worn, it does two things: it makes the wearer more susceptible to sleep spells (disadvantage against sleep), and the wearer can't be awakened unless the earring is removed.

5. **Summer Song, Weapon (Greataxe 1d8):** When the bearer is outdoors, harmless creatures such as squirrels and birds flock to them when they sing songs for a minute or longer.

6. **The Navigator's Bane:** A slightly oversized captain's hat with blue cloth and golden yarn trim. Underneath the top bill of the hat is a spinning compass made to look like a mug of grog, so only the wearer can determine the location of booze. The only thing this hat does is tell you where the closest alcoholic drink is.

7. **Ring of Sticky Fingers:** Your hands are sticky while wearing this ring. Items under five pounds require a Strength check of d8 to remove the item from your hands. Failure increases the roll needed by +2.

8. **Sweet Tooth:** A magic tooth from an unknown creature, discolored, with a sweet smell. While channeling this item, you can make any edible object taste like any other edible object. The effect stops if not being channeled.

9. **Giant's Toenail, Shield (2 AC):** While holding, you have +2 intimidation towards any creature larger than you. Must be painted after every battle, otherwise the first strike will destroy the shield.

10. **Spirit Balloons:** A bag of five balloons that can be turned into a balloon animal of any small creature with a DC 14 Performance check. If you succeed, a DC 14 Wisdom check will animate the balloon. It will mimic the nature of the animal it was based on and is alive for one hour, after which it deflates and dies. Horribly.

II.) STRUCTURE

"Structure" is a scary word. As a writer, it's basically the whole story. Without a structure, I don't have a story; I have a series of random events strung together by common participants.

So how do you structure your campaigns and what is a healthy mix of story moments and character moments?

Part of structure is knowing what your players' expectations are, and this applies to other kinds of writing as well. Typically, a healthy mix of conversational bits, getting to know new, interesting characters, and what I'd call the "discovery" phase of any particular story. So things like finding a key item, or hitting a particular moment that would trigger a set piece like a kraken, would be a part of the discovery. Letting players flounder for a bit as they experience the world you built them is a great way to kill a bunch of birds with one stone.

The other side to the structure of a campaign is battles! Tailoring the intensity, the frequency, and the length of your battles to the group you're playing with will help a ton. You may want lengthy, epic battles, but maybe your players aren't ready for that, or they haven't earned it in

Illustrated by Ahmara Smith

the campaign. Having a three-year endurance test against some low-level goblins may sound intense, but it can turn boring quickly.

Finding a balance between these two aspects of structure can help you navigate building your world and story in a way that flows.

What things need to be in every campaign?

- Rad, interesting NPC characters
- Unique stories and quests
- A mix of homebrew items and traditional Dungeoneering items
- A mix of fights that are challenging and rewarding for your player mix

III.) DIRECTION

Direction is the culmination of taking all your creative endeavors, all the character and story moments, shaping them into a coherent thread of events, and then being okay with tossing it out the window. You share this responsibility of direction with the players. Yup, it's a joint effort.

Directing can be boiled down to cause and effect, that happened and now this will happen. Having connective language tie together in a way that makes sense reinforces this "cause and effect" way of writing. Typically, you as a GM are the "cause," and the "effect" transfers to the players. You put a bugbear in a suit as a shopkeeper, now it is up to the players to turn this thing into a story moment if they want.

How do you take creativity and structure and tie them together? How do you take the strange items and characters and mesh them with meaningful moments to move the story forward?

Your primary goal as a Game Master is to ensure that your players are having fun, and a large part of that is being flexible with your script. Let events flow and direct the course of action so that your players feel as though they have agency and control, while still maintaining your own control.

The importance of player choice can't be understated. I made an effort in writing certain sections of our campaign to fill it with strange, unconnected objects: the decomposing skeleton of a deer that was thrown in a hole, a magic hairpin, a variety of wigs, magic clothes, and some basic rules for an NPC character that was essentially a reanimated gnome skull who required attachment to a magic item to retain its consciousness. These items give the players ample opportunities to be creative and experiment with different solutions to your puzzles. They ended up creating a damn monstrosity too, so that was fun.

The players taking these items into their own hands helped me truly understand how writing these campaigns, acting out these characters, and letting the players do some of the creative legwork is beyond planning and also part of the fun. These are the moments that have helped me explore the depths of my creativity, both as a structural tool (how do I get to those moments?), and then how to let them happen naturally as not to overdirect things (how do I let it play out?).

You don't have to worry about whether or not something will work because the stakes are contained between you and your group, and generally your players will figure out a way to rebound if you've made a storytelling "judgment error."

Creating is stressful. We all do it because we love it, though, and you must make sure to nurture that love. For me, when between projects, with the accompanying bouts of stress and anxiety, I can count on writing my campaigns to remind me that I truly do love writing, and it is always beautiful, fun, and exciting. ⊘

RUNNING THE GAME: ON-THE-FLY NPCS

E.L. THOMAS

If you are a less than prepared GM like me, you know the woes of your PCs wandering in a way different direction than you had planned on, and they will run into NPCs you have nothing made up for. Oh, and yes, they will want to have an in-depth interaction with the on-the-fly NPCs and test you with everything from their name to asking about the NPC's hobbies, family, or even life story. They will want a distinct voice, mannerisms, or something memorable about every sell sword, waitress, shopkeeper, and bartender.

Unless you are a genius and a voice actor, you might fall short of the mark from time to time. I like to give my players as immersive an experience as I can, but more than once I've either nailed it or just hand-waved through it with, "It's a dwarf. He has a beard, He talks about mining, axes, and beer between telling you that the guy you are looking for can be found down the road at the stables." While sometimes the above mentioned less-than-stellar dwarf description just gets the adventure rolling, it takes players out of the game. To prevent this (and still not do much in the way of prep), I have six simple rules for making on-the-fly NPCs that make the game just a little more immersive, though far from perfect.

RULE #1: WHAT'S IN A NAME?

Your players are always going to want a name (even if they spent zero effort themselves on their own PC's name—like a dwarf named after their favorite beer), so here are my basic bullets:

- At the beginning of the game session, I pick six random letters and just have the NPCs names start with those. It's quick, dirty, and from time to time is all you will need to get through a session.

- Try to stick with a single name or nickname, unless it is a noble. If it's a semi-powerful NPC or your player characters insist, use these tricks listed below.

  - **HUMANS**: Go with a common name and an added moniker that describes their job or a characteristic. *Examples: Thom Flagon (for a bartender), Red Sally (for a redheaded thief), Bill Long Arrow (for a hunter), Gray Hugo (for an old man).*

  - **ELVES:** I use any name ending in an -us, -ill, -anna, or -ond sound, followed by a combination of a color, distance, state of being, something from nature, or an elfish weapon. *Examples: Loreond Yellowmoon, Vistus Silverbow, Glieus Loneleaf, Rillanna Nightstar, Kuill Farwind.*

  - **DWARVES:** I do anything Tolkien-sounding, without it being a complete rip-off. Or a one- or two- syllable name for the first name, one being ideal. For the clan name, I do combo of a color, metal, gem, stone type, or something angry or work sounding. *Examples: Mogin Grimgranite, Yorie Steelhack, Gerta Goldsanrl, Folkin Redaxe, Dobin Diamondig.*

  - **HALFLINGS:** Go with something relating to nature for the first name. For the family name or title, I go with a combo of food, something homey sounding,

MEMORABLE MONSTERS: SHADOW

E.L. THOMAS

TAKE AN OLD SCHOOL MONSTER, TWEAK IT AND SURPRISE YOUR PLAYERS. WHETHER THEY ARE RULES LAWYERS, LONG-TIME DUNGEON CRAWLERS, FELLOW GAME MASTERS, OR THOSE OH-SO-ANNOYING MONSTER-MEMORIZING SPOILSPORTS TRY OUR TWISTS ON THIS DUNGEON DENIZEN.

Whether delving in the deepest of dungeons, darkened sanctums, haunted crypts, or befouled tombs, I love using shadows. They make every scouting thief or ranger wary when skulking near any areas of gloom. Nothing scares an axe-toting barbarian or a sword swinging fighter than creatures that weaken you, draining your strength as you fight them. If a shadow drains all a character's strength, they don't only die, but also have a good chance of spawning another shadow. And there's something so creepy about trying to fight such an undead monster.

The shadow is an undead thing of sentient darkness that, with only its touch, saps the vitality from a living creature. If the shadow drains enough strength from a non-evil humanoid creature, the humanoid creature then rises as another shadow. A monster that makes more monsters when it kills is a dangerous thing, and rare in 5E. The shadow has been around since the first supplements in 1975, before it became the world's most popular roleplaying game. In prior editions, the shadow was a truly horrible enemy.

In 5E, this latest incarnation of the shadow is very nasty at challenge ½ because of its strength drain attack. The strength attack not only does 9 (2d6 + 2) necrotic damage, but it also reduces the target's strength by 1d4. If a non-evil

humanoid is dropped to 0 strength, it dies and rises as a new shadow 1d4 hours later. Additionally, that shadow will have a good amount of resistances and immunities. When in dim light or darkness, they can hide as a bonus action and they can slip through a space only one inch wide. You have quite a nasty monster for first-tier adventures. Like most of the good low-tier foes, they are front loaded, meaning they aren't much to fight against as a character higher than 2nd-tier unless you encounter them in large numbers. But the shadow is still a bit dangerous even against higher than third-level characters because of the strength drain.

The weaker aspects of the 5E shadow are its vulnerability to radiant damage, low armor class (AC 12), low intelligence (Int 6), and its low hit point total (16 hp), and they have only a single +4 to hit melee attack. Lastly, shadows are undead and subject to clerical turning and destruction abilities because of their low CR and +0 wisdom saving throw.

We can ramp up the shadow as it is listed in the core rulebooks with a couple of simple tweaks to make it a much more fearsome monster (even at 2nd or 3rd tier). Increase the Dexterity from 14 to 16, thus increasing the AC to hit and damage by +2 each. Then give the shadow an ability like Pack Tactics (see below).

PACK TACTICS

The shadow has advantage on attack rolls against a creature if at least one of the shadow's allies is within 5 feet of the creature, and the ally isn't incapacitated.

With just the above-mentioned tweaks, you've made any encounter with multiple shadows much more dangerous, though still not too dangerous for any characters of 5th level and above. To challenge characters of 5th level or above, you can consider using more than six shadows, or by making a higher challenge shadow that not only is tougher, but can control and or enhance normal shadows, such as the umbral puppeteer. The umbral puppeteer is a shadow that controls or leads other shadows. Umbral puppeteers are what a normal undead shadow transforms into when its "un-life" lingers on for more than a century without interaction with a living creature. Umbral puppeteers serve a grim purpose, only existing to feast upon the strength of the living. The vile creature's pull on darkness is so powerful that lesser shadows fall under its control, just by encountering it.

UMBRAL PUPPETEER

Medium undead (shadow), chaotic evil

Armor Class 13
Hit Points 39 (6d8 + 12)
Speed 40 ft.

STR	DEX	CON	INT	WIS	CHA
16 (-2)	16 (+3)	14 (+2)	12 (+1)	14 (+2)	14 (+2)

Skills Perception +4, Stealth +5 (+7 in dim light or darkness)

Damage Immunities radiant

Damage Resistances acid, cold, fire, lightning, thunder, bludgeoning, piercing, and slashing from nonmagical weapons

Damage Immunities necrotic, poison

Condition Immunities exhaustion, frightened, grappled, paralyzed, petrified, poisoned, prone, restrained

Senses darkvision 60 ft., passive Perception 14

Languages –

Challenge 3 (700 XP)

Gloom Aura. Any nonmagical light sources within 30 feet of the umbral puppeteer are immediately extinguished. Any magical light sources are reduced to only dim light while within the aura.

Amorphous. The umbral puppeteer can squeeze through a space as narrow as 1-inch wide without squeezing.

Shadow Calling. Any non-evil humanoid that is slain using any shadows strength drain ability within 120 feet of an umbral puppeteer rises as a new shadow within 1d4 rounds instead of 1d4 hours, as is the norm.

Shadow Puppet. As a bonus action, the umbral puppeteer grants a number of ally shadows equal to its charisma modifier and within 60 feet an immediate action.

Shadow Stealth. While in dim light or darkness, the umbral puppeteer can take the Hide action as a bonus action.

Sunlight Weakness. While in sunlight, the umbral puppeteer has disadvantage on attack rolls, ability checks, and saving throws.

ACTIONS

Multiattack. The umbral puppeteer makes two melee attacks.

Greater Strength Drain. *Melee Weapon Attack:* +5 to hit, 5 ft., one creature. *Hit:* 10 (2d6 + 3) necrotic damage, and the target's Strength score is reduced by 1d6. The target dies if reduced to Strength 0 or lower. Otherwise, the reduction lasts until the target finishes a short or long rest.

If a non-evil humanoid dies from this attack, a new shadow rises from the corpse 1d4 rounds later.

Dark Recovery (Recharge 5-6). The umbral puppeteer regains 7 (2d6) hit points while in dim illumination or darkness. This ability does not function in sunlight or on any round the umbral puppeteer suffered radiant damage.

REACTION

Birth Shadow. As a reaction, when the umbral puppeteer suffers 10 or more non-radiant damage from a single attack, it gives birth to a shadow.

LESSER SHADOW

Small undead, chaotic evil

Armor Class 11
Hit Points 7 (2d6)
Speed 40 ft.

STR	DEX	CON	INT	WIS	CHA
6 (-2)	12 (+1)	10 (+0)	6 (-2)	10 (+0)	6 (-2)

Skills Stealth +3 (+5 in dim light or darkness)

Damage Vulnerabilities radiant

Damage Resistances acid, cold, fire, lightning, thunder, bludgeoning, piercing, and slashing from nonmagical weapons

Damage Immunities necrotic, poison

Condition Immunities exhaustion, frightened, grappled, paralyzed, petrified, poisoned, prone, restrained

Senses darkvision 60 ft., passive Perception 10

Languages –

Challenge 1/8 (25 XP)

Amorphous. The lesser shadow can squeeze through a space as narrow as 1-inch wide without squeezing.

Shadow Stealth. While in dim light or darkness, the lesser shadow can take the Hide action as a bonus action.

Sunlight Weakness. While in sunlight, the lesser shadow has disadvantage on attack rolls, ability checks, and saving throws.

ACTIONS

Strength Drain. Melee Weapon Attack: +3 to hit, 5 ft., one creature. *Hit:* 4 (1d6 + 1) necrotic damage, and the target's Strength score is reduced by 1d4. The target dies if reduced to Strength 0 or lower. Otherwise, the reduction lasts until the target finishes a short or long rest.

Another way to elevate a shadow encounter is to add a few support creatures to round out the ranks of your newly tweaked shadows. For that, we make a lesser version of the shadow from the core rulebooks. ◈

MEMORABLE MONSTERS: MONSTER COUTURE: A BOOK REVIEW

BY SHANNON CAMPBELL AND DILLON MACPHERSON

The enemy is vanquished: melee and magical combatants alike stand glistening with monster guts, and naturally, it's time to loot the bodies. Sure, you can sell a giant eyeball to the highest bidder, but you killed the beast yourself, so why shouldn't you get down, dirty, and DIY with the spoils?

Luckily the dwarven monster hunter Bartha Buart has recently published her notes in the acclaimed best-selling HIDE ACTION: How to Live and Make a Living. *Anyone within earshot of a bard has likely heard the stories of Buart's myriad monster maimings, but this publication marks the first time she's shared her techniques on making the most of any kill.*

HIDE ACTION *is available from most magic shops and fine booksellers, and is priced at 15 gold pieces in leatherbound edition or five gold pieces in folio.*

A sample of Buart's new must-read book has been made available by the publisher.

CHAPTER FIVE: ABOLETH IS MORE

Aboleth, psionic deep-sea alien.

In the last chapter, I mentioned how only a foolish adventurer lets any part of the monster go to waste, and this likely summoned a bark of protest from any reader who has been on the receiving end of a monster's worst quality, be it rancid breath or acid barf. Case in point, anyone who's faced an aboleth has likely done the math on when they last honed their weapons— if your blade's not wicked sharp, it runs the risk of just sliding down its squelching hide. But an aboleth corpse is ripe for plundering, as the buoyant and yielding flesh often leaves components in good, clean condition, assuming you haven't pulverized it into a fishy paste. (Remember, folks: when harvesting, slicing is nice, bashing is bad.)

HIDE

Working from a fresh source is a must. Like jellyfish, aboleth mucus begins to decompose into liquified sludge the second it dies, and it'll take the leathery skin with it. A quick slap of *gentle repose* will do the trick until you can get to a clean workstation and scrape down the hide. Unfortunately, the hide needs to be fully moistened at least once a day or it'll grow brittle and begin to flake. Fortunately, this isn't my first attempt at aboleth armor, and I was able to whip up something pretty dang satisfactory:

ABOLETH HIDE ARMOR

Medium armor (unique), rare (requires attunement)

This magical, medium armor grants AC 17 + Dex, weighs 40 pounds, and does not impose disadvantage on Stealth. The armor has 10 durability. Each day the aboleth hide armor needs to be soaked in water for 10 minutes. Failure to do so reduces the armor's durability by 1d6 + 1. Soaking the armor returns the durability back to 10. If the durability ever reaches zero it disintegrates.

MUCOUS MEMBRANE

This membrane needs to be immediately submerged in oil, and you'll want protective gloves to handle it. However, slicing the skin of the membrane open and stretching it out, while keeping it submerged in an oil bath over the course of a week, will give you enough material to make an entire cloak— perhaps even a *cloak of water breathing*! But it is also a *cloak of air choking*. Fortunately, the side effects end when you lower the hood. Bonus: convert a dilution of the tainted oil into an aerosol and *bam*, a quick way to tell your enemies they can choke on it.

ABOLETH *CLOAK OF WATER BREATHING*

Wondrous item, uncommon (requires attunement)

This slick, pale cloak is perpetually tacky (in both ways) and often clings to your body as if it were wet. While wearing this cloak with the hood up, you gain the following benefits:

- You can breathe underwater.

- You have a swimming speed of 40 feet.

- You gain advantage on saving throws against disease.

And the following drawbacks:

- You cannot breathe out of water.

- Pulling the hood up or down requires an action.

BUBBLEKILL SPRAY

Potion, uncommon

As an action, this potion can be thrown up to 30 feet and shatters on impact, creating a 10-foot sphere of aerosol contamination. This sphere lasts one minute before dissipating harmlessly. When a creature enters this sphere for the first time on their turn, or starts their turn there, they must succeed on a DC 16 Constitution saving throw or take 1d6 necrotic damage and begin to suffocate on a failed save. These effect last for an additional 1d4 rounds after the creature has left the sphere. A creature can submerge themselves in water to negate the suffocation, but not the damage. Creatures who do not need to breathe are immune to the effects of this potion.

EYES

WARNING: ADVANCED CRAFTERS ONLY. I hope I don't have to remind anyone that psionics are literally *mind-blowing*. Aboleth eyes are certainly the most dangerous component (aside from the brains). I recruited my frequent collaborator Richter, so a good deal of time was spent arguing over exactly what we should do with this piece before getting to work. We settled on a gauntlet design, having both agreed that putting an item with that much psionic energy on a headpiece would be misguided. But I will, someday, make the codpiece that stares back, and we'll see if Richter gets an honorable mention for being on the wrong side of history, then.

ABOLETH GAUNTLET OF EYES

Wondrous item, very rare (requires attunement)

This smooth, rubbery gauntlet features a single closed eye on the wrist. The eye opens once the Enslave feature is used and, once the effect ends, it turns milky white until it closes and resets at dawn the next day.

ENSLAVE

As an action, you can target one creature you can see within 30 feet. The target must succeed on a DC 14 Wisdom saving throw or be magically charmed by you for one hour, or until you die or travel to a different plane of existence from the target. The charmed target is under your control and can't take reactions, and you and the target can communicate telepathically with each other over any distance. Whenever the charmed target takes damage, the target can repeat the saving throw. On a success, the effect ends. You can perform this action once per day.

PROBING TELEPATHY

If a creature communicates telepathically with you while within your line of sight, you learn the creature's greatest desires. The target is unaware of this connection.

ABOLETH CODPIECE THAT STARES BACK

Wondrous item, very rare (requires attunement)

WARNING: THIS DESIGN IS HYPOTHETICAL AND HAS NEVER BEEN TESTED.

This magical belt is likely an object of tremendous power. For each eye affixed to the codpiece, add 1d4 charges to be replenished at dawn each day.

The codpiece contains a max of five charges at a time. When worn, you can expend a charge to use the following feature:

- **MY EYES ARE DOWN HERE**: You may present a distraction to any creature who can see you, as long as line of sight is not broken with the belt. The creature must make a Wisdom saving throw vs DC 18 or your spell save DC (whichever is higher), or become stunned for the duration. During this time, your target will be completely transfixed, unable to respond to any stimulus other than the sound of your voice. They can, and will, truthfully answer any yes or no question to which they know the answer. They are incapable of answering questions that require more complicated responses.

Any creature that can't be charmed or stunned succeeds on this saving throw automatically, and if you or your companions are fighting a creature, it has advantage on the save. You can transfix up to three creatures at a time, expending a charge for each one. The effect ends on any of the following conditions: after an hour, once line of sight is broken, if the creature is touched, or if the creature takes damage. The creature will be unable to remember anything afterwards but the sight of the codpiece.

TENTACLES

Every time I mention I worked with aboleth tentacles at a party, the first thing anyone ever says is, "Oh, you should make a whip." Obviously, I tried that. The whips were too thick to wield conventionally and

Illustrated by KikiDoodle

too slippery to be used for adventurous swinging. But in our efforts we did discover that the tentacles could be, unpleasantly enough, milked.

ABOLETH SLIME
Potion, very rare

This sticky slime can be applied to one melee weapon. Applying the slime takes an action. A creature hit by the slimed weapon must make a DC 14 Constitution saving throw. On a failed save, the creature takes 1d12 acid damage, its skin becomes translucent and slimy, and it can't regain hit points unless it is underwater. At the end of its turns, it can make another Constitution save. Each time the creature fails, the save DC is decreased by 4. The effects of the slime end when the creature makes a success save or the DC reaches 0. Damage dealt while the creature is affected this way can only be healed while the subject is submerged in water, or by *heal* or another disease-curing spell of 6th level or higher. Creatures immune to disease are immune to this slime.

LESSONS TO LIVE BY:

Of course, no project is perfect. There's always a cleaner kill on the horizon, and a superior blueprint to work from. Learn from my mistakes:

I prefer medium, but the aboleth armor could be trimmed to be lighter or reinforced to make heavy armor.

- Infusing a water rune or other water elemental power item into the armor could keep it permanently wetted, but it might also make you drip. It won't have any consequence if you're a drip, however.

- A more powerful version of the gauntlet could be created with all three eyes studded in all the way up to the elbow. But the risk of accidentally charming yourself seems high and unpredictable.

Despite the aboleth's natural properties, the design for *shoes of sliding* continues to slip through my fingers. Just wish I could get a grip on the concept.

When all is said and done, the thing I find most satisfying about salvaging after a kill (or, as I like to call it, *monster couture*) is how applicable the ideas can be from one thing to the next. An aboleth is an abundant source of materials, but the monster world is so full of devious abominations and freakish mutants that there's no limit to your creativity;

you could surely fashion a *cloak of waterbreathing* from any water-dwelling creature. Likewise, an aboleth isn't the only creature with a transfixing gaze. Monster couture is perhaps the most infinite of canvases. You're limited only by your own genius...and possibly by how many healers you know who are capable of regrowing limbs. You can't rip the nerve endings out of a severed pincer without losing a few arms.

Which reminds me that this book is dedicated to Richter, who always has my back, and has, in fact, literally regrown it more than once.

—

Our preview of *HIDE ACTION* ends here, but thank you once again to Bartha Buart and the publishers at Winter Coast Kindling for allowing us to reprint it in a limited capacity for your perusal. ⬡

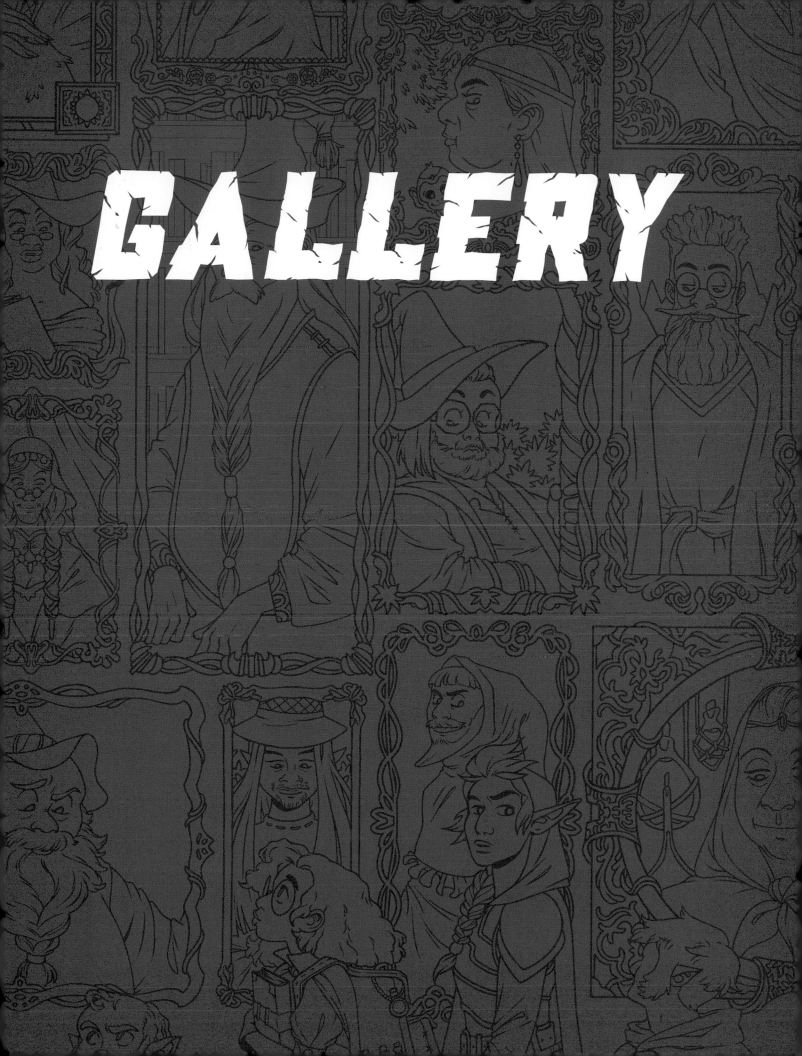

GALLERY

ISSUE 7 | MARCH 2019 | COVER | ALANE GRACE

ISSUE 7 | MARCH 2019 | SPLASH | TYRA KURTZHALS

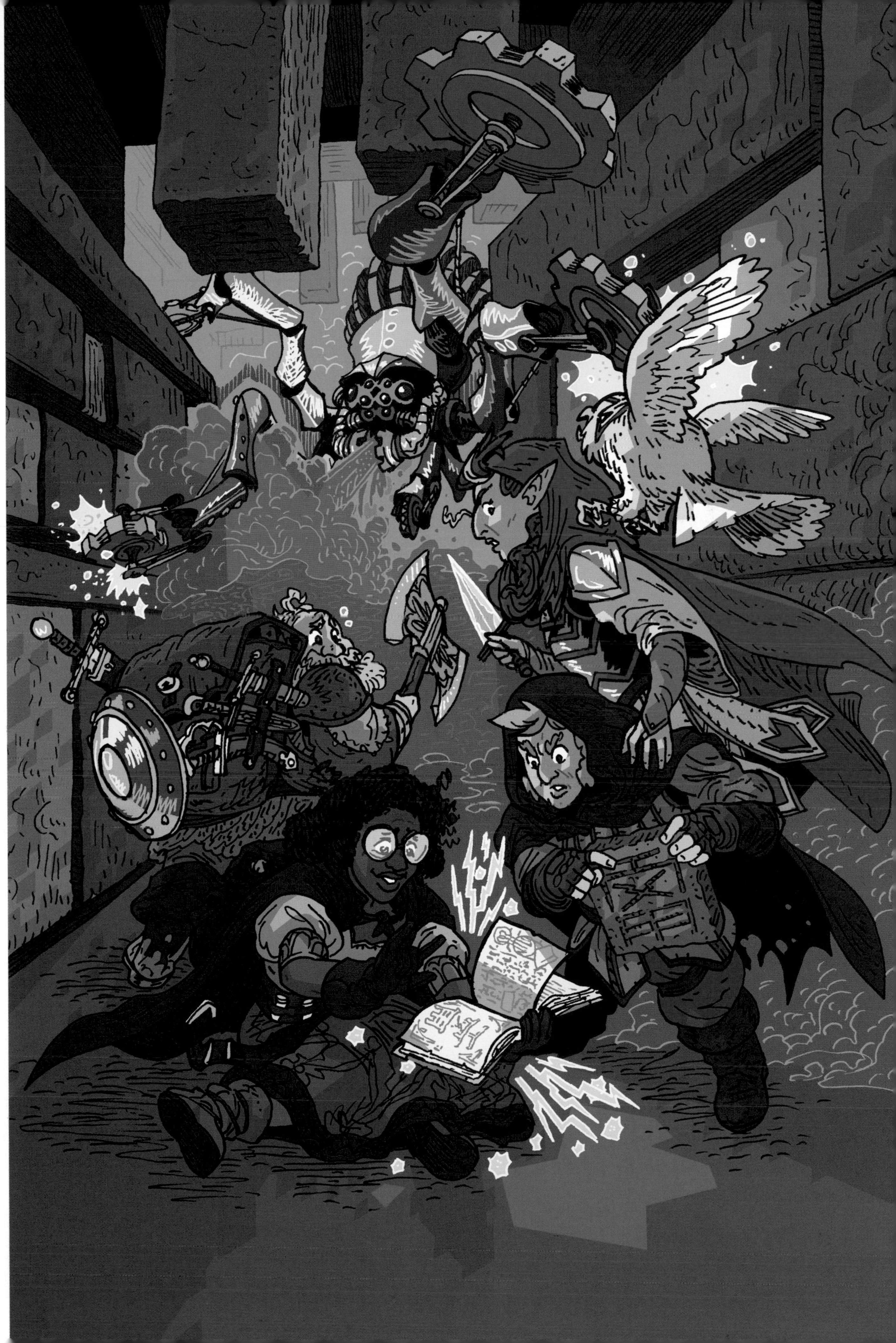

ISSUE 8 | APRIL 2019 | COVER | TIM SIEVERT

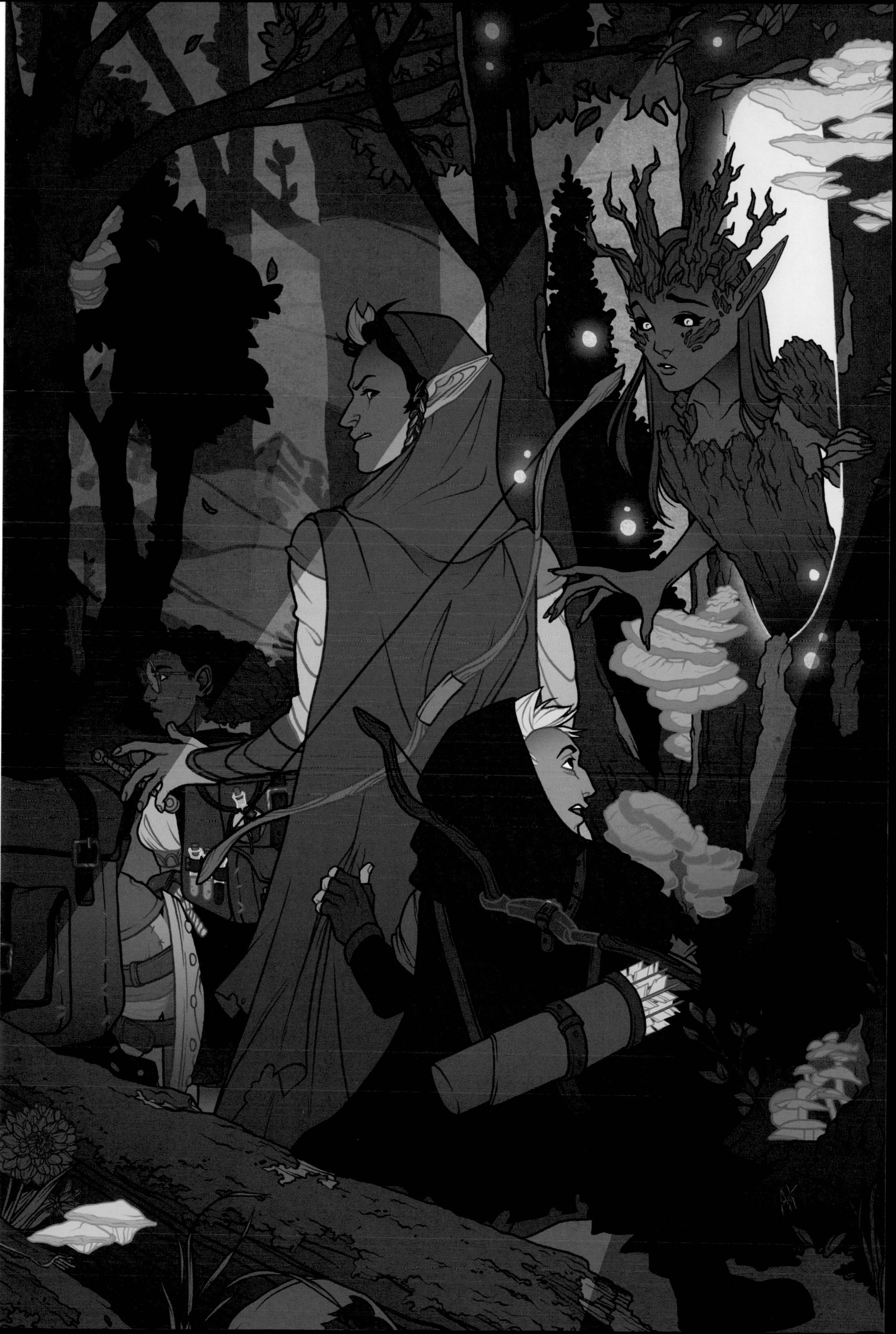

ISSUE 9 | MAY 2019 | COVER | MACI HASS

ISSUE 9 | MAY 2019 | SPLASH | RACHEL DUKES

ISSUE 10 | JUNE 2019 | COVER | BEX GLENDINING

ISSUE 10 | JUNE 2019 | SPLASH | BEX GLENDINING

ISSUE 10 | JUNE 2019 | SPLASH | AHMARA SMITH

ISSUE 10 | JUNE 2019 | SPLASH | KIKIDOODLE

ISSUE 10 | JUNE 2019 | SPLASH | KAREN KO

ISSUE 11 | JULY 2019 | COVER | SARAH BOLLINGER

ISSUE 11 | JULY 2019 | SPLASH | ALEXA SHARPE

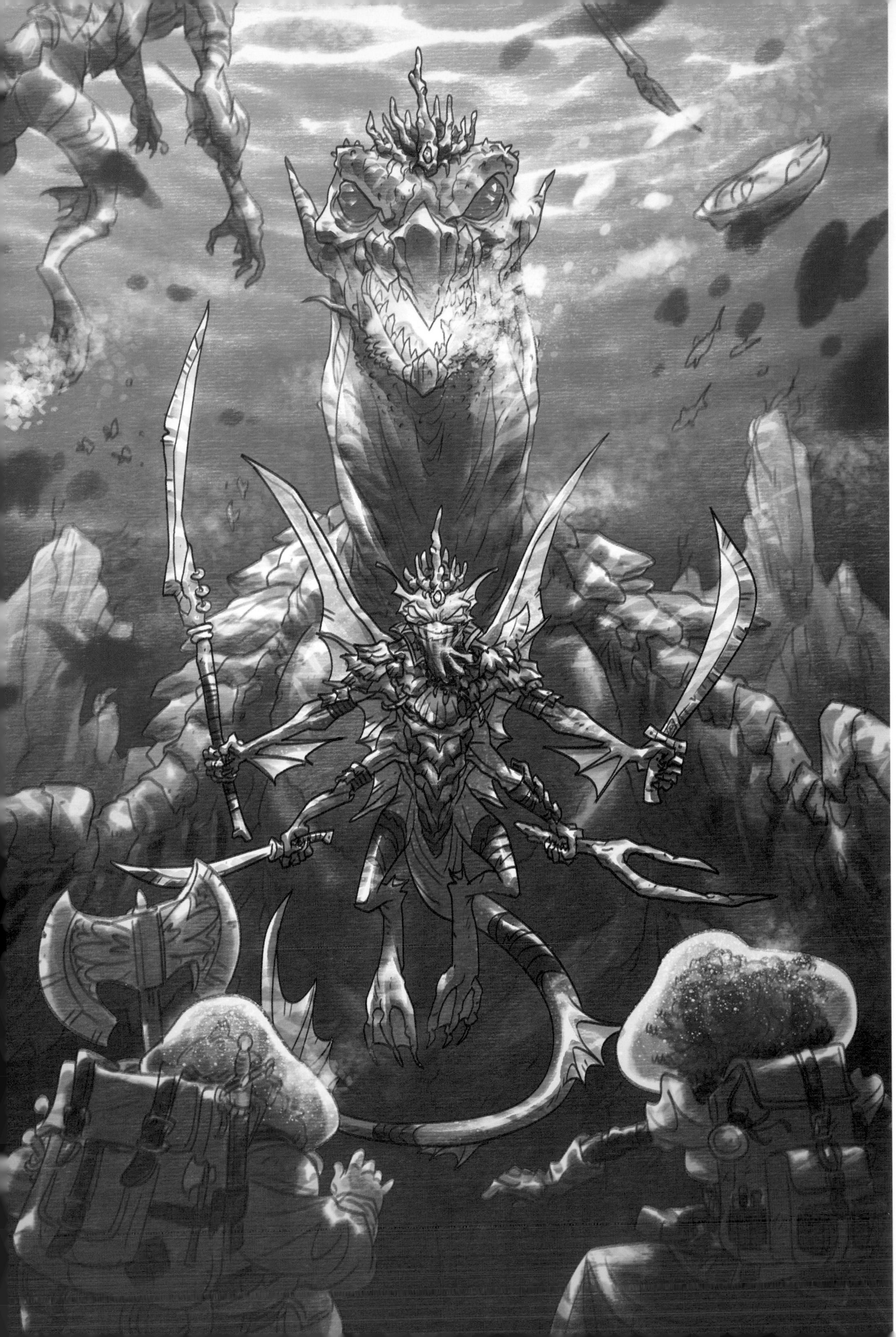

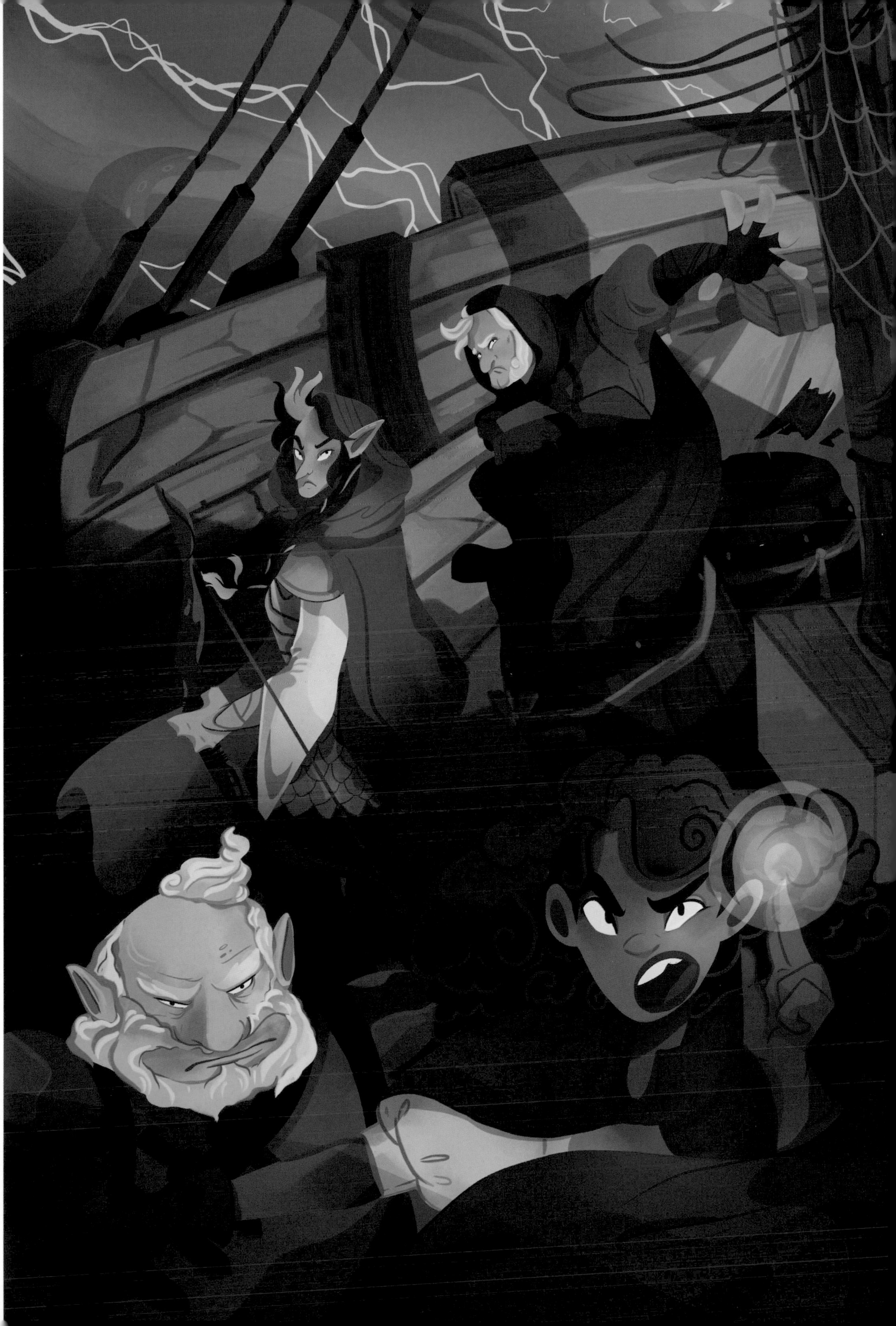

ISSUE 11 | JULY 2019 | SPLASH | BEX GLENDINING

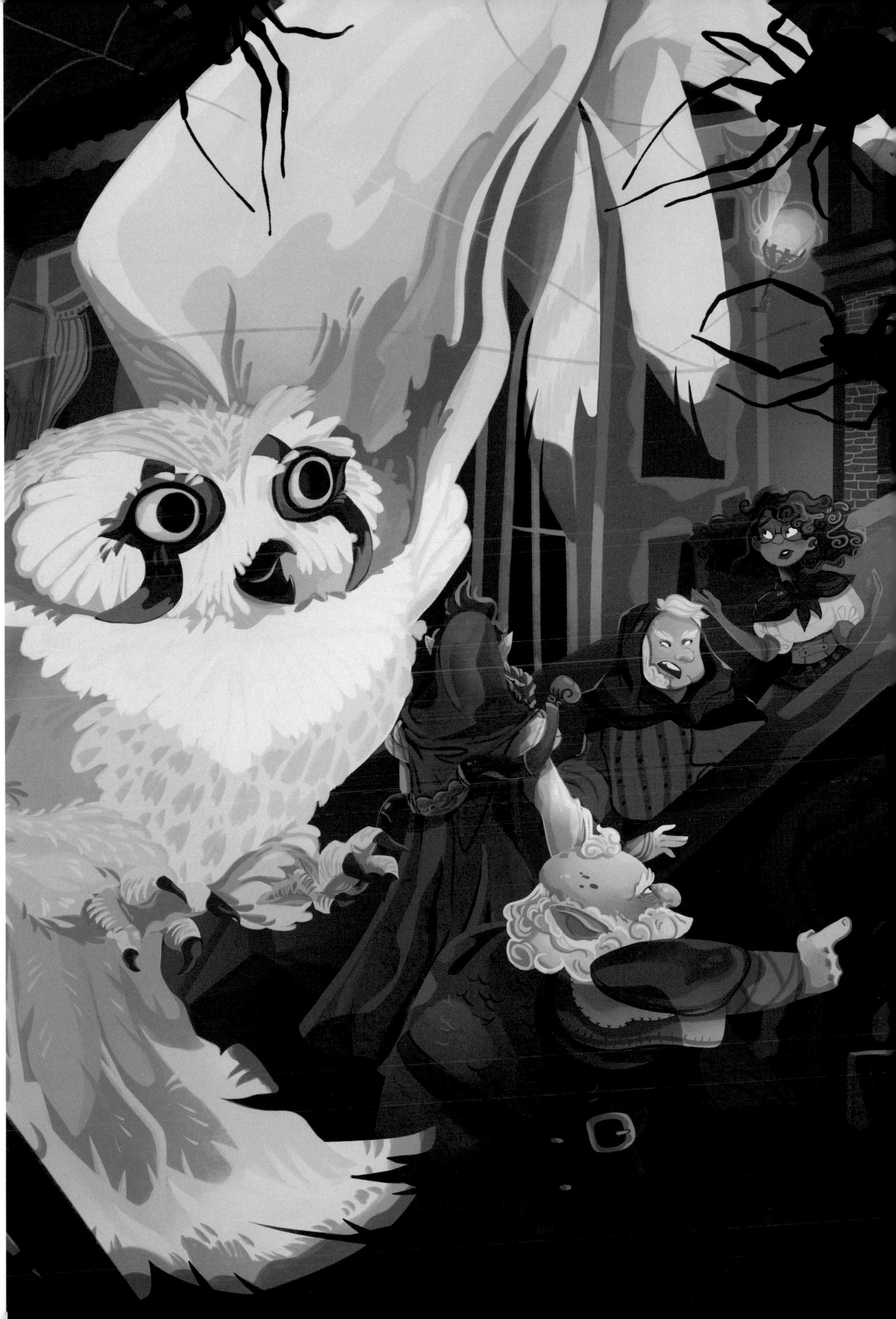

ISSUE 12 | AUGUST 2019 | COVER | VANESSA MORALES

ISSUE 12 | AUGUST 2019 | SPLASH | CAROLYN NOWAK

ISSUE 12 | AUGUST 2019 | SPLASH | MARTIE ADBURRASHEED

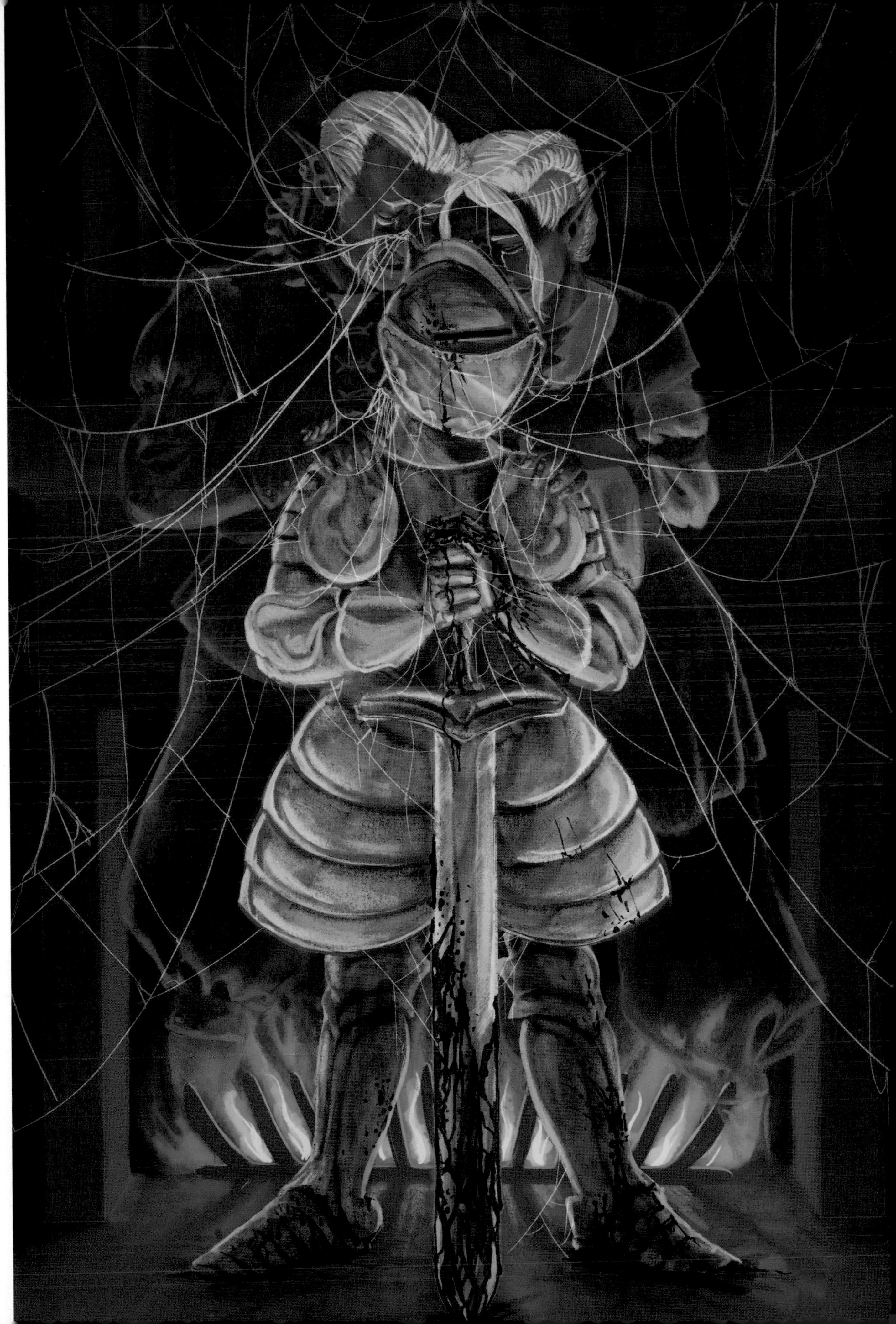

MUGG PIGIRON

FIGHTER Level 4 • Medium humanoid (hill dwarf), lawful good
Armor Class 20 (plate & shield) | **Hit Points** 52 (4d10 + 24) | **Speed** 25 ft.

STR	DEX	CON	INT	WIS	CHA
18 (+4)	10 (+0)	20 (+5)	8 (-1)	14 (+2)	12 (+1)

Saving Throws Str +6, Con +7
Skills Animal Handling +3, Athletics +6, Intimidation +3, Perception +3
Senses darkvision 60 ft., passive Perception 14
Languages Common, Dwarvish
Tool Proficiency Smith's Tools, Gaming Set, Vehicles (land)
Fighting Style Dueling (PHB page 72)
Second Wind (PHB page 72)
Dwarf Traits (see PHB pages 19-20 for details)
Action Surge (see PHB page 72 for details)
Martial Archetype Champion
Improved Critical (see PHB page 72 for details)

ACTIONS

Battle Axe. Melee Weapon Attack: +6 to hit, reach 5ft., one target. *Hit:* 10 (1d8 + 4 +2 dueling) slashing damage or 9 (1d10 + 4) slashing damage if used with two hands.

Heavy Crossbow. Ranged Weapon Attack +2 to hit, ranged 100/400 ft., one target. *Hit:* 5 (1d10).

ROLEPLAYING INFORMATION

Background: Soldier (support staff)
Personality Trait: "I always mind my manners...unless ya hurt my friends."
Ideal: Greater Good. "I'll fight for what is right, every time!"
Bond: "Those who call me friend are worth killing or dying for."
Flaw: "I suppose everybody is trustworthy, till they ain't..."

EQUIPMENT

- (1) sturdy but old traveling clothing
- (1) scale armor
- (1) shield
- (1) oversized backpack (counts as both an Explorer's Pack and Dungeoneer's Pack)
- (1) battleaxe
- (1) heavy crossbow
- (1) case of (10) crossbow bolts

- (2) daggers
- (2) shortswords
- (2) longswords
- (1) greataxe
- (1) Warhammer
- (2) handaxes
- (1) net
- (1) small steel mirror
- (1) signal whistle

- (10) sacks
- (1) soap
- (1) iron pot
- (1) shovel
- (1) deck of cards
- (1) small pouch containing 10 gp

Trinket: A silver locket with a badly depicted portrait of his beloved Heartha inside

Magic Item: *Helm of Omens* (see item card for details)

HELM OF OMENS *Wondrous item, very rare (requires attunement by a dwarf)*

The dented and grim looking half-helm once sported two stubby dragon claws as horns. Now it looks to have seen more battles than can be counted. When worn, the *helm* grants the wearer the merest glimpse into the future. This gives an attuned wearer advantage on initiative rolls. In addition, when the attuned wearer finishes a long rest, roll two d20s and record the results. The attuned wearer can replace any attack roll, saving throw, or ability check made by the wearer or a creature the wearer can see with one of the previously rolled d20 results. The wearer must choose to replace the result before a roll is made. Each of the two results granted by the *helm* can be used only once and are lost if not used before the wearer takes another long rest.

ZELLA VADE

WIZARD Level 4 • Medium humanoid (human), chaotic good
Armor Class 11 | **Hit Points** 22 (4d6 + 4) | **Speed** 30 ft.

STR	DEX	CON	INT	WIS	CHA
11 (+0)	12 (+1)	12 (+1)	18 (+4)	15 (+2)	12 (+1)

Saving Throws Int +6, Wis +4
Skills Arcana +6, History +6, Investigation +6, Medicine +6
Senses passive Perception 12
Languages Common, Draconic, Dwarvish, Elvish, Gnomish
Arcane Tradition School of Divination
Divination Savant (see PHB page 116)
Portent (see PHB page 116)

SPELLCASTING

Zella is a 1st-level spellcaster. Her spellcasting ability is Intelligence (spell save DC14; +6 to hit with spell attacks). She has the following wizard spells prepared:

Cantrips (at will): *fire bolt, light, mending, true strike*

1st level (4 slots): *comprehend languages, expeditious retreat, feather fall, identify, mage armor; magic missile, shield, seep, thunderwave*

2nd level (2 slots): *locate object, misty step, shatter*

ACTIONS

Staff. Melee Weapon Attack: +2 to hit, reach 5 ft., one target. *Hit:* 3 (1d6) bludgeoning damage, or 4 (1d8) bludgeoning damaging if used with two hands.

ROLEPLAYING INFORMATION

Background: Sage (Discredited Academic)
Personality Trait: "I'm a bit awkward in social situations outside of academia."
Ideal: Knowledge. "The true power in life is knowing all the answers."
Bond: "My word is my bond, and I shall not willingly break it."
Flaw: "My temper sometimes gets away from me if I am pushed to anger."

EQUIPMENT

- Common Clothing (robes)
- Component Pouch
- Explorer's Pack
- Pen, ink & parchment
- Quarterstaff
- Spellbook
- A small pouch containing 10 gp

Trinket: A strange, knobby, oily, hide-bound tome, scribed in what appears to a be ever-shifting non-Euclidean shapes

Magic Item: *Spectrum Spectacles* (see item card for details); *Robe of Useful Items* (see DMG page 195); *Wand of Magic Missiles* (see DMG page 211)

SPECTRUM SPECTACLES *Wondrous item, very rare (requires attunement)*

These oversized, wire-rimmed and crystal-lensed *spectacles* grant the attuned wearer a variety of magical sight options (see below). While wearing the *spectacles*, an attuned wearer can expend the needed amount of charges as a single action to gain access to a single chosen magic effect. Only one effect may be active at any time and if another effect is produced by the *spectacles*, it dismisses any previous effect as it takes effect. The *spectacles* have seven charges.

Darkvision 60 ft., duration 8 hours (2 charges) | **Detect Magic** duration 1 minute (1 charge)
Find Traps duration instant (3 Charges) | **True Seeing** duration 1 hour (7 charges)

HUCK SNIPESHADOW

ROGUE Level 4 • Small humanoid (lightfoot halfling), chaotic neutral

Armor Class 17 (leather + ring of protection)
Hit Points 27 (4d8 + 4) | **Speed** 25 ft.

STR	DEX	CON	INT	WIS	CHA
10 (+0)	20 (+5)	12 (+1)	14 (+2)	16 (+3)	16 (+3)

Saving Throws Dex +7, Int +4
Skills Acrobatics +7, Deception +5, Investigation +5, Perception +5, Sleight of Hand +7, Stealth +7
Senses passive Perception 13
Languages Common, Halfling, Thieves' Cant
Tool Proficiency Thieves' Tools, Gaming Set (cards)
Expertise Stealth, Thieves' Tool (see PHB page 96)
Sneak Attack 2d6: (see PHB page 96)
Cunning Action (see PHB page 96)
Halfling Traits (see PHB pages 27-28 for details)
Roguish Archetype Thief
Fast Hands (see PHB page 97)
Feat Dungeon Delver (see PHB page 166)

ACTIONS

Dagger. Melee or Ranged Weapon Attack: +7 to hit, reach 5ft., one target. *Hit:* 10 (1d4 + 5) piercing damage or +7 to hit. Ranged (20/60), 7 (1d4 + 5) piercing damage.

Short Bow. Ranged Weapon Attack +7 to hit, ranged 80/320 ft., one target. *Hit:* 8 (1d6 + 5).

ROLEPLAYING INFORMATION

Background: Criminal (Burglar)
Personality Trait: "I'll never pass up a dare."
Ideal: Greater Good. Independence. "I truly listen to just one person...Me."
Bond: "I never steal from a friend...lucky for me, I only have three of those."
Flaw: "If it's worth something to someone, it's worth me stealing it."

EQUIPMENT

- (1) dark traveling clothing with a deep hooded cloak
- (1) leather armor

- (1) shortbow
- (1) quiver of (20) arrows
- (5) throwing knives (daggers)

- (1) Thieves' Tools
- (1) Burglar's Pack
- (1) small pouch containing 15 gp

Trinket: A jackalope's foot

Magic Item: *"Lady Sharps" the jeweled dagger* (see item card for details)

"LADY SHARPS" THE JEWELED DAGGER *Wondrous item, very rare (requires attunement)*

This magnificent and perfectly balanced weapon is made of adamantine. The handle is wrapped in braided black leather. The pommel is made in the image of a grinning skull, its sockets and teeth set with tiny gemstones. The cross guard and blade are intricately decorated with a skull motif, giving the long-bladed dagger a fearsome appearance.

This +1 dagger scores a critical hit on a roll of 19 or 20 for the attuned wearer. In addition to a critical hit, the wearer causes automatic maximum damage of any weapon damage dice you would roll on the attack.

VESSKA MOONWYND

RANGER Level 4 • Medium humanoid (wood elf), chaotic good
Armor Class 16 (leather armor)
Hit Points 36 (4d10 + 8) | **Speed** 35 ft.

STR	DEX	CON	INT	WIS	CHA
14 (+2)	20 (+5)	14 (+2)	12 (+1)	16 (+3)	12 (+1)

Saving Throws Str +4, Dex +7
Skills History +3, Nature +3, Perception +5, Persuasion +3, Stealth +7, Survival +5
Senses darkvision 60 ft., passive Perception 15
Languages Common, Dwarvish, Elvish
Tool Proficiency Gaming Set
Favored Enemy (Giants)
Natural Explorer (Mountains)
Elf Traits (see core rulebooks for details)
Fighting Style Archer
Primeval Awareness (see PHB page 92)
Spell Casting (Wis) +5 to hit/ Save DC 13
1st-level spells (3 Slots): *good berry, hunter's mark, longstrider*
Ranger Archetype Hunter
Hunter's Prey Horde Breaker
Feat Sharpshooter

ACTIONS

Short sword. Melee Weapon Attack: +7 to hit, reach 5ft., one target. *Hit:* 8 (1d6 + 5) piercing damage.

Longbow. Ranged Weapon Attack +7 to hit, ranged 150/ 600 ft., one target. *Hit:* 9 (1d8 + 5)

ROLEPLAYING INFORMATION

Background: Noble
Personality Trait: "One's birth station does not make one noble."
Ideal: Change. "I will not be satisfied until I have seen every corner of the world."
Bond: "I will gladly give my life for those that follow my lead."
Flaw: "I tend to forget that not everyone is as long lived as an elf."

EQUIPMENT

- (1) fancy clothing (rolled up in her pack)
- (1) signet ring
- (1) sturdy traveling clothing
- (1) leather armor
- (1) explorer's pack
- (1) longbow
- (1) quiver of (20) arrows
- (1) dagger
- (2) short swords
- (1) small pouch containing 25 gp

Trinket: A smooth stone, taken from the river near her former mountain home. The stone always feels cool to the touch.

Magic Item: *The Grayghost Cloak* – (see item card for details)

Unique Ability: Soul-Bound Familiar Owl – See "Flake the Owl" entry for details.

GRAYGHOST CLOAK

Wondrous item, rare (requires attunement)

While wearing this *cloak* with its hood up, you have advantage on Dexterity (Stealth) check to hide or move quietly. The *cloak* has two additional abilities; each can be used once per long rest. The cloak allows the wearer to cast the following spells as the same action listed in their spell descriptions, with no need of components—*misty step* and *pass without trace*.

FLAKE THE OWL

Flake functions similarly to the celestial owl produced by the *find familiar* spell with the following exceptions: It can only ever summon a celestial owl. Vesska can use the spell only once per long rest for each character level she has, and doing so requires no material components (so at 2nd level she can use it twice per long rest). Also, unlike a normal familiar produced by the spell, Flake can take the Attack Action and his melee attacks count as magic. Use the "Owl" stat block in the core rulebooks for Flake.

CONTRIBUTORS

E.L. THOMAS
ADVENTURE WRITER

- "Vault of the Mad Crafter"

ARTICLE WRITER

- "Memorable Monsters: Shadow"
- "Running the Game: On-the-Fly NPCs"

LEAD GAME DESIGNER

- "Running The Game: Ten Rules to Follow when Running Games for First-Time Players"

ALANE GRACE
ILLUSTRATOR

- *Rolled & Told Vol 2* Cover Artist
- March 2019 Cover
- May 2019 Spot Illustrations

PHIL MCCLOREY
ADVENTURE WRITER

- "The Dragon, the Witch, and the Dryad"

HADEEL AL-MASSARI
ADVENTURE WRITER

- "A Tale of Two Gnomes"

SHARANG BISWAS
ADVENTURE WRITER

- "A Tale of Two Gnomes"

SHANNON CAMPBELL
ARTICLE WRITER

- "Memorable Monsters: Monster Couture: A Book Review"

DILLON MACPHERSON
ARTICLE WRITER

- "Memorable Monsters: Monster Couture: A Book Review"

KAT KRUGER
ADVENTURE WRITER

- "Alone Time"

ARTICLE WRITER

- "Adventure Craft: Nobody Said There'd Be Math Involved!"

COMFORT LOVE
ADVENTURE WRITER

- "Ship of The Dead"

CARTOGRAPHER

- August 2020 Map

ADAM WITHERS
ADVENTURE WRITER

- "Ship of The Dead"

CARTOGRAPHER

- August 2020 Map

FINLAY LOGAN
ADVENTURE WRITER

- "The Secret of the Spiderplague"

ARTICLE WRITER

- "Running the Game: Adventures with Kids"

TELINE GUERRA
ADVENTURE WRITER

- "Reginald's Closet"

ARTICLE WRITER

- "Random Nonsense: Spiritually Speaking"

GEOFFREY GOLDEN
ADVENTURE WRITER

- "Forest of Delusion"

ARTICLE WRITER

- "Random Nonsense: Party of One"

CRYSTAL FRASIER
ADVENTURE WRITER

- "The Matchmakers"

JOSHUA TRUJILLO
ADVENTURE WRITER

- "Keeper of Urough's Flame"

JEFF ELLISH
ADVENTURE WRITER

- "Ride the Deep Currents"

ADAM MA
ADVENTURE WRITER

- "The Demon of Queen's Haven"

TIM SIEVERT
ILLUSTRATOR

- April 2019 Cover

MACI HASS
ILLUSTRATOR

- May 2019 Cover

VAL WISE
ILLUSTRATOR

- March 2019 Mini Adventure Comic

BEX GLENDINING
ILLUSTRATOR

- June 2019 Cover
- June 2019 Splash Illustration
- July 2019 Splash Illustration

SARAH BOLLINGER
ILLUSTRATOR

- July 2019 Cover
- March 2019 Spot Illustrations

VANESSA MORALES
ILLUSTRATOR

- August 2019 Cover
- July 2019 Splash Illustration

NICKY SOH
ILLUSTRATOR

- March 2019 Full Adventure Comic

CAROLYN NOWAK
ILLUSTRATOR

- April 2019 Full Adventure Comic
- August 2019 Splash Illustration

CARTOGRAPHER

- March 2019 Map

EA DENICH
ILLUSTRATOR

- May 2019 Full Adventure Comic
- May 2019 Splash Illustration

SAVANNA GANUCHEA
ILLUSTRATOR

- July 2019 Fully Adventure Comic
- May 2019 Mini Adventure Comic
- August 2019 Spot Illustrations

KAYLEE PINECONE
ILLUSTRATOR

- June 2019 Full Adventure Comic
- April 2019 Mini Adventure Comic

CARA MCGEE
ILLUSTRATOR

- June 2019 Mini Adventure Comic

COURTNEY HAHN
ILLUSTRATOR

- July 2019 Mini Adventure Comic
- August 2019 Character Sheets

MELANIE KIM
ILLUSTRATOR

- August 2019 Full Adventure Comic

CARTOGRAPHER

- July 2019 Map

RUDY MORA
ILLUSTRATOR

- August 2019 Mini Adventure Comic

TABBY FREEMAN
ILLUSTRATOR

- March 2019 Spot Illustrations

HARI CONNER
ILLUSTRATOR

- March 2019 Spot Illustrations

RACHEL DUKES
ILLUSTRATOR

- April 2019 Spot Illustrations
- May 2019 Splash Illustration

ARTICLE WRITER

- "Sites & Settings: Setting the Environment – Tips to Brighten Your Burrow and Host Your Party's Next Adventure"

ANNA LIISA JONES
ILLUSTRATOR

- April 2019 Spot Illustrations
- May 2019 Splash Illustrations

Tara Kurtzhals
ILLUSTRATOR

- March 2019 Splash Illustrations
- April 2019 Spot Illustrations

Jonathan Hill
ILLUSTRATOR

- May 2019 Spot Illustrations

Kikidoodle
ILLUSTRATOR

- May 2019 Spot Illustrations
- June 2019 Splash Illustration

Amelia Allore
ILLUSTRATOR

- June 2019 Splash Illustration

Max Dlabick
ILLUSTRATOR

- June 2019 Spot Illustrations

Ahmara Smith
ILLUSTRATOR

- June 2019 Spot Illustrations
- June 2019 Splash Illustrations

Martie Abdurrasheed
ILLUSTRATOR

- July 2019 Spot Illustrations
- August 2019 Splash Illustrations

Ashanti Fortson
ILLUSTRATOR

- July 2019 Spot Illustrations

Geneva Benton
ILLUSTRATOR

- July 2019 Spot Illustrations

Katie Green
ILLUSTRATOR

- August 2019 Spot Illustrations

Michael Harris
ILLUSTRATOR

- August 2019 Spot Illustrations

Brandon Reese
CARTOGRAPHER

- April 2019 Map

Shing Yin Khor
CARTOGRAPHER

- May 2019 Map

ARTICLE WRITER

- "Adventure Craft: Adventure Crafting"

Kyle Latino
CARTOGRAPHER

- June 2019 Map

ILLUSTRATOR

- March 2019 Splash Illustration

Phil McAndrew
CARTOGRAPHER

- August 2019 Map

Aubrie Warner
CARTOGRAPHER

- August 2020 Map

Becca Farrow
ILLUSTRATOR

- March 2019 Splash Illustration

Matt "TytoAlba" Martines
ILLUSTRATOR

- March 2019 Splash Illustration

Reimena Yee
ILLUSTRATOR

- April 2019 Splash Illustration

Andrea Kendrick
ILLUSTRATOR

- April 2019 Splash Illustration

Maia Kobabe
ILLUSTRATOR

- April 2019 Splash Illustration

Amanda Castillo
ILLUSTRATOR

- April 2019 Splash Illustration

Rii Abrego
ILLUSTRATOR

- May 2019 Splash Illustration

Karen Ko
ILLUSTRATOR

- June 2019 Splash Illustration

Alexa Sharpe
ILLUSTRATOR

- July 2019 Splash Illustration

Ron Chan
ILLUSTRATOR

- July 2019 Splash Illustration

Lisa Sterle
ILLUSTRATOR

- August 2019 Splash Illustration

Rachel Kahn
ILLUSTRATOR

- August 2019 Splash Illustration

Shel Kahn
ARTICLE WRITER

- "Sites & Settings: The Five Senses and the Sweating Swamp"

MK Reed
ARTICLE WRITER

- "Running the Game: Night Moves"

Jeremy Melloul
ARTICLE WRITER

- "Sites & Settings: The Adventure Comes to You"

Brooke Jaffe
ARTICLE WRITER

- "Random Nonsense: Homebrew Homeschool – A Crash Course in Content Creation"

Steve Kenson
ARTICLE WRITER

- "House Rules: Reimagining Classes"

Matthew Erman
ARTICLE WRITER

- "Random Nonsense: Sharpening Your Swords When Your Pen Is Dull"

Gareth-Michael Sharka
ARTICLE WRITER

- "Sites & Settings: The Trans-Kingdom Skyway Company, LTD."

Grace Thomas
ARTICLE WRITER

- "Running the Game: MMORPG IRL"

Andrew G. Schneider
ARTICLE WRITER

- "Memorable Monsters: Roleplaying Dragons Great and Small"

Ben McFarland
ARTICLE WRITER

- "Sites & Settings: Roadside Shrines"

Lisa Olson
ARTICLE WRITER

- "Running the Game: Comics for Dungeon Enthusiasts"

Renee Rhodes
ARTICLE WRITER

- "Running the Game: Bridging Generations: Family Game Night"

Alina Pete
ARTICLE WRITER

- "Random Nonsense: Underwater Adventurer's Guided"

Max Bare
ILLUSTRATOR

- "May 2019 Instant Encounter Illustration"

Haley Rose-Lyon
LETTERER

- June 2019 Full Adventure Comic

Melanie Tingdahl
ILLUSTRATOR

- August 2019 Full Adventure Comic

WIZARDS OF THE COAST OPEN GAMING LICENSE

Permission to copy, modify and distribute the files collectively known as the System Reference Document 5.1 ("SRD5") is granted solely through the use of the Open Gaming License, Version 1.0a.

This material is being released using the Open Gaming License Version 1.0a and you should read and understand the terms of that license before using this material.

The text of the Open Gaming License itself is not Open Game Content. Instructions on using the License are provided within the License itself.

The following items are designated Product Identity, as defined in Section 1(e) of the Open Game License Version 1.0a, and are subject to the conditions set forth in Section 7 of the OGL, and are not Open Content: Dungeons & Dragons, D&D, Player's Handbook, Dungeon Master, Monster Manual, d20 System, Wizards of the Coast, d20 (when used as a trademark), Forgotten Realms, Faerûn, proper names (including those used in the names of spells or items), places, Underdark, Red Wizard of Thay, the City of Union, Heroic Domains of Ysgard, Ever-Changing Chaos of Limbo, Windswept Depths of Pandemonium, Infinite Layers of the Abyss, Tarterian Depths of Carceri, Gray Waste of Hades, Bleak Eternity of Gehenna, Nine Hells of Baator, Infernal Battlefield of Acheron, Clockwork Nirvana of Mechanus, Peaceable Kingdoms of Arcadia, Seven Mounting Heavens of Celestia, Twin Paradises of Bytopia, Blessed Fields of Elysium, Wilderness of the Beastlands, Olympian Glades of Arborea, Concordant Domain of the Outlands, Sigil, Lady of Pain, Book of Exalted Deeds, Book of Vile Darkness, beholder, gauth, carrion crawler, tanar'ri, baatezu, displacer beast, githyanki, githzerai, mind flayer, illithid, umber hulk, yuan-ti.

All of the rest of the SRD5 is Open Game Content as described in Section 1(d) of the License.

The terms of the Open Gaming License Version 1.0a are as follows:

OPEN GAME LICENSE VERSION 1.0A

The following text is the property of Wizards of the Coast, Inc. and is Copyright 2000 Wizards of the Coast, Inc ("Wizards"). All Rights Reserved.

1. Definitions: (a)"Contributors" means the copyright and/or trademark owners who have contributed Open Game Content; (b)"Derivative Material" means copyrighted material including derivative works and translations (including into other computer languages), potation, modification, correction, addition, extension, upgrade, improvement, compilation, abridgment or other form in which an existing work may be recast, transformed or adapted; (c) "Distribute" means to reproduce, license, rent, lease, sell, broadcast, publicly display, transmit or otherwise distribute;(d)"Open Game Content" means the game mechanic and includes the methods, procedures, processes and routines to the extent such content does not embody the Product Identity and is an enhancement over the prior art and any additional content clearly identified as Open Game Content by the Contributor, and means any work covered by this License, including translations and derivative works under copyright law, but specifically excludes Product Identity. (e) "Product Identity" means product and product line names, logos and identifying marks including trade dress; artifacts; creatures characters; stories, storylines, plots, thematic elements, dialogue, incidents, language, artwork, symbols, designs, depictions, likenesses, formats, poses, concepts, themes and graphic, photographic and other visual or audio representations; names and descriptions of characters, spells, enchantments, personalities, teams, personas, likenesses and special abilities; places, locations, environments, creatures, equipment, magical or supernatural abilities or effects, logos, symbols, or graphic designs; and any other trademark or registered trademark clearly identified as Product identity by the owner of the Product Identity, and which specifically excludes the Open Game Content; (f) "Trademark" means the logos, names, mark, sign, motto, designs that are used by a Contributor to identify itself or its products or the associated products contributed to the Open Game License by the Contributor (g) "Use", "Used" or "Using" means to use, Distribute, copy, edit, format, modify, translate and otherwise create Derivative Material of Open Game Content. (h) "You"or "Your" means the licensee in terms of this agreement.

2. The License: This License applies to any Open Game Content that contains a notice indicating that the Open Game Content may only be Used under and in terms of this License. You must affix such a notice to any Open Game Content that you Use. No terms may be added to or subtracted from this License except as described by the License itself. No other terms or conditions may be applied to any Open Game Content distributed using this License.